Building VRML Worlds

Ed Tittel
Claire Sanders
Charlie Scott
Paul Wolfe

Osborne **McGraw-Hill**

Berkeley   New York   St. Louis   San Francisco   Auckland   Bogotá   Hamburg   London
Madrid   Mexico City   Milan   Montreal   New Delhi   Panama City   Paris   São Paulo
Singapore   Sydney   Tokyo   Toronto

Publisher
Brandon A. Nordin

Acquisitions Editor
Megg Bonar

Project Editor
Mark Karmendy

Associate Editors
Cynthia Douglas, Heidi Poulin

Editorial Assistant
Gordon Hurd

Technical Editor
Daniel B. Levine

Copy Editor
Marcia Baker

Proofreader
Stefany Otis

Indexer
Rebecca Plunkett

Computer Designer
Peter Hancik

Illustrator
Leslee Bassin

Series Design
Lance Ravella

Quality Control Specialist
Joe Scuderi

Cover Design
*Timm F. Sinclair,
Red Rooster Design*

Osborne/**McGraw-Hill**
2600 Tenth Street
Berkeley, California 94710
U.S.A.

For information on translations or book distributors outside the U.S.A., or to arrange bulk purchase discounts for sales promotions, premiums, or fundraisers, please contact Osborne/**McGraw-Hill** at the above address.

Building VRML Worlds

1234567890 DOC 9987

ISBN 0-07-882233-5

Information has been obtained by Osborne/**McGraw-Hill** from sources believed to be reliable. However, because of the possibility of human or mechanical error by our sources, Osborne/**McGraw-Hill**, or others, Osborne/**McGraw-Hill** does not guarantee the accuracy, adequacy, or completeness of any information and is not responsible for any errors or omissions or the results obtained from use of such information.

About the Authors...

Ed Tittel has written 25 PC-related books. He is the co-author, with Deni Connor, of the best-selling IDG book, *NetWare for Dummies,* and of *HTML for Dummies* and *MORE HTML for Dummies*, both co-authored with Steve James. More recently, he co-authored *The Foundations of WWW Programming, Web Programming Secrets,* and *The 60 Minute Guide to Java.*

In a past life, Ed was Director of Technical Marketing for Novell, Inc., where he worked from 1988 to 1994, in a variety of networking-related technical positions. Ed has been a regular contributor to the computer trade press since 1987, and has written over 200 articles for a variety of publications, with a decided emphasis on networking technology. These publications include *Infoworld, LAN Times, LAN Magazine, BYTE, Iway, MacWEEK, MacWorld, MacUser, Maximize, NetGuide,* and *Windows NT* (where he's a columnist and contributing editor) magazine.

> ## Ed Tittel
>
> 5810 Lookout Mountain Drive
> Austin, TX 78731-3618
> Ofc: (512) 452-3768
> FAX: (512) 452-8018
>
> CompuServe ID: 76376,606
> Internet: etittel@lanw.com

Claire Sanders was a double major in comparative literature and French at Indiana University, where she obtained her degree in 1993. A Phi Beta Kappa graduate, she moved on to the University of Illinois, where she authored *The Right Foot Guide to the University of Illinois*, a 200-page introduction for new students. A recent transplant to Texas, she spent two semesters as a graduate student at the University of Texas, where she took courses in electronic music composition and studied the relationship between architecture, music, computers, and VR with Marcos Novak. She's now a full-time Web writer and researcher for LANWrights, Inc. Claire has written about Electronic Commerce, Intranets, and Java, and about her favorite Web phenomenon, VRML, in two other books. In her spare time, she composes synesthetic music and dreams about altering reality through the Web.

Charlie Scott has been working with computers and networks for many years. His career path has put him in front of terminals at a variety of technology companies, including Texas Instruments, IBM, Wayne-Dresser, and Tomorrow's Technologies. Most of his experience lies with system and network analysis for the Windows, OS/2, and UNIX platforms. Charlie is currently the vice-president of Client Services at OuterNet Connection Strategies, where he oversees the development, administration, and promotion of Internet application services, such as the World Wide Web. In addition, he also provides consulting services for LAN and WAN administration, systems administration, and Internet connectivity. One of his current interests is technical writing, and he is a co-author (with Ed Tittel and others) of *Internet World's 60 Minute Guide to VRML*, *WWW Programming Secrets*, and *More HTML For Dummies*, all for IDG Books.

Charlie Scott

8235 Shoal Creek, #105
Austin, TX 78758
 Ofc: (512) 345-3573
 FAX: (512) 206-0345

Internet: charlie@outer.net

Paul Wolfe has done everything from driving an M1A1 tank in Operation Desert Storm to flipping computer chips for Motorola. For the last ten years, he has served in various marketing and operations positions for technology companies, many of his own devising. He has worked on and with the Internet for ten years, and on and with computers for 15. He has racked up several hundred hours in various colleges around the world (Germany, Maryland, and Texas), though he never decided on a degree.

Paul currently serves as vice-president of marketing and communications for OuterNet Connection Strategies, Inc., where he provides Internet services to corporations worldwide. He has edited a couple of IDG Internet books, and is currently co-writing the following titles: *Building Virtual Worlds* and *Electronic Commerce for Web Developers,* with Ed Tittel and Charlie Scott.

Paul Wolfe

8235 Shoal Creek, #105
Austin, TX 78758
 Ofc: (512) 345-3573
 FAX: (512) 206-0345

Internet: info@outer.net

CONTENTS

The Building Blocks of VRML

9 VR Tools 215

10 VRML Extensible Rendering Packages 235

A Self-Extending VRML Resource Kit

IV Appendixes

Foreword

by Rick Denny, Director of Product Marketing, OZ Interactive

At start-ups, like OZ Interactive (a six-year-old start-up), it's easy to get caught up in a rat-a-tat series of deadlines: products to ship, worlds to build, demos to perform.

Every once in a while, usually on a Friday evening over beer, we try to remember the big picture. Collectively, with baby steps, we are starting to build the Metaverse. In 5, 10, 20, or 50 years, we'll look back on this period with wonder and amusement over the new Microsofts and Edsels that are being created now.

3-D will change the face of not just the World Wide Web, but of the world itself. Social 3-D over the Internet—VRML and its extensions—is the first step towards full-on virtual reality for everyone, at least everyone who can afford it. Animating texture-mapped spheres in VRML will no longer be cool (at least not after your first time). It's not just that things need to look and sound good; that's just the minimum.

We are entering a time when people will ask, maybe only once, "what's it good for?" The challenge is to harness the vast creativity of people and companies to create not just killer content, but entertainment, utility, community. A cool world, like a pretty Web site, ages faster than a super-model if there's nothing to do or learn, no one to meet, play or work with, nothing that changes and causes you to change.

So, as you learn about the concepts discussed in *Building VRML Worlds*, and learn to use the tools on this CD, reserve a few clock cycles of your CPU to think about what kind of world you want to build. As we say at OZ, what's your dream?

- A scripted, directed user experience like a real-time 3D movie?

- An anarchic free-for-all where participants are gods?

- A sentient world that develops according to its own scheme?

- A "just"or a "cruel" world?

Astound us, not only with your technical execution, but also with your creativity, vision, and humor. Infect us with your memes. And, most of all, have a blast—is there anywhere else you'd rather be?

Rick Denny
OZ Interactive

Acknowledgments

All of the authors would like to thank William Hurley and Don Parsons of Infinite Media for letting us borrow their Silicon Graphics Indy system for the chapter on that product. Thanks also to Mark Owens at WebMaster for his thoughts and ruminations about this project, and to Mark Meadows for his technical expertise on the early chapters.

Ed Tittel

Nobody ever does anything entirely by themselves. This is especially true when a book names four co-authors! Let me start by thanking this talented team of writers, programmers, and researchers, without whom this project could never have happened. Next, I'd like to thank my colleagues at LANWrights, Inc., the newly minted corporate version of our five-year-old company. Thanks, Dawn and Michael, for all your services in pulling this book together. Next, I'd like to thank the staff at Osborne, especially Megg Bonar, who helped get this project going and kept it on track when we got a little too close to the wall at one point. Finally, I'd like to thank my family for putting up with the distractions and disturbances of a home-based business while we chugged our way through the many worlds, virtual and real, that found their way into this book!

Claire Sanders

Thanks go to Shawn Gough and Sonia Feigenbaum for their support. Thanks to Brian for his inspiration. And special thanks to my family.

Charlie Scott

First, I would like to thank my wife Mary for letting me do another one. Special thanks to my co-authors Ed, Claire, and Paul, for their interest and insight into this book, and to Dawn Rader and the LANWrights staff for pulling everything together and reminding us of deadlines. Finally, thanks to the folks at OuterNet for being understanding when I came in late.

Paul Wolfe

I bow before my wife, Brenda, my sons, Nikolaus and Lukas, and the as yet undetermined fifth addition to the Wolfe family for their patience and support in the many nights away from home necessary to write this book. Thanks to Ed Tittel for cracking the whip, and Dawn Rader for her gentle reminders. To my OuterNet brothers, Mike Erwin, Sebastian Hassinger, and Charlie Scott, who have all labored hard to build a bullet-proof network, without which my contribution to this book would not be possible. Finally, to all those who assisted in gathering material for this book: Stan Ziel at Caligari for coming through in a pinch, Paragraph International (great app guys!), and all those who've endeavored to make virtual reality an Internet reality...

Introduction

Welcome to *Building VRML Worlds* (*BVW*)! In this book, we'll explore what we think is one of the most exciting new advances in Web technology—the Virtual Reality Modeling Language (VRML, pronounced "vermil" or "vee-arr-em-ell,"according to your taste). VRML offers Web designers an unparalleled opportunity to create three-dimensional environments for users to explore. It's entirely up to you whether those worlds resemble the one we've come to know in everyday life, or whether they resemble nothing like anyone has ever seen before.

Because the three-dimensional spaces you can build with VRML reside within a mathematical model on a computer, and may be rendered on computer display devices, we call them "virtual worlds," to distinguish them from the one we ordinarily occupy "in real life," as it were. As you learn more about the power and capability of VRML, and its rich representational capabilities, we believe you'll find the virtual worlds it can sustain every bit as absorbing and compelling as any other phenomenlogical world you might care to inhabit. In fact, if there's one thing we learned in researching this book, it's that there's no limit to the amount of time and energy these virtual worlds can consume, especially if you want to endow them with a sufficiently large and diverse population of spaces and objects.

We believe that you'll find VRML offers tremendous potential to expand the kinds of experiences you can provide to visitors to your Web site, and improve their ability to interact with your ideas, products, or information. Even though VRML is a relatively recent technology (it was born in 1993), a sufficient body of work and experience has been developed to permit us to identify good design principles, best implementation practices, and to identify a variety of platforms and budgets to pursue realizing your own virtual VRML worlds.

Thus, the aim of this book is twofold:

1. To provide sufficient background and information about VRML terminology and technology to enable you to understand its intellectual underpinnings, and exposure to design principles and

practices, to enable you to apply what you've learned to the act of construction.

2. To examine available software, including authoring environments and related construction equipment, and available resources, including predefined virtual objects, textures, and components, to help you decide not only what to construct, but how to go about the act of construction.

That's why you'll find us discussing particular software packages for popular desktop environments, including several varieties of MS Windows and the Macintosh, as possible alternatives for your work. In addition, we'll touch on higher-end systems and solutions, like those provided by Silicon Graphics, Inc. (a major contributor to the technology that underlies VRML), but more as an illustration of what's possible with VRML, rather than as a definite focus within this book.

How this Book Is Organized

The main body of *BVW* is divided into three parts, and includes a handful of appendixes and supplementary materials. The book also includes a CD-ROM which features some of the software that we discuss throughout its contents (especially Part 2, which deals with VRML software and related tools).

Part 1 is entitled "The Building Blocks of VRML." It's intended to provide background information on VRML, including its inception and development history, a discussion of terminology and technology related to thinking in three dimensions. This is followed by an examination of the VRML language itself, including its many reserved words, and the all-important set of relationships that must exist between objects within any VRML world. Part 1 concludes with a discussion of VRML design approaches, and covers the pros and cons of realism versus performance, the various foundations upon which a virtual world can rest, and explores the elements of good VRML style and execution.

Part 2 is entitled "The VRML Toolbox." It abandons the largely theoretical and abstract approach used in Part 1 in favor of an examination of the options for building VRML that are available for the most popular desktop platforms in use today. Starting with an exposition of the kinds of features and functions you should look for in any VRML tool, we establish a set of minimum requirements that any decent VRML development environment should support. In the chapters that follow, we examine Paragraph International's Home Space Builder, Caligari Corporation's Pioneer, Virtus Corporation's Walkthrough Pro and 3-D Web Space Builder, plus a set of server tools and related graphics development packages that support either the operation or development of VRML worlds. Throughout, the focus is on explaining each product's capabilities, and exploring its installation and use.

Part 3, entitled "A Self-Extending VRML Resource Kit," builds on the foundation created in Part 2, and covers a variety of extensions, add-ins, and component sources suitable for enriching the content of any VRML world. Beginning with an examination of texture tools, used to imbue the surfaces of 3-D objects with realistic or fanciful visual characteristics, you'll learn about techniques to improve and enhance the looks of any virtual world. From there, we explore a variety of VRML and other 3-D object libraries, then explore what's involved in bringing VRML and the World Wide Web together. We conclude this section, and the book, with a guided tour of some stunning VRML Web sites, and a discussion of what makes VRML sites so compelling to end users.

The various appendixes to *BVW* are intended to document its contents, and to provide additional pointers to other resources. We've included a comprehensive Glossary that provides definitions for the many technical terms you'll find in this tome, as well as expansions of its numerous acronyms. To help you obtain additional information about products and services, we've included a comprehensive vendor list. Finally, we include a comprehensive index of the book, to help you locate information by keyword or concept.

Conventions Used in This Book

Wherever possible, we've tried to flag important or noteworthy elements in the text of the chapters. To that end, we've incorporated some catchy icons to call attention to a variety of tips, tricks, warnings, and potential gotchas throughout.

TIP   *The Tip icon is meant to alert you to the presence of a potential time- or effort-saving pointer in the text that it accompanies. This will flag recommendations for best practices, improved ease of use, and effective applications of tools or techniques.*

REMEMBER   *The Remember icon is meant to inform you that certain common behaviors (things you might do, unless instructed otherwise) or omissions (things you might neglect to do, unless forewarned) may have unintended consequences. When you see this icon, it's intended that you should pause and reflect on its accompanying information: it could save you time, trouble, or lost work at some point in the future!*

WARNING *The Warning icon is meant to alarm you! It's placed only where there's a possibility that dire consequences could result from ignoring its admonitions. When you see this one, you'd better pay attention!*

As far as wayfinding tools go, we strongly recommend using the Table of Contents to locate major topics of interest, or discussions of those elements where you seek general information or enlightenment. When it comes to dealing with specific terms or concepts, we suggest using the Glossary for definitions, and the Index to help you locate specific references within the text of the book.

How to Use This Book

BVW has been constructed to act both as a reference and a guide to VRML. For those with little experience in this area, we'd recommend reading Parts 1 and 3 in their entirety, with an exploration of Part 2 as it pertains to your desktop of choice. If you're interested in purchasing a desktop specifically for VRML development, however, a sequential read of Part 2 will make good sense.

As you acquaint yourself with the subject matter of VRML, and begin your own development experiments, we believe you'll find the book useful as a source of inspiration and experiment during the learning process. During this phase, we believe you'll find Chapters 2 and 4 quite useful, since the former lays out the structure of VRML as a language, and the latter covers the basics of good VRML design and coding style. Likewise, you should find the chapter in Part 2 that covers your development tool set of great interest. We've deliberately constructed Part 3 so that it can explain VRML add-ins and related tools for anyone, and have included discussions of building related Web sites to make your work easy to bring to others. You should find the sites on our VRML tour in Chapter 14 a constant source of inspiration, at all phases of your involvement with VRML.

Once you've familiarized yourself with VRML and your tools, Chapter 3 should help you import materials from other sources into your virtual worlds. Also, Part 3 should remain a constant source of information for embellishments and improvements to your creations, as you build on your initial efforts to create more full-blown, interactive spaces for your users to visit.

We sincerely hope you'll find our efforts to be both informative and entertaining. To make sure they're as clear and accurate as possible, we welcome your feedback on any and all of its contents. Feel free to e-mail any of the authors with your comments and criticisms (you'll find all our addresses in the "About the Authors" section). Or, write us care of the publisher, Osborne/McGraw-Hill at 2600 Tenth Street, Berkeley, CA, 94710, USA. We will respond to all mail, and thank you in advance for your feedback!

Using the CD-ROM

We've tried to include as much useful material and software about VRML as possible on the CD-ROM that accompanies this book. We approached all the vendors whose products we mentioned in the book for demonstration copies of their software; many of them were kind enough to oblige us by granting permission to reproduce their materials on the CD. You'll find a page near the back of this book (opposite the CD-ROM itself) entitled "About the CD-ROM" that covers these materials in detail; right now, we only want to alert you to its presence and tantalize you with some discussion of its contents.

In addition to a set of subdirectories that contain software, organized by vendor name, you'll also find a small set of HTML documents on the CD. Using any Web browser that can open local files (either Netscape Navigator or MS Internet Explorer should work admirably), you can point it at the CD-ROM drive, and open the document named bvw.htm. This provides a brief description of the CD's contents, and includes pointers to a hotlist of all the URLs we mention in the book, plus a set of links to the source code and software elements elsewhere on the CD-ROM. In short, we provided these documents to give you a simple, easy way to explore its contents, and to visit the many Web sites we mention throughout the book.

Where to Go from Here

Since it's your book, that's entirely up to you. If you're a relative newcomer to VRML, you could do worse than sitting down and reading Part 1 in its entirety. If you're already familiar with the terms and technology related to VRML, skip around to your heart's content. Once you start developing, we hope you'll make this book a part of your reference arsenal, ready to assist with pointers, design tips and techniques, and development advice.

Whatever you do, we insist you try your best to enjoy yourself. With an exciting and appealing medium like VRML, this should be pretty easy to do!

part 1

The Building Blocks of VRML

ELCOME to the introductory section of *Building VRML Worlds*. In this section, we cover a broad variety of topics ranging from general VRML information to VRML language specifics. This section begins with Chapter 1, "An Introduction to VRML," which covers VRML's history and evolution, talks about VRML's precursor systems and formats, and examines the selection of Open Inventor as base format. After a thorough review of VRML's past, we move on to take a look at VRML's relation to the Web and the need for specialized browsers or plug-ins to view VRML worlds. Chapter 1 concludes with an in-depth foray into the VRML specifications, including: VRML 1.0, VRML+, VRML 1.1, and VRML 2.0.

From there, we move on to Chapter 2, "Thinking in 3-D," which explains the basics of three-dimensional graphics development, including origins, coordinate systems, solids modeling, wireframe modeling, and rendering techniques. After we cover the basics, we investigate how to start "moving" in 3-D, through the coverage of VRML orientation and translation. We also explore 3-D objects, from points to polygons, and frames to surfaces. Then, we take a look at the brighter and darker sides of VRML programming by examining the various methods to produce light and shading in a VRML world, including: directional lights, spotlights, point lights, rendering, flat shading, Gouraud shading, Phong shading, and raytracing. Finally, Chapter 2 concludes with an overview of textures and texture mapping.

Next, in Chapter 3, "The Basics of VRML Files," we examine the use of VRML as a MIME type, the VRML file header, comments in VRML files, and the VRML coordinate system. Chapter 3 concludes with thorough coverage of nodes, the true building blocks of VRML. Node topics cover node structure, the parent-child relationship, instancing, and an overview of node types, including shape nodes, geometry nodes, material nodes, transformation nodes, camera nodes, lighting nodes, and group nodes.

Part 1 closes out with Chapter 4, "Creating Good VRML." In this chapter, we explore some specific ways to successfully serve up VRML at your site, including: how to keep file sizes to a minimum, how to create worlds that neither neglect the low-end user nor insult the users with powerful systems. We also explore the pros and cons of WWWInline, explain how to avoid creating "movie set" worlds that look good from only one point-of-view, and, most important, how to make your world functional rather than just cool.

building

VRML

World

chapter 1

An Introduction to VRML

V

IRTUAL Reality Modeling Language (VRML) is one of the hottest, most promising technologies around. Using VRML allows you to create navigable, hyperlinked 3-D spaces (called "worlds") on the World Wide Web. VRML has quickly joined the ranks of Java and HTML as an essential Web technology and has been heralded as a catalyst to lead the Web's next stage of evolution. People have been fascinated by VRML's potential to stretch the boundaries and definitions of cyberspace since its introduction in 1994 and by the way that it will allow us to restructure our relationship with the Web.

Although VRML is not the only technology that allows spatialization of the Internet, it's regarded as today's most promising one. The radical possibilities that this technology opens for computer use, and for human interactions, are both wild and wonderful. In this book, we'll take you on a tour of what these worlds hold, and give you the tools and resources that enable their creation.

How VRML Can Change Your Web Experience

The Web's foundation is built around the Uniform Resource Locator (URL), which is usually a string of indecipherable pseudo-words (these can be particularly daunting for neophytes). But with VRML, the Web is significantly more tangible and directions to a site can be given in much more human terms, such as "take a right past the lobby and walk into the mirror bordered by pink flamingoes." As Mark Pesce, one of VRML's creators, says, "Information made sensual makes sense." VRML succeeds at putting information navigation into a sensual realm.

VRML has the sizzling power to allow 3-D Web navigation through a virtual body. The ramifications that spring from this are definitely ground-breaking and perhaps even somewhat overwhelming: The language's 3-D faculties are seen as an entree into an entirely new dimension of the Web's potential to promote human interaction. In addition, VRML's ability to present a convincing graphical take on the online world will make the Web more accessible, more visually stimulating, and more realistic. Tomorrow's Web may be written largely in VRML, allowing its users to navigate through its resources minus the need for an interface as we know it.

For example, when you walk into an Italian restaurant in a Moving Worlds scene, you'll see much of what you do In Real Life (IRL)—tables, chairs, mood lighting, people, bottles of wine, an espresso machine, etc. This scene is described in the VRML file in terms of polygons and 3-D coordinates. When you download a file to your local machine, your VRML browser determines what the restaurant should look like from the perspective of your location, and it renders the view multiple times per second, so it changes constantly, just as IRL. The content of Moving Worlds scenes isn't predetermined; what transpires can depend on your action. If you want a nice glass of Chianti in the restaurant, touching the wine bottle can launch a Java applet that lets you hear the wine splashing gently into your glass and see the rosy glow it emanates as it's being poured. The way these changes transpire differs from other 3-D formats like QuickTime VR, in which a scene's content is predetermined and your movement only allows you to look at different parts of the file. Because VRML files are the most compact type of multimedia files that can be added to Web sites, navigating through them quickly is also efficient.

Although VRML's critics chide it for trying to take a 2-D viewing screen experience into the third dimension, the Webbed interactivity that VRML promises can't be paralleled by classic VR technology, replete with pounds of headgear.

In this chapter, we'll cover the elements of VRML that make it such an welcome addition to the Web. We'll give you an overview of how VRML came into existence, the various stages of its development, descriptions of its browsers and plug-ins, and ideas about where VRML will lead the future of cyberspace.

If you want to explore VRML on your own before you continue reading, try the following important VRML Web sites.

The original VRML Web site:

```
http://vag.vrml.org/www-vrml/
```

The large and valuable VRML Repository:

```
http://www.sdsc.edu/vrml/
```

VRML from HELL's monster link resource:

```
http://www.well.com/user/caferace/vrml.html
```

Construct's ultra-cool site:

```
http://www.construct.net
```

Bob Crispen's VRML page:

```
http://fly.hiwaay.net/~crispen/vrml/
```

The VRML FAQ:

```
http://www.vrml.org
```

ZD3D Terminal Reality:

```
http://www.zdnet.com/~zdi/vrml/
```

Pondering VRML

VRML can be regarded as a catalyst for a third wave of computing. Computing's first wave, centered around industrial production and control systems that promoted greater corporate productivity, began around 1955 and lasted until 1980. The advent of the IBM PC in 1981 and the subsequent release of the Apple Lisa, succeeded in eradicating the barriers that had kept computing apart from individuals during the first wave. The personal computers of the 80s represented an entirely new watermark in accessibility and allowed users to manipulate data through much friendlier techniques. With this new freedom came the realization that computers could be used for sensory stimulation, mental recreation, and entertainment. The development of this orientation toward the computer has been seminal in fostering the growth of technologies like VRML, which take computer users beyond the personal, toward collective experiences.

VRML and similar technologies that use computers to enter another dimension of perception and, therefore, another construct of reality, are both exciting and provocative. As Mark Pesce, VRML's co-creator, says in *VRML: Browsing and Building Cyberspace*, "The power of VRML lies in its abilities to create a bridge between the two primary methods of human communication: cerebral imagination and visceral sensation." One of the hottest issues centering around VRML today is how these powers will be used in the future. By allowing you to experience interactive virtuality in three dimensions, VRML is flushed with one of today's most radical technological potentials.

Pesce characterizes VRML 2.0 as being "all about interactivity"—that is, how objects in VRML worlds can affect and be affected by other objects or external applications.[1] In VRML worlds, the "objects" he mentions can be people as easily as things, and these people or things can interact with each other in realms that have never before existed.

The ability to sensually, emotionally, quickly, transform yourself into another thing, person, or place, and be able to experience from that perspective is beginning to exist. Although the results are still crude at this point, using a VRML browser such as WorldView gives you the power to create your own avatar (a graphical representation of your persona), determine its characteristics, talk in its voice, and interact with others through its perspective. Transforming into another identity has never been easier or more intriguing.

We are undoubtedly tapping into potential our ancestors could only have conceived in terms of magic or supernatural power. Pesce, an avowed pagan, recognizes VRML's connection with magic and recognizes cyberspace and magical space exist in the realm of the imagination, where their spaces are constructed by the individual's beliefs and thoughts. This site features an article chronicling VRML's importance in the technopagan belief structure:

```
http://www.eor.com/pages/ftp/Techpgns.htm
```

How VRML Works

VRML operates in accordance with the general Web browser-server setup. The browser sends requests to a server, which ideally returns the requested document, complete with its Multipurpose Internet Mail Extension (MIME) type. If the server is configured correctly, it will detect that VRML documents

1. Pesce, Mark. "VRLM 2.0: For Living, Breathing, Moving Worlds." *Web Developer* 2, no. 2 (May/June 1996): 25.

have an associated MIME type of "x-world/x-vrml." The browser parses this content type and, as long as it has access to a VRML helper application or plug-in, displays the VRML scene. A VRML world's components don't have to be kept on a single server; it's OK to have parts of a scene at different servers and locations (in fact, for performance reasons, it's often more efficient to distribute them this way).

A VRML document describes geometric models and these models' relationships and properties within that document. VRML objects are called *nodes*. Nodes, which could be considered the building blocks of VRML, are used to describe how a document's 3-D objects should be shaped, what its properties are, and how it should move or be grouped. Nodes are employed to represent texture, lighting, rotation, scale, positioning, geometry, and perspective data, which is called a scene description. Nodes can include MIDI sound data, JPEG images, and (importantly) links to other items on the Internet, including VRML documents. This ability to link to other VRML sites provides the opportunity for 3-D Web travel.

note   *VRML's initial release contained some limitations (such as a lack of interpolators or API bindings) that made segments of the Web community question whether or not it would realize its hype. Although VRML 2.0 doesn't fully realize the language's potential, its innovations (as well as those that it's inspired) have somewhat placated those doubts. In addition to VRML 1.0's lack of interpolators or API bindings, its browsers were infested with bugs and its graphics were on the crude side (especially on machines that weren't state-of-the-art graphics workstations). VRML 2.0, though, is a different story. VRML 2.0 features interactive behaviors for 3-D objects, is powered by scripting abilities (priming it for collaboration with Java), and its more sophisticated syntax provides a welcome increase in descriptive capabilities. In addition, its navigation is significantly smoother, and it runs more efficiently and effectively.*

The real-time multi-interaction that this new version brings is eagerly awaited because the cyberspace contact it promises to deliver will be the most "realistic" to date. VRML 2.0's interactive behaviors enable you to "see" other participants in a chat room or a MOO—or whatever identity they use to represent themselves (MOOs, like MUDs and MUCKs, are real-time interactive, text-based fantasy lands that transpire over the Net—watch for their popularity to combine powerfully with VRML). In addition, the choices of VRML browsers, plug-ins, and development tools continue to become more and more impressive, as do Web galleries that feature VRML creations.

If you're expecting video game or slick CD-ROM quality from VRML files you download from the Web, don't. Although VRML's potential is enormous, even its most rabid devotees admit it is in its infancy and the best is yet to come. Expect to encounter bugs—many of the files you'll find will not have been thoroughly tested with all the available VRML browsers (especially the few Macintosh ones) and may cause the occasional crash. But, hey, that's part of the excitement of being involved with such new technology!

At the viewing end, the vantage point of a VRML browser is similar to that of a camera's eye. Most VRML browsers feature joystick-type controls, handlebars, or directional buttons. It's also possible to navigate simply by dragging and clicking the mouse through the VRML scene. Clicking your mouse on a link loads the corresponding document, whether it be audio, video, or an HTML page. If you select a link that requires a helper application, the viewer will bring up the necessary program (provided the proper association exists, of course).

VRML currently still works best on high-end graphics machines (which is probably one of the reasons it's a darling of the companies that make them). If you don't have a modem that's 28.8 or faster, or at least 16 MB of RAM, expect your VRML experience to be slow, jagged, and buggy. Although browsers and their plug-ins have increased in number and in quality for most platforms, only scant capability still exists on the Macintosh, especially for non-PowerPC users.

Comparing HTML and VRML

If the distinction between HTML and VRML is still a little blurry, perhaps this list will lend some clarity:

- VRML was designed as a common visual and graphics delivery system for the Web. HTML's role is similar, but deals primarily with textual data.

- Both VRML and HTML are written in plain text and provide descriptions, not representations of formats and layouts.

- HTML is pretty easy to code by hand, but it's difficult to code VRML without an authoring tool (although it is possible to do so). The reasons behind this aren't too complex—VRML produces graphical objects through numbers and text, while HTML uses text alone to create its textual documents.

- HTML displays graphics and text in 2-D, while VRML documents work against a 3-D background.

Here are some examples of VRML's manifold uses:

■ **Music**   Imagine how it will change your perception of music to *walk* through a musical composition. Debussy never dreamed of this kind of ambient setting. Check out Bluebonnetspace to see how audio files can be converted into VRML:

`http://www.ar.utexas.edu/students/graf/bluebonnet/bonnet.html`

■ **Urban Planning and Architecture**   With VRML, cities and buildings can be planned, examined, and experimented upon. Builders and architects can easily realize their ideas in 3-D space without ever breaking ground, with obvious environmental benefits.

■ **Virtual Shopping**   The ability to examine a product from 3-D angles before buying is appealing to many consumers. As our "concrete infrastructure" becomes increasingly clogged, shopping in VRML may become preferable to driving to a mall.

■ **Art**   The possibility to create entire worlds in VRML takes artistic expression into a new realm. Artists can now represent the intricacies of their minds in 3-D and lead viewers through a trip that can restructure perceptions of "art." Translating existing artworks into VRML gives them a completely different orientation, as evidenced at this site, where you can navigate through works from Dali, Miro, and Van Gogh:

`http://www.lindenmedia.com/web/vrml/vrml.htm`

This site, the Abulafia VRML Gallery, contains VRML pieces:

`http://www.cgrg.ohio-state.edu/~mlewis/Gallery/gallery.wrl`

The Arc VRML Gallery is a 3-D representation of 1995's Interactive Media Festival:

`http://www.construct.net/gallery95/`

■ **Entertainment**   This is one of the most obvious realms for VRML development (and don't think the sex and gambling industries are unaware, either). Games take on completely new meanings when coupled with interactivity, not to mention other forms of distraction. Here's a rather benign VRML mystery game:

```
http://www.itp.tsoa.nyu.edu/~student/yorbClass/Web/hotel/
```

■ **Virtual Communities** Mark Pesce's dream of creating a "space" on the Web that feels real and human has been enthusiastically received by denizens of online "places" (such as MOOs and MUDs). Although such interfaces are still on the cheesy side, the possibilities for character creation (and transformation) and interaction with others in these spaces are truly enthralling. Worlds Chat is one of the first multiuser communities (it sported over 10,000 users at press time)—investigate it at:

```
http://www.worlds.net/products/wchat/index.html
```

■ **Geographical Navigation** VRML allows its users to visit and trek through all kinds of locations. This means you could walk through a national park before you book a camping reservation or examine a mountain's trails before you climb it.

■ **Education** The profoundly powerful idea of VRML use in education has barely begun to germinate. While virtual classrooms have yet to be widely implemented, VRML can already be used at an obvious, pragmatic level. For example, students who squirm at the idea of dissecting a frog or cat need never be disgusted again; VRML allows such tasks to be "realistically" undertaken, with no blood or unnecessary loss of life. In more complex realms, a great deal of scientific research exists that can use VRML's capacities. Chemistry is one field that's eagerly espoused VRML's modeling abilities. The VRML Chemistry site at:

```
http://ws05.pc.chemie.th-darmstadt.de/vrml/
```

is one example.

The CSSJ Software World page contains a section on "VRML in Chemistry" that contains links to several interesting scientific applications using VRML:

```
http://cssj.chem.sci.hiroshima-u.ac.jp/ftp/indexe.html
```

You can learn the American Sign Language Alphabet in VRML:

```
http://holodeck.gsfc.nasa.gov/sign/sign.html
```

This site contains information about the Egyptian tomb of Menna, as well as a VRML model of the tomb:

```
http://reality.sgi.com/employees/nigelj_manchester/Mattz/
```

Walk through chunks of the galaxy by downloading this site's VRML astronomy models:

```
http://imagelib.ncsa.uiuc.edu/imagelib/VRMLHighlights.html
```

- **Online Conferencing** The new interactivity of VRML 2.0 readies future venues for telecommunication (although it's really VRML 3.0 that's expected to make it viable). This possibility has not been overlooked by the telecommunications industry, which is already developing "virtual phone booths."

- **Network Mapping** VRML 2.0's interactivity brings the possibility of network mapping in 3-D because objects can now run their own Java scripts in response to events. Just think—with a little headgear, flying through a network and checking for problems might be fun!

- **Instruction Manuals** Assembling a complicated piece of equipment will be considerably simpler when you can hit a button and see its components assemble themselves in 3-D.

Here are some additional URLs that should give some great ideas about VRML's many implementations.

Clay Graham of SGI's Virtual Architecture page takes your mind on a trip:

```
http://reality.sgi.com/employees/clay/virarch.html
```

Multimedia Gulch is San Francisco's foray into virtualhood:

```
http://www.hyperion.com/planet9/vrsoma.htm
```

Here's MIT's Urban Planning and Design in Cyberspace site:

```
http://alberti.mit.edu/arch/4.207/homepage.html
```

VRML's History and Evolution

VRML's germination occurred in 1994 at the initial W3 conference in Geneva, Switzerland. Tim Berners-Lee, the visionary creator of the Web, had become intrigued by Mark Pesce's programming work and invited him to present his paper entitled "Cyberspace." The article explained a prototype VRML browser called Labyrinth, which he and Tony Parisi, another programmer, had finished writing in January of 1994. Pesce, who had been kicked out of MIT in the early 1980s, was a programmer with a mystical bent who found intrigue in William Gibson's ideas about the existence of space in virtual worlds in his sci-fi classic, *Neuromancer*. "Cyberspace" reflects Pesce's desire to realize Gibson's idea of a "consensual hallucination" in 3-D worlds on the Web.

Lots of buzz occurred at that W3 conference about Labyrinth, because it was the first interface able to render 3-D on the Web. It was there VRML assumed its acronym, which, at the time, stood for "Virtual Reality Markup Language" (it was changed several months later to "Virtual Reality Modeling Language," because this was a more accurate description of its function). The paper met with such enthusiasm that a mailing list—*www-vrml*—was created for further discussion; Brian Behlendorf, the technical brains behind HotWired, arranged to have some of *Wired*'s computer space donated to the VRML development effort. Pesce served as the list's moderator and drafted the first VRML requirements document. Over a thousand subscribers joined in the first week; this group was ultimately responsible for debating and deciding many of VRML's components. If you're interested in viewing the list's archives, they're available at:

```
http://vag.vrml.org/www-vrml/
```

The *www-vrml* list proved a seminal part of VRML's development. Gavin Bell, a programmer at Silicon Graphics, Inc., was an important voice in the VRML community and a leading advocate of adopting Open Inventor as the official VRML file format. The question about format was crucial and one that garnered considerable debate. Some members of the list wanted an entirely fresh format created for the new technology but others, like Pesce, were convinced that VRML had a better shot at success if its specification was described by an existing graphics file format, rather than one developed specifically for VRML. The ideal structure was conceived of as being accessible, analogous to HTML, and capable of meeting professional 3-D designers' demands.

In fact, SGI's Open Inventor was ultimately selected (Pesce and Parisi credit Bell for having done much of the technical writing for the ensuing VRML 1.0 spec), but it did meet with some competition before being chosen. Here are descriptions of the other file formats considered, followed by a description of the Open Inventor format.

Cyberspace Description Format

Cyberspace Description Format (CDF) is a VRML proposal from VR hotshots Autodesk, who created AutoCAD, the leading 3-D software design tool. CDF is based on its Cyberspace Development Kit, and although it has many more extensions than VRML, its basic structure is similar. Both VRML and CDF are declarative rather than procedural, meaning they aren't algorithms that create virtual worlds, but rather they describe them. CDF is platform-independent, expandable, syntactically concise, and object-oriented. One of CDF's most intriguing features is its ability to delegate the parsing of various file formats, including OOGL, Open Inventor, DXF, and 3-D Studio.

A File Format for the Interchange of Virtual Worlds

A File Format (AFF) for the Interchange of Virtual Worlds sports a format fairly similar to VRML's existing specifications, although it isn't as detailed. AFF has specific tags that actually compose a 3-D virtual world by functioning as texture maps, materials, shapes, etc. AFF's ASCII format ensures it's platform-independent, readable by humans, and transmissible through a variety of means, including network delivery, e-mail, and applications via TCP/IP. AFF was proposed in May 1994, by Kerry Bonin and Bernie Roehl; a draft of its proposal is available at:

```
http://www.immersive.com
```

Labyrinth-VRML Specification Version 1.3.1

Mark Pesce and Tony Parisi saw the Labyrinth working specification as a simple language to describe polygons. They didn't believe it was sufficiently complex to accomplish all they wanted VRML to do; so basically, it acts as a parsing algorithm for the VRML files that drive a VRML browser's engine. Labyrinth's 1.3.1 working specification is available at:

```
http://vag.vrml.org/www-vrml/proposals/labspec.html
```

Web OOGL

The Object-Oriented Graphics Language (OOGL) for the World Wide Web was created at the University of Minnesota's Geometry Center. Its textual file format permits geometric visualization of mathematics, engineering, and physics, and it has a fairly straightforward, simple syntax. Many elements of its syntax, such as color control, textures, polygons, and its hierarchical structure, overlap with VRML. Included in the OOGL proposition is the idea URLs from anywhere on the Web can be accessed to create a VRML world. The Geometry Center offers a free browser for Web OOGL, which is a nonproprietary format. Its specification can be found at:

```
http://www.geom.umn.edu/software/geomview/docs/ooglman.html
```

and additional information on Geomview can be accessed at:

```
http://www.geom.umn.edu/software/geomview/docs/geomview_toc.html
```

Manchester Scene Description Language (MSDL)

The Manchester Scene Description Language (MSDL) was created to facilitate portability between applications used by graphic developers, as well as to reduce redundancy. Initially coded for UNIX, MSDL has also been ported to DOS. MSDL, which fundamentally parallels VRML, is actually used at the University of Manchester, giving it some real-world exposure that several of the other contenders didn't have. The MSDL is available at:

```
ftp://ftp.mcc.ac.uk/pub/cgu/MSDL
```

Multitasking Extensible Messaging Environment (Meme)

Multitasking Extensible Messaging Environment, or Meme, from Immersive Systems, Inc., is an interactive development package that runs solely on DOS systems with 80386 processors or better. With Meme, programmers can create virtual worlds, which can then be acted within. Meme's programming language is similar to VRML in the sense the virtual worlds are created by "modules" written by programmers. These modules can then be created and loaded when you're in a certain world. In Meme, users also use "cyberspace deck modules" (a term lifted from William Gibson's science fiction) to provide the code for I/O devices and interact with the created environment.

Unlike some other VR languages, Meme was built from the bottom up for networked, multi-user virtual worlds. Meme's overview can be examined at:

```
http://www.immersive.com
```

And the Winner: Open Inventor (OI)

Although many anticorporate hackers were savagely disappointed when Silicon Graphics Inc.'s Open Inventor (OI) was chosen as the basis for VRML, Pesce believed it was the correct choice. He was convinced OI's established status ensured a strong user base, which would translate into market success. Joining with OI made VRML instantly reach mainstream areas of the market that might have otherwise been missed. SGI was similarly excited about the union because a boom in 3-D development would benefit the company.

Open Inventor is an object-oriented 3-D tool kit, which lets you control objects like trackballs, cubes, materials, polygons, cameras, and text through its programming libraries. Its file format supports complete descriptions of 3-D scenes with lighting, ambient properties, polygonally rendered objects, and realism effects. OI's ASCII file format gives it the power to work seamlessly with HTML. At the demand of Pesce and other democratically inclined Netizens, SGI agreed to place OI in the public domain. This means anyone can use Open Inventor without having to pay royalties or worry about lawsuits.

Here are some of OI's most important characteristics:

- Window system and platform-independent
- Allows high-performance object picking
- Supports PostScript printing
- Built on top of OpenGL
- Defines a standard file format for 3-D data interchange
- Encourages the creation of new customized objects
- Makes a simple event model viable for 3-D interaction

The following site contains a summary created by and for members of the *www-vrml* mailing list of *The Inventor Mentor*, a book written by Josie Wernecke, which explains how OI is used to program object-oriented, 3-D graphics.

```
http://www.sgi.com/Technology/Inventor/VRML/TIMSummary.html
```

The VRML 1.0 Specification

After Open Inventor was accepted, it was tweaked into what we now recognize as the VRML 1.0 specification. Its creators crafted it for platform independence, extensibility, and the ability to work well over low-bandwidth connections. Clearly, VRML was designed as a standalone language, not merely as an HTML extension. VRML demands a more finely tuned network than HTML, it employs a greater number of servers than HTML, and its worlds consist of many more inline objects. Because HTML is already an accepted standard, with implementations to match, VRML 1.0's developers steered away from intermingling the design processes of the two languages. By declaring independence from HTML, VRML also protects itself against automatic failure should HTML someday be superseded.

VRML 1.0's creators had to decide between excluding interactivity from VRML 1.0 or making it cross-platform compatible. Because the Web wasn't interactive, they decided VRML's first version didn't have to be interactive either, although they always anticipated interactivity for the second version. Languages that describe interactive behaviors are complex, especially given the issues inherent in network communication.

In fact, Pesce and other developers thought using an existing language with the capacity to express such behaviors might prompt a "language war," which would impede development. Leaving out interactivity made VRML 1.0 more streamlined and easier to implement. Installing a VRML viewer without interactive behaviors is easier than installing one that includes them. Although this was the most criticized element of the technology, it's been fixed in VRML 2.0 by the inclusion of Java. Even though VRML 1.0 doesn't support interactivity, users' virtual worlds can contain objects that hyperlink to HTML documents, VRML worlds, or valid MIME types. Through the use of authoring tools, these worlds can be created without knowledge of a complex programming language. VRML 1.0's linking out feature (WWWAnchor) parallels the function of the HREF anchor in HTML. Another one of the language's critical features is the level of detail (LOD), which allocates the right amount of data to an object, based on its placement in the scene or on the browser's rendering capabilities.

VRML 1.0, unlike its successor, is completely ASCII-oriented and, therefore, restricted to control characters and 127 symbols. This limitation is problematic for non-Roman languages, such as Chinese and Japanese, because they employ thousands of different characters. VRML 1.0's lack of standards for browsers dealing with avatars proved another problem—browsers represented avatars with a great deal of (unwanted) variation.

From its inception, VRML 1.0 was perceived as a minimal starting point. This is recognized in its specification at this site:

```
http://vag.vrml.org/vrml10c.html
```

The History Continues . . .

The second WWW conference, in November 1994, witnessed the presentation of VRML 1.0. Many segments of the Web community, including vendors and distributors, were quite enthusiastic about VRML's potential (thoroughly unveiled by SGI's 2.2 billion dollar marketing machine). VRML even merited a cover story from *Newsweek*.

Parisi founded his own company, Intervista, after the conference and he began building WorldView, the first VRML browser. SGI announced its VRML browser, WebSpace, in April 1995. By that summer, 17 companies, including Netscape, NEC, Spyglass, and DEC, had announced support for VRML. In August 1995, the VRML Architecture Group (VAG) was founded in an attempt to bring structure and focus to the ideas being bounced around in the *www-vrml* mailing list. The VAG's members were selected from leading VR and Internet companies, as well as from mailing list leaders. The VAG's goal is to foster consensus within the VRML community. Initially, VAG was most concerned with technical design but, at its second meeting in October 1995, its members decided to shift their focus to process guidance. From this shift came a Request-For-Proposals (RFP) for a new version, called VRML 2.0.

The VRML and Java communities' initial rendezvous occurred at the Third W3 conference in 1996, where both entities clearly saw a collaboration would be mutually beneficial. Fusing the two technologies would endow VRML with much coveted interactivity, while bringing 3-D capabilities to Java. The Moving Worlds specification recognizes VRML's need for Java and is primed to fully incorporate its power.

For an insider's glimpse at VRML's development and the role that sushi played, check out Rikk Carey's notes at:

```
http://webspace.sgi.com/Archive/Sushi/index.html
```

VRML +

IBM announced a VRML extension named VRML+ in August 1995. Although the company touted this extension as technology that would facilitate VRML's range of services, the technology behind this statement has yet to be presented. VRML+ was going to feature avatar-like "Digital Actors" in scenes and it promised support for the type of interactivity that VRML 2.0 incorporates. Little other information about VRML+ remains, although the *www-vrml* archives are sure to turn up some material for the interminably curious.

VRML 1.1

VRML 1.1 is a set of extensions to VRML 1.0, which were intended to extend the initial version's functionality. Slated for release in November 1995, the VRML 2.0 specification development progressed so quickly, these extensions were simply integrated into VRML 2.0. Extensions included multilingual text, audio support, and geometry enhancement, among other things.

VRML 2.0

In the summer of 1995, the VAG began creating a new set of specifications for VRML's next version and, as was just explained, these specifications—originally called VRML 1.1—were integrated into VRML 2.0. The VAG put out a RFP for VRML 2.0 in January 1995. They debated the merits of the six proposals (from Microsoft, IBM Japan, Apple, GMD, SGI, and Sun) that resulted from this call for about two months. Although all 2000 subscribers to the www-vrml and www-vrml-digest mailing lists were technically eligible to vote in the election, the VAG requested that only members who felt authentically qualified to make an informed decision cast votes. Only 300 members ultimately cast their ballots, and this group voted the Moving Worlds proposal in by a landslide. The VRML 2.0 specification, based on this proposal, became official in August 1996. The latest version is at:

```
http://vag.vrml.org/VRML2.0/
```

VRML 2.0's selected moniker (Moving Worlds) provides insight into what this release is about—literally moving our perception of what constitutes worlds, both inside and outside cyberspace. Moving Worlds is truly an evolution of VRML: It moves beyond simple geometry and introduces behavior, opening up a blank canvas for growth and experimentation. Like Open Inventor, Moving Worlds was created by Silicon Graphics and was also supported by a range of other companies, including Sony, Black Sun, Visual Software, Intervista Software, and Integrated Data Systems. SGI played its homecourt advantage well—and the fact that it offered a parser, a license-free standard, and a huge pre-existing user base didn't hurt, either.

VRML 2.0 won't work with a VRML 1.0 browser and it isn't backward-compatible with its predecessor. A program called **vrml1to2** will let you translate VRML 1.0 files into VRML 2.0. It works on SUN, IRIX 5.3, and Windows 95, and is available for download at:

```
http://vs.sony.co.jp/VS-E/works/util/vrml1to2E.html
```

While VRML 1.0 lacked interactivity, VRML 2.0 is defined by that very characteristic. When you enter a VRML 1.0 world, it's completely still, devoid of any noise or movement. Entering a Moving Worlds 'scape is a different experience because it allows you to interact and affect information, not just look at it.

VRML 2.0 solves VRML 1.0's problems with consistent representation of avatars by the addition of the NavigationInfo node. This new node nonambiguously defines the information that characterizes an avatar, so little cause for inaccurate representations exists. Despite this node, the Moving Worlds specification still lacked some elements used for specific avatar information than some of the other proposals offered. As the following section explains, there are both benefits and drawbacks to standardized avatars.

VRML 2.0 and Avatar Use

This Web page contains a proposal about VRML avatar standardization, written by members of Chaco Communications (distributors of the VRScout plug-in) and Worlds Inc., among others:

```
http://www.velocitygames.com/avatar/avatar.html
```

The proposal discusses the need for standard avatar descriptions in VRML worlds. Users of MOOs and MUDs (etc.) are familiar with the idea of a user profile. The authors of this proposal advocate the adoption of a standard avatar description so that users moving between worlds can carry identities with them; this would allow not only characteristics to be maintained between environments, but also "persistent" accompanying objects, such as pets. Standard descriptions would also enable avatars to be located easily with search engines, either by name or unique characteristics.

Not surprisingly, there's money to be made from people sticking with one identity that can be easily tracked in its journey across the Web's wires, and strategically hit up by savvy marketing tailored to demographics, established buying patterns, and other semi-private preferences. With an established identity, an avatar can also conduct electronic commerce transactions much more securely and conveniently—from the vendor's viewpoint.

So although the idea of avatar standardization may be useful at certain levels, it can also compromise the freedom of identity that so many Web explorers have found to be exhilarating and liberating.

Because ASCII was a hindrance for VRML 1.0, VRML 2.0 switches from ASCII encoding to UTF-8 (and has a new file header "#VRML V2.0 utf8"). The AsciiText node will be replaced with the Text node, which is more flexible. Other neat new nodes include the Fog node, which lets you dim the background lights and darken the scene for atmospheric conditions, and the Background node, which uses texture maps to create a more realistic meeting between ground and sky. For more information on new VRML 2.0 nodes, refer to Chapter 3.

VRML 2.0 offers support for Musical Instrument Digital Interface (MIDI), which is essential for the development of truly impressive VRML worlds. MIDI is the language of control codes that instructs a computer how sounds are to be played—it's the format for a great deal of music on the Web. MIDI files are ideal for use with VRML because they're compact. The possibilities of fully integrated sound capabilities for VRML worlds has limitless possibilities. New VRML browsers will probably include built-in support for spatialized audio, which can be controlled through a VRML 2.0 Script node. With the addition of audio, VRML worlds can lead their users into realms of synesthetic perception, intensifying their feelings of being in a different world.

The addition of *video streaming* to VRML is an important one, as well. With video streaming, you can "wrap" a video image onto an object. This capacity will be especially exciting when integrated with spatialized audio.

We're going to take a brief look at each of the proposals, then return to analyze why Moving Worlds emerged as the overwhelming winner.

ActiveVRML

ActiveVRML was Microsoft's proposal for VRML 2.0. The fact that Microsoft's leverage didn't translate into a win (this time) reflects the strong-minded essence of the VRML community who voted it down. Many VAG members found the proposal itself to be more appealing than the politics it enshrouded.

Here are some of ActiveVRML's chief proposals:

- Modeling of behaviors and interactions, which it calls *temporal modeling*

- Application of the power of the modeling principle to 2-D images and sound

- Recognition of VRML's rich, expressive language capabilities that need to be considered beyond the limitations of programming

Microsoft has removed its ActiveVRML reference manual from its site, and although this site is its supposed link to ActiveVRML information, there's little there:

```
http://www.microsoft.com/intdev/avr
```

This site contains more detail about the specification:

```
http://www.research.microsoft.com/research/graphics/elliott
/ActiveVRML/Essence.htm
```

Dynamic Worlds

The creators of the Dynamic Worlds proposal anticipated the acceptance of Moving Worlds as the VRML standard; however, they still submitted the Dynamic Worlds proposal to throw a little variety into the selection process.

The Dynamic Worlds proposal includes support for object reusability, arbitrary scripting languages, the interactive modeling of interactions and behavior, and special mechanisms to support shared interactions and behavior. It has added nodes such as Avatar, for character representation; Artifact, which represents entities or objects and replaces VRML 1.0's Separator node; and Behavior, which groups a set of behavior components.

Link here to read the Dynamic Worlds proposal:

```
http://wintermute.gmd.de:8000/vrml/dynamicWorlds.html
```

HoloWeb

HoloWeb was Sun's VRML 2.0 proposal. One of its most salient features is its limited support of geometry; it assumes that advanced 3-D authoring packages and digitizing services address the needs for complex 3-D geometry, and therefore support only compressed 3-D dots, textured triangles, lines, and text. By doing so, it acts as an efficient transporter of pre-created geometry (it uses 3-D geometry compression as a universal geometry format).

As the creator of Java, Sun was eager to see Java's run-time animation abilities incorporated into VRML, which this proposal neatly accomplishes. Since it uses Java as the animation language, no complex preprogrammed object behavior needs to be written. It includes a "simple set of low level preprogrammed behaviors," called *elemental animation operators*, as a foundation for building Java code.

The HoloWeb proposal also addresses avatar issues; users connect to HoloWeb worlds by "jacking in" to an AvatarSoul object. These objects are lower-level primitives that prompt applets to create plug-ins that act as user vehicles. AvatarSoul's locations are affected by TeleportTargets, which determine the viewing platform.

To read the HoloWeb proposal, venture here:

```
http://www.sunlabs.com/research/tcm/holoweb/holoweb.html
```

Out of this World

Out of this World's main characteristic is its file format—it's based on the 3-D Metafile Format, which is the specification that Apple's QuickDraw 3D (a cross-platform 3-D graphics API) employs. 3DMF supports all types of objects and geometries, as well as lights, textures, active renderers, cameras, material properties, shaders, and hierarchical information; it acts as a "container" for such information, and can include multimedia attributes as well. The 3DMF file format is significantly smaller than the Moving Worlds file format (or the VRML 1.0 file format), and effectively reduces the need for file compression. 3DMF is also backward-compatible with VRML 1.0—a nice feature that Moving Worlds lacks.

By not requiring VRML information to be presented as a processor-intensive Scene Graph, Out of this World saves memory and data jams. Its database is noncentralized, meaning that the browser isn't responsible for all parsing and communication with the VRML world. The browsers promulgated by this proposal are wholly dynamic, as they're automatically downloaded in tandem with the 3-D world. You're therefore always equipped with a totally fresh, updated browser for viewing your worlds. Of course, this fresh download also translates into an increase in download time.

See this site for additional information on Apple's proposal:

```
http://www.webmaster.com/horizonpr/apple/Out_Of_This_World.html
```

Reactive Virtual Environment

Unlike many of the other proposals, IBM Japan's VRML 2.0 proposal, Reactive Virtual Environment, doesn't support scripting languages. Arguing that scripts can be too burdensome for real-time rendering, RVE instead incorporates pragmatic scheduled motions. These scheduled motions can be altered through user interactions; RVE uses a model of events and *callbacks* (objects' reactions to particular events) to accomplish this feat. The world is therefore time-dependent; motion engines can be connected to fields' nodes to assign time-dependent behaviors.

Refer to this URL for additional information about RVE:

```
http://www.ibm.com.jp/trl/projects/rve/world.htm
```

Moving Worlds Emerges Victorious!

Moving Worlds is the only VRML 2.0 proposal influenced by the Web community at large. Microsoft and Apple's proposals hadn't been open to any outside collaboration, which didn't correspond well to the open spirit of VRML's history. Once Moving Worlds' initial specification was completed, it was posted on the Web and a discussion group was formed, enabling hundreds of companies and individuals to contribute feedback. This open forum gave Moving Worlds a huge advantage, both in terms of popularity and in development, and contributed to the support it received upon becoming the standard.

Moving Worlds' event model is an important part of its structure. Nodes in VRML worlds can generate events or events can perform actions upon nodes. Either way, the event model functions as a series of components that work together to create a virtual machine. This ability to trigger events through nodes is exciting, for it addresses actions, such as turning light switches on and off, that will make the worlds far more credible. Developers who want to create extremely complex behaviors have new options with VRML 2.0, which allows the provision of an interface between VRML and any programming language. Java is the obvious language to fill this slot, although Moving Worlds' team was sure to leave it open to languages and interfaces such as C++, OLE, Visual Basic, and others.

We cover the Moving Worlds specification in greater detail in Chapter 3; this SGI site takes you through a tour of Moving Worlds' various capabilities:

`http://reality.sgi.com/employees/frerichs_esd/im/mw_index.html`

This site, The SIGGRAPH Introduction to VRML 2.0, contains an extremely helpful tutorial:

`http://www.sdsc.edu/siggraph96vrml/`

Mark Pesce gave an interesting speech in Paris about the collective intelligence and the politics behind the VRML 2.0 specification process— link to it at:

`http://www.hyperreal.com/~mpesce/www5.html`

VRML and the Web: A Stellar Partnership

The connectivity the Web brings to VRML is a big part of the 3-D language's appeal. And the possibilities of interactivity and radical new perspectives VRML introduces to the Web will have a huge impact on the Web's future. The future success of the Web and of VRML are intimately connected; the question of how VRML will be used within the Web's structure is fascinating.

To view VRML on the Web, you must use either a VRML browser or a plug-in. VRML browsers are quite similar to their HTML counterparts; plug-ins are software programs that merge with a Web browser and provide extra features as if they were integrated into the host program. Plug-ins aren't a wholly new invention—crude plug-ins actually existed a decade ago for Lotus 1-2-3, and Adobe Photoshop's excellent plug-ins came into existence in the early 90s. Netscape astutely recognized Netscape Navigator 2.0 would benefit from plug-ins (as has Navigator's 3.0 version, which comes equipped with Live 3D for both Mac and Windows platforms). The proliferation of VRML plug-ins attests to the interest this technology commands.

The earliest browsers were oriented toward the UNIX camp (and func- tioned especially well on SGI machines), though development for the PC market was quick to follow.

VRML for the Macintosh

VRML development for the Macintosh has definitely lagged behind other platforms' development. But Macheads, take heart—VRML browsers and authoring tools for Macs are growing in number and in quality, and the marvelous MacVRML page exists as a reward for your suffering:

```
http://www.rain.org/~da5e/macvrml.html
```

Only several VRML browsers/plug-ins currently exist for the Macintosh (Whurlwind, Voyager, and VRML Equinox), although the ExpressVR plug-in as well as the Live 3D plug-in that accompanies Netscape Navigator 3.0 have made VRML viewing much easier for Mac users. Most VRML browsers are helper applications, meaning they operate in conjunction with a Web browser. VRML standalone browsers exist, although they're not very useful for Websurfing because you can only use them to view VRML content. By the time you read this, Netscape Navigator and Internet Explorer will probably have created completely adequate VRML plug-ins, which should eliminate any need for standalone VRML browsers.

Although recent VRML browsers are significantly more stable than their early prototypes, remember VRML is still a new technology. Because it's effecting an enormous amount of change and it is designed to be receptive to external enhancements, VRML appears somewhat unstable at times. The bottom line remains: Be prepared for bugs and crashes, especially when you're in beta territory! If you're able to use a test machine for such code, do so; if you must work on a production machine, be sure to make frequent backups!

This URL contains information and offers downloads for the entire range of VRML browsers and plug-ins:

```
http://www.sdsc.edu/vrml_repository/browsers.html
```

The VRML Update page features the latest information about VRML and includes an up-to-date table that compares browsers:

```
http://cedar.cic.net/~rtilmann/mm/vrmlup.htm
```

The following sections provide descriptions for a selection from the range of VRML browsers and plug-ins.

InterVista's WorldView

WorldView was the first standalone browser for Windows NT and Windows 95; InterVista also plans to develop a version for Power Macs. WorldView is a browser for the people (unlike most hardware-greedy browsers), and was created to run on a standard PC with only a 14.4 modem. WorldView requires at least a 50Mhz 80486, loaded with a minimum of 8 MB of RAM (12 MB is more realistic if you're using Windows 3.1 or 3.11; if you're using Windows 95, try 16 MB). WorldView is a standalone browser that can also be configured as a helper application to an HTML browser.

You can download WorldView from:

```
http://www.intervista.com
```

Cosmo Player

Cosmo Player has superseded WebSpace, the first commercially available 3-D viewer, as SGI's VRML browser. Cosmo, the first VRML 2.0 browser for the World Wide Web, is freely distributed by SGI, Open Inventor's creators. Cosmo Player runs on Windows 95, Windows NT, and IRIX 5.3; it requires at least 8 MB of RAM, a 66MHz 486 processor, and a 256-color SVGA display system (a Pentium 90MHz is preferable). Some of Cosmo Player's abilities include constant frame rates for smooth interaction, spatial audio, and embedded audio and video. Visit the Cosmo Player page at:

```
http://webspace.sgi.com/cosmoplayer/
```

CyberGate

CyberGate offers the exciting capacity to navigate through VRML worlds with a custom-built avatar, rather than one selected from a list (its avatars are human-sized. . . and must act accordingly). It also lets you completely ignore any avatar during your entire online session. CyberGate includes e-mail integration, fast rendering, a card-exchange option, and a public chat thread. CyberGate recommends a Pentium to run its browser, although any processor over a 486 will work. It runs only on Windows NT and Windows 95 and it can operate either as a plug-in or as a standalone VRML browser.

Here's the CyberGate download site:

```
http://www3.blacksun.com/products/cybergate.html
```

GLView

In addition to VRML, GLView can view a variety of file formats, including DXF, RAW, OBJ, GLView, and the following texture formats: VRML inline, RGB, JPEG, GIF, TARGA, BMP/DIB. GLView features texture mapping support and hardware shading and supports native OpenGL rendering on Windows NT and Windows 95, which are the platforms it supports. GLView implements VRML features like multiple Viewpoints, nested inlines, level of detail (LOD), ASCII Text, convex/concave faces, texture transformation, and color per vertex.

Visit this site to download GLView:

```
http://www.snafu.de/~hg/
```

Liquid Reality

Liquid Reality from Dimension X has lots to offer in addition to its cool name. It was developed to address the lack of interactivity in VRML 1.0 and uses Java to imbue VRML with interactivity it couldn't achieve by itself. This concept has been warmly received by the Web community and VRML 2.0 rests on an essential relationship with Java. Liquid Reality isn't a browser, but rather a VRML toolkit you can dynamically extend using Java. It runs inside a Java-enabled browser (such as Sun's HotJava or Netscape 2.0), which allows smooth movement between the 2-D realm of HTML and the added dimension offered by VRML. Mac, Windows NT, and IRIX versions are forthcoming. Liquid Reality is currently available for Windows 95, Solaris/SPARC, and Linux/x86 platforms that run under the current 1.0.1 Java Development Kit (Windows 95 can run it as a plug-in, too).

Grab a download of Liquid Reality from:

```
http://www.dnx.com/products/lr/download/index.html
```

Caligari Pioneer

Pioneer is a browser that heralds itself as "the world's first VRML tool that lets anyone browse and build three-dimensional home worlds on the World Wide Web." It's significantly less dependent on HTML browsers than some other VRML viewers, and it doesn't require a Web browser to download VRML files. Pioneer is the only VRML browser that includes 3-D creation tools and VRML authoring. It can read in VRML files, as well as import 3-D objects from AutoCAD, TrueSpace, 3D Studio, Wavefront,

LightWave, and Imagine formats. Pioneer's authoring tools let you build and edit shaded solid objects instead of wireframes, and its completely interactive interface lets you see the changes you make to a world's object manipulation, lighting, and textures in real-time. It has nice sound capacities as well; you can create 3-D sound with Pioneer, which takes the aural experience into another realm along with the visual.

Pioneer, unfortunately, is not free, although you can try a thirty-day trial period that runs tutorials only. You'll find the Pioneer information page at:

```
http://www.caligari.com/com/products/pfeat.html
```

Virtus Voyager

Voyager bills itself as the premiere VRML Web browser for the Macintosh/Power Macintosh; it also works with Windows 95. Voyager now incorporates advanced features, such as 3-D stereo support, collision detection, and OpenDoc compliance, and has been expanded to import Virtus' proprietary file format, as well as other 3-D rendering and modeling formats. Voyager's download page is at:

```
http://www.virtus.com/voyager.html
```

Whurlwind

Whurlwind is one of the few Mac browsers, and it also works with Windows 95. It lets you view 3-DMF and VRML models, and uses Quick-Draw 3-D for navigation, rendering, and linking to other sites.

You can read about and download Whurlwind at Apple's QuickDraw site:

```
http://quickdraw3d.apple.com/viewer.html
```

VRweb

VRweb doesn't require any special graphics hardware to run, although you can run an OpenGL version of VRweb, which takes advantage of graphics hardware on SGI, Windows NT, and DEC Alpha. It can run on all platforms as a software-only implementation using the Mesa library, which works like OpenGL. VRweb's currently supported platforms include: HP-UX, IBM AIX, SGI IRIX, Windows 95, Windows NT (Intel), Windows 3.*x* (with Win32S), SUN Solaris, Sun OS, DEC ULTRIX, DEC Alpha, and

LINUX, with promises of forthcoming versions for the Macintosh Power PC and Macintosh 68000.

`http://www.iicm.tu-graz.ac.at/vrweb/`

Live3D

Live3D is Netscape's contribution to the selection of VRML plug-ins. When used with Netscape Navigator 3.0, it's available for Windows 3.1, Windows 95, Windows NT, and Power Macintosh. Development is underway for 68K Macintosh and UNIX versions.

Live3D was one of the initial VRML plug-ins; it's pretty advanced. It lets you access distributed 3-D spaces with adaptive rendering, background processing, hardware acceleration, and GZIP compression. You can select the camera viewpoint, choose to point, walk, or fly through virtual worlds, and even arm yourself with gravity and collision detection, if you like. The Live3D plug-in has full integration with LiveMedia for streaming video and audio in 3-D spaces.

Live3D initially ingratiated its way into the hearts of VRML users through early extensions to VRML 1.0. Some of the nifty Live3D extensions currently include Motion Blur, a mode which brings a psychedelic effect to your viewing experience, and sound nodes that let you control the audio effects in your world. For a listing of Live3D extensions, refer here:

`http://home.netscape.com/eng/live3d/live3d_extensions_index.html`

You will soon be able to run 3-D applications written for the Live3D platform. Examples of these applications will include chat environments, geographical information systems, authoring environments, multiuser 3-D games, interactive advertisements, database visualizations, and online presentations. Live3D replaces the WebFX browser since Netscape acquired Paper Software.

Download the Live3D Plug-in at:

`http://home.netscape.com/comprod/products/navigator/live3d/index.html`

Topper

Topper is a plug-in from Kinetix, a company intimately involved with VRML development. Kinetix has created a new specification for extending the current capabilities of VRML worlds, called Virtual Reality Behavior

Language (VRBL). VRBL allows viewers to see animations within VRML worlds and supports trigger animations and behaviors. The trigger ability lets viewers trip off behaviors and animations in a VRML world. VRBL is an open standard and it can be freely incorporated into development tools. Topper, the VRML plug-in offered by Kinetix, supports VRBL worlds, enabling users to experience dynamic 3-D interactive worlds.

To use the Topper plug-in, you need to have Netscape 2.0 (or a newer version), Windows 95 or Windows NT 3.51, at least 20 MB of hard disk space, and a minimum of 16 MB of RAM. To run Topper, you also must install the Reality Lab renderer. If the installation program doesn't find the Reality Lab renderer during the download, it will automatically launch the Reality Lab install located inside the Topper download.

Kinetix's download site is located at:

```
http://www.ktx.com/products/hyperwire/download.htm
```

The Future of VRML: To Be Determined . . .

How VRML's power will be used and whom it will benefit are the essential questions surrounding its future. Will VRML be most advantageous to monopolistic telecommunications corporations? Or will it bring an increase in shared experience between groups of people previously unconnected because of location or identity? Will VRML transform human sexuality? Or will it create new forms of artistic expression that lead to an expansion in human consciousness? We don't know, but we're sure it'll be fun to find out!

In fact, VRML could be one of the most wonderful creations of our age. It could be a technology that enables new forms of experience, communication, and conceptualization, that actually contributes to human evolution. With its ability to combine the intellectual and the sensual, the musical and the visual, with shadows, light, color, form, and essence, VRML can literally change the way we look at our world. This technology could revolutionize the way we learn and, in conjunction with the Web, the access we have to what we learn. VRML brings the opportunity to experiment with how worlds are built. This privilege has previously been restricted to gods or to those with fecund imaginations and a great deal of spare time.

Now, however, the mortal computer user can create a world in which reality can be mutated, dreams reproduced in surreal color, the subconscious uncovered and exhibited for others to explore. And artists, who are traditionally society's visionaries, have a wholly fresh set of tools with which to unleash their memes. In *Art & Physics: Parallel Visions in Space, Time, and*

Light, Leonard Shlain writes, "Relativity, Cubism, and psychoanalysis share this feature: Profound distortions of everyday time and space occur regularly in each theory." [2] VRML shares the potential to give rise to the same type of profound distortion; to what extent this promise will be used is a separate question. Television had a great deal of original potential as well, and many cultural critics now classify its societal influence as negative (of course, perhaps its true glory days lie ahead—in a union with the Web—and with VRML).

Although it's somewhat hard to predict exactly how pervasive VRML's impact will be, it could be as monumental as the Web's—and who knew anything about the Web ten years ago? Well, nobody, because it didn't exist (an obvious but, somehow, slightly shocking fact for devoted Websurfers). When Mosaic turned the public onto the Web in 1993, it altered paradigms of how information was gathered and distributed. VRML has the power to do the same thing, and pondering online life before VRML may be just as difficult as imagining a Webless existence in a few years. If that's true, it prompts other questions—how will VRML affect the way we perceive life and our current version of reality? What affect could spending hundreds of hours a month interacting in virtual spaces have upon our real-life interactions (not to mention our eyesight)?

For links that investigate these and other ideas of VRML's future, venture to SGI's VRML experts page at:

```
http://webspace.sgi.com/experts/
```

Ponder how collaborative VRML art spaces such as stratus may affect art as we know it:

```
http://www.construct.net/perihelion/gallery/
```

Or venture into the VRML guru's homepage, Outside the Light Cone:

```
http://www.hyperreal.com/~mpesce/
```

2. Shlain, Leonard. *Art & Physics: Parallel Visions in Space, Time, and Light.* New York: William Morrow and Company, Inc., 1991.

building

VRML

World

chapter 2

Thinking in 3-D

T

E X T U A L interfaces were once the standard means for user-computer interaction. That approach, however, is rapidly disappearing; likewise, the velocity of this change is increased by the impetus to use VRML. Graphics now allow us to create environments within the computer world, which can transport us beyond the limitations of text. An entire new level of stimulation exists that now accompanies computer graphics. When the element of interactivity is thrown into the brew, as it has been with VRML 2.0, that stimulation grows still more profound.

Until the late 1980s, computer graphic applications dealt mainly with 2-D objects. Today's 3-D objects are a great deal more complex and, therefore, more demanding in terms of processing power. It wasn't until the advent of very large-scale integration (VLSI) semiconductor technology that 3-D graphics started becoming more viable. VLSI sunk the price of microprocessors and memory and, by doing so, opened the floodgates for subsequent 3-D development. Now it only takes several chips to perform real-time 3-D animation and the future looks bright for 3-D applications.

In VRML, it's the graphics system that intermediates between output devices and the application model. The application program itself monitors what needs to transpire according to the user's actions. With the addition of interactivite behaviors to VRML 2.0, VRML is a more viable means of human communication. Although real-time communication has been available in text-based formats for years and it has deeply affected many of its users, the possibilities of real-time communication that's centered around graphic interfaces is uncharted territory. For this reason, new paradigms must be considered as this ground is broken. Because the 3-D graphics system is endowed with an entirely new dimension, its potential cannot be realized if the structure and assumptions used with 2-D graphics are transferred intact.

In this chapter, the information and ideas that can help you to create earth-shattering 3-D worlds will be discussed. You'll learn about the complexity of the third dimension and how to navigate through it, the specifics behind the construction of 3-D objects, and techniques of lighting, shading, rendering, and texture mapping, which you can use to make killer 3-D worlds.

Origins and Axes

In the "real world," having an idea of where you are and how you got there is always useful. As Mark Pesce discusses in *VRML—Browsing and Building Cyberspace*, the idea of connecting to the *axis mundi* (or foundation of the world) has been an important theme in many human cultures because it serves as the reference point for places and events. It's no less important to define a place in a VRML world: Before you can process data about places, it's imperative to have your origins straight.

The VRML Coordinate System

VRML's coordinate system is based on the typical mathematical representation of 3-D space—it's a right-handed system that projects its x-, y-, and z-axes in Cartesian form. While the 2-D realm defines its origin as the point where two axes (X and Y) cross, when you're dealing with 3-D VRML worlds, you have three axes to think about: the X, Y, and Z axes.

On the X axis, numbers increase from left to right, on the Y axis, numbers increase from bottom to top, and on the Z axis, numbers increase as they come toward you. The higher the value a shape has on the Z axis, the closer it is to you. When you're interacting in 3-D space, X is positive to the right, Y is positive upward, and Z is positive toward you.

Within this system, meters are the standard units for lengths and distances, and radians are the standard units for angles (this is an example of applying a real-world measurement system, as discussed in the following). The default settings of this system render objects onto a two-dimensional display device by projecting them in the direction of the positive Z axis. The positive X axis lies to the right of the Z axis, while the positive Y axis is up from the positive Z axis.

VRML Units

VRML worlds are measured in VRML units. Because these units are completely generic and unattached to any outside system of measurement, you can apply a real-world measurement system if you find this useful. You can also think of them simply as neutral units, without any affiliation to feet, centimeters, etc. However you choose to perceive these units, if you maintain a consistent approach when dealing with them, this will help to ensure your scene's perspective doesn't go askew.

Moving in 3-D

When you're situated in a three-dimensional virtual world, it's important to understand how to maneuver within this space and how to plot your course. In the sections that follow, a brief tutorial will be provided on the all-important concepts of orientation, viewpoint, and translation.

Orientation

When you're using a VRML browser, you can often choose how you want to be oriented in a scene and from what perspective you'd like to view it. Browsers such as WebSpace give you multiple navigation choices: WebSpace offers Walk Mode, which features a joystick, tilt knob, arrow pad, and seek tool as navigation guides for your cruise through a virtual world. WebSpace also has an Examination Mode, which lets you navigate with a trackball, arrow pad, and thumbwheel for more in-depth investigation of a scene's objects. You can also control a scene's view by employing viewpoints.

Viewpoints

In creating a VRML world, you can choose where you'd like its viewpoints to be located. Viewpoints are the sites (ideally selected for their interesting vantage points) from which users can view the world.

The point of view in VRML 2.0 assumes a real person exists at the other end of the computer, viewing the VRML world and interacting with it. In VRML 1.0, the Viewpoint node's job was performed by a Perspective Camera. As with this former camera node, the viewpoint can be altered (through the Viewpoint node), so a world can contain an array of interesting viewpoints. Only one of them can be active at any time, though.

Browsers can provide user interfaces that will permit the viewer to alter a scene's viewing position. Usually, a number of preprogrammed positions exist that you can set up in a VRML world for your viewer to experience. For example, many browsers offer a "home" position, which is your initial viewpoint upon entering a scene. If you get lost in VRML space, you can revert back to this original viewpoint.

When a viewpoint becomes active, the browser orients its view into the scene graph under whatever viewpoint is currently in operation. For that reason, when you're teleporting to a viewpoint in motion, you should move right along with the viewpoint.

Newer browsers support user-interface mechanisms, which let you "teleport" between viewpoints. This Star-Trekkian action can set off a scripting-language mechanism at the viewpoint to which you teleport and connect your teleport actions to the playing of a script. If you happen to teleport to a moving viewpoint, then you'll just move along with it!

Translation

When you think about how the "real world" is organized, it's clear all objects have a position. The same thing applies to VRML worlds. These positions define the relationships that exist among objects—why your bed is in your bedroom, for example, and why there's a table in your dining room—and these relationships illuminate these objects' functions.

Because you have the choice of placing shapes anywhere in the world, in any position, this concept of relationships is important. The act of positioning your VRML shapes is called *translation*. The Translation node centers around moving or transporting something from one place to another. By using it, you can position the origin in a location of your choice, any distance in any direction, before you add text or draw shapes. The Translation node's single translation field contains three floating-point values and describes the distance to move the origin before it assumes a new position. The Translation node's three values refer to the X, Y, and Z directions (either positive or negative) relative to the true origin (at Cartesian coordinates 0,0,0 expressed in VRML as 0.0 0.0 0.0).

The VRML Repository contains helpful examples of translation; you'll find them at:

```
http://www.sdsc.edu/vrml
```

Objects

Anything you see within a VRML world is an object of some kind. In the sections that follow, what kinds of objects you might encounter in a virtual space will be explored.

Points to Polygons

When you're creating a VRML world, your computer creates objects out of clouds of points. These points are used to create a scene's framework of objects and these collected points are called a *point cloud*. Were the framework linking these points removed, you'd see a mass of points that look somewhat like a cloud—hence, the name "point cloud." But points are connected within frames, and frames are covered with surfaces, and surfaces are composed of objects called *polygons*. That's why what you see looks like a collection of objects, not a cloud of points.

You can think of polygons as surfaces that are infinitely thin or absolutely flat. Polygons are the most fundamental components inside computer-generated 3-D worlds. Shapes such as triangles, quadrilaterals, pentagons, hexagons, etc., are all examples of polygons because they consist of sets of points. Lines can't ever be polygons because polygons are required to contain some area, and lines don't.

All polygons have faces or sides. Because they're mathematical constructions with only a single side, however, they're only visible from that one side. Determining which side will be visible is taken care of by the polygon's normal, a synonym for "right angle." A polygon's *normal* is a line that passes through its surface at a right angle; this inherently points out from the polygon's surface. Thus, the side with the line sticking out is the one viewers will see.

From Frames to Surfaces

In linking a scene's points together, the computer frames the objects within a structure. Although this framework (called a *wireframe rendering*) increases the objects' realism, they're still hollow and skeletal in their representation. By applying a surface to an object, you make the surface look as if it's actually solid and, therefore, take it another step closer toward achieving realism. A surface is rather like a skin that coats the object; this skin can vary widely in its color, shininess, reflectivity, texture, etc.

Working with Light Sources

Creative, convincing lighting can be one of the best ways to add mood and realism to your scene, so after the points you've established in your VRML space have been connected to a frame and wrapped in a surface of polygons, shining a little light on the world is the next step. You can do so by adding light sources to create effects, such as shadows, shininess, and reflectivity, just like you would see in the real world. Human eyes cannot see where there's no light and neither can the VRML camera's perspective. The only way you can see an object in your VRML world is if it's illuminated.

There is a light, frequently referred to as a headlight, that the VRML browser automatically includes in every world. The *headlight* moves with you as your perspective changes—almost as if it's attached to your eyes or your head, like a miner's helmet. But the light provided by a headlight only shines in front of you, so it's not sufficient for advanced lighting of VRML worlds. For that, you'll want to endow your scenes with extra lights. You'll never actually see the lights you add to your scene because they don't possess a form or shape unless you give them one. Instead, you'll only see the effect these lights have on your worlds as they are apparent from your perspective.

You can add three types of light sources in your VRML worlds: PointLight, SpotLight, and DirectionalLight. These three sources have different capabilities, which will be discussed shortly. *Ambient* light sources are another source of a scene's light—they're the accumulated light of the worlds' surfaces. *Ambient* light sources can provide uniform lighting and create diffuse lighting effects. Because their light is diffuse, the angle from which ambient lights are viewed is irrelevant.

To light your scene, you'll need to determine how much light you want striking the scene's objects and how much light should be reflected. The more a shape is oriented toward a light, the more brightly it will be shaded. This is apparent when you use the headlight to light a scene—the shapes it faces are always bright, while the shapes that face away are less strongly illuminated. You can select the locations for your light sources, as well as the directions in which you want them directed.

Just like their real world counterparts, lights in VRML scenes create different ambiance. Employing spotlights highlights those features their beam illuminates, while using a bare light can light up an entire room. To create a pale evening glow, choose the Moon; for intense radiation, try the Sun. You can also remove light from a scene; most VRML browsers and graphic boards support negative light intensities, which let you create antilights in a scene. *Antilights* actually darken your scene, so you can add a threatening, dungeonlike atmosphere to part of a world or simply darken backgrounds and corners to give the foreground greater eminence.

Ambient Light

A scene's ambient illumination comes from the reflection and scattering of light that originates with its various light sources. Each of the scene's lights has an AmbientIntensity field, which acknowledges the relationship between the direct and ambient lighting. Here's the way a single light's contribution to the overall ambient lighting is computed:

```
if ( light is "on" )
      ambientLight = intensity * ambientIntensity * color
   else
      ambientLight = (0,0,0)
```

Using this setting allows you to change a light's overall brightness by controlling its intensity. If you're using a renderer that doesn't support per-light ambient illumination, you can use this information to create ambient lighting parameters at the time when you load the world.

Directional Lights

Use the *DirectionalLight* node when the objects in your scene require precisely controlled lighting. Directional light doesn't randomly diffuse—instead, it lets you direct light at particular objects in your world, just like track lighting would IRL. The light rays of directional lights always point in the same direction and they are always parallel, as well. This type of light has both a location (expressed in x, y, and z coordinates) and an orientation (expressed in pitch, yaw, and roll degrees). These specifications determine where in the world the light will be located, as well as in which direction it will point. Traffic lights are examples of directional lights because they are controlled lights that always diffuse in the same direction.

To create a directional light, specify an aim direction for the light. *Aim directions* are created like rotation axes—you can think of them as a line that starts at the origin point of 0.0 0.0 0.0. and connects to a point of your choice. By moving the flexible point, the line linking the points changes directions. Employing aim directions allows you to point a directional light in any direction. Using an aim direction of 0.0 0.0 -1.0 produces a directional light that shines straight down the negative Z axis. The aim direction 0.0 1.0 0.0, however, points a light up to the Y axis.

Directing the light in this manner doesn't bring a wholly natural look; this is because of the light rays' parallelism and the light's lack of a true point of origin (because it exists as a vector and doesn't vary in length). In using a directional light, you're illuminating only the objects contained by the light's parent group node (which includes any descendent children of the group node). As an example of how a lighting node looks, here's the Directional-Light node's public interface and file format:

```
DirectionalLight {
exposedField SFFloat ambientIntensity  0
exposedField SFColor color             1 1 1
exposedField SFVec3f direction         0 0 -1
exposedField SFFloat intensity         1
exposedField SFBool  on                TRUE
}
```

Here's an example from the VRML 2.0 specification, which demonstrates how a directional light can be used in a scene. This scene, lit by a directional light, consists of a view of a blue box and a red sphere.

```
#VRML Draft #2 V2.0 utf8
Transform {
children [

    DirectionalLight {          # First child
        direction 0 0 -1        # Light illuminating the scene
    }

    Transform {                 # Second child - a red sphere
      translation 3 0 1
      children [
        Shape {
          geometry Sphere { radius 2.3 }
          appearance Appearance
            material Material { diffuseColor 1 0 0 }   # Red
        }
      ]
    }

    Transform {                 # Third child - a blue box
      translation -2.4 .2 1
      rotation     0 1 1  .9
      children [
        Shape {
          geometry Box {}
          appearance Appearance
```

```
            material Material { diffuseColor 0 0 1 }   # Blue
      }
   ]
 }

] # end of children for world
}
```

Spotlights

Spotlights can be used like lasers or stage lights—they're useful for directing your light in a cone shape, which shapes your scene with maximum realism and control. SpotLight and PointLight both light any and all objects that fall within the boundaries of their influence, regardless of where they may be located in the file. For SpotLight, the volume of this influence is defined as a solid angle, defined by a radius and a cutoff angle. A SpotLight's source is fixed at a three-dimensional coordinate whose illuminating rays are cast into a cone. This cone runs along a 3-D vector and, as each ray moves farther from its center, the illumination's intensity diminishes exponentially.

Spotlights have a direction toward which their light rays project. Spotlights also have an umbra, which is a focus to determine the beam of light's width and how quickly it will widen during its passage through space. A point light's rays emanate within a light cone and whatever shapes are included in this cone of light are illuminated.

As the ray of light moves away from light's direction to the cone's edges, the intensity of the illumination may decrease. How this illumination decays with distance is determined by the spotlight's attenuation coefficients, expressed in this equation:

$$1/(\text{attenuation}[0] + \text{attenuation}[1]*r + \text{attenuation}[2]*r^2)$$

where r is the distance of the light to the surface being illuminated. The default setting for spotlight is no attenuation.

Spotlights are defined as:

```
SpotLight {
exposedField SFFloat ambientIntensity  0
exposedField SFVec3f attenuation        1 0 0
exposedField SFFloat beamWidth          1.570796
exposedField SFColor color              1 1 1
exposedField SFFloat cutOffAngle        0.785398
exposedField SFVec3f direction          0 0 -1
exposedField SFFloat intensity          1
```

```
exposedField SFVec3f location          0 0 0
exposedField SFBool  on                TRUE
exposedField SFFloat radius            1
}
```

Point Lights

Point lights are the simplest of all the lights (you can think of them as incandescent light bulbs) and are omnidirectional. The PointLight node creates light that comes from a fixed 3-D location—to create it, you specify its 3-D location in your world, along with its color and intensity. Point lights are useful for imbuing a scene with a sense of realism. To provide adequate lighting in your virtual worlds, add point lights wherever you include a lamp. Like spot lights, point lights can be dropped at any point in a VRML world.

Whether or not you place a spotlight near an object or far away is up to you but, remember, this light illuminates equally in all directions (hence, its omnidirectional characteristic). To create the impression that light is coming from far away, it's often useful to try parallel point lights. They send out light rays that run parallel to each other, just as the light rays we receive from the sun's rays do here on Earth. Here's the point light's definition:

```
PointLight {
exposedField SFFloat ambientIntensity  0
exposedField SFVec3f attenuation        1 0 0
exposedField SFColor color              1 1 1
exposedField SFFloat intensity          1
exposedField SFVec3f location           0 0 0
exposedField SFBool  on                 TRUE
exposedField SFFloat radius             1
}
```

Lights, Sensors, and Scripts

The Sensor and Script nodes are the two nodes most likely to generate events. By employing them, you can add interesting complexity to your scenes, making them either more unpredictable or closer to "real-life" existence.

Sensor Nodes

You can use *Sensor* nodes to generate events, such as turning lights on or off. Sensors act like triggers that fire off a message in response to some activity. Sensor nodes can be based upon user input: the Geometric Sensor nodes (ProximitySensor, VisibilitySensor, TouchSensor, CylinderSensor, PlaneSensor, and SphereSensor) are the ones affected by user actions. When they're used with lighting, they can be set to go on when a user moves close to them or when a mouse is clicked on them. Sensor nodes can also be set to predetermined time; the TimeSensor can function either as a ticking clock—by firing off events at predetermined, regular intervals—or as an alarm clock, which will make it go off at a specific time.

If you want to place a sensor in front of a door and trip off lights this way, use the BoxProximitySensor. Whenever a user enters the region defined by this sensor's box, it will send out a message from isActive, which is defined as the node's eventOut interface. As long as the sensor has been wired to another node's eventIn, the node will receive the message and activate the script. Using other nodes, like ClickSensor as a light switch and DragSensor as a dimmer control, are obvious ways to enhance your lighting.

Using Sensor nodes in conjunction with lighting will make Moving Worlds scenes much more lifelike than their predecessors. Just as in the outside world, VRML 2.0 scenes will have lights that vary, depending on what's happening around them, and patterns that change, based on actions such as an avatar entering a room and touching an object, which will illuminate the light.

The following TouchSensor's enabled exposedField is routed to the SpotLight's on exposed field. All four of the following routing examples are legal syntax:

```
DEF CLICKER TouchSensor { enabled TRUE }
DEF LIGHT SpotLight { on   FALSE }

ROUTE CLICKER.enabled TO LIGHT.on
or
ROUTE CLICKER.enabled_changed TO LIGHT.on
or
ROUTE CLICKER.enabled TO LIGHT.set_on
or
ROUTE CLICKER.enabled_changed TO LIGHT.set_on
```

Script Nodes

One of the hottest new features of Moving Worlds is its ability to use Script nodes. A *Script* node can be triggered by a certain event (such as turning on a light or making contact with an object). When the event transpires, the browser executes a program in the Script node's URL field (if necessary, the program can be passed on to an external interpreter). Although Script nodes can be written in any language, Java's interactive potential is particularly applicable to Script nodes. Script nodes, written in a language like Java, can be put to excellent use with lighting because they have the power to change a scene's lighting both effectively and realistically.

The Script node was defined to provide an interface between VRML and any programming language. Like many other Moving Worlds nodes, the Script node functions by defining eventIn and eventOut interfaces, as well as by giving the definition information required to bind to an external script or program. By doing so, a Script node has the ability to both send and receive messages to nodes inside VRML worlds.

Rendering

Rendering computes the scene from a graphics database. In plain English, this means when you choose a rendering type in your browser, you're telling the computer how you want your graphics displayed.

Most VRML browsers have a rendering menu from which you can choose the type of rendering you desire. Which level of rendering you choose depends on several factors, most importantly the choice between speed and graphics quality. If you're navigating through a VRML world and you want to do so quickly, then wireframe is ideal. But if you must study the detail of the shapes surrounding you, you'll need to render them as solids.

Wireframe Rendering—for Quick Results

Wireframe rendering, as shown in Figure 2-1, displays only an object's frame. It shows you an object's skeletal structure with a minimum of CPU demand. It's often used on low-end computers, which aren't endowed with top-of-the line graphics capabilities. Wireframe rendering works by connecting the dots in an object's point cloud with wires or lines; then the crude outline is displayed. It makes objects appear as if they're created from wire, with only the edges showing.

If you want to see an object in its fully rendered glory (as well as the time and the processor power), solid rendering, as shown in Figure 2-2, is your ideal format. The polygons of an object that's solidly rendered are fully colored in, which makes the object look as if it's a solid. Because this type of rendering shows the greatest detail, it's the most enriching graphically. Depending on how powerful your computer is, solid rendering may be rather tedious to wait for, though.

FIGURE 2-1

Although wireframe rendering is the fastest way to render something, it's also the least realistic.

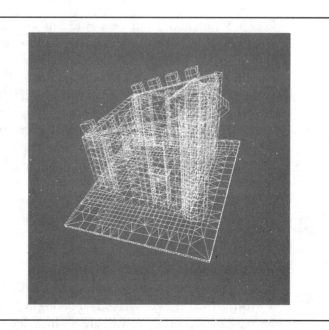

FIGURE 2-2

Choose solid rendering for detailed results.

Shading Techniques

Shading determines how much light is spread across the surfaces of a scene's polygon faces; it is the key to making your shapes truly look 3-D. Calculations you can perform determine how an object is to be shaded, some of which are quick, while others are painfully slow. How an object is shaded often determines the level of believability it will achieve. Hollywood films with big computer graphics budgets often set the high end of the shading standard—the ray traced models they employ are complicated and realistic. Video games, on the other hand, will sometimes use less complicated shading models because they allow the games to run more quickly.

Flat Shading

Flat shading is the simplest form of shading. In flat shading, each face is seen in the same color. The computer determines a single value between the light source and the polygon's normal (the light ray that could project from an object's face) and shades the whole polygon's face according to this value. When an object is flat shaded, all of its vertices are assigned the same color, which is the color of the vertex that created the primitive. When you're dealing with points, this is the color associated with the point; when you're dealing with line segments, it's the color of the vertex's second (final) vertex. If you're flat shading a polygon, the color is selected depending on how the polygon was generated. Although flat shading is fast, its simplicity also makes it look less believable.

Gouraud Shading

By using more of the computer's mathematical ability to smooth an object's shading, *Gouraud shading* achieves a smoother look than flat shading. Gouraud shading averages the shading among a scene's polygon faces by using the normal of a polygon's face, as well as those of its neighbors. Because of the mathematical power necessary to average all those numbers, Gouraud shading may run several times slower than flat shading. It does, however, allow objects to achieve a better level of realism.

Phong Shading

Phong shading addresses some of the weaknesses that accompany Gouraud shading, such as Gouraud-shaded objects' tendency to show banding (lines where the math couldn't create sufficient shading). Phong shading uses even more math than Gouraud shading—the computer calculates a greater number of normals for the polygon's face, as well as those surrounding it. Phong shading is ten times more demanding on your computer than Gouraud shading, but it's far superior in terms of realism.

Ray Tracing

Ray tracing is the ultimate in shading (see Figure 2-3). It's extremely processing-intensive; it could take days to ray trace a complicated scene on a desktop computer. It produces excellent results, which is why it's the form of shading used in movies, TV commercials, and high-end graphics. Ray tracing works by tracing the paths of all the light rays that travel through a scene. Each pixel's rays are usually traced backward from the object and other polygons until a boundary is reached. In a complex VRML world, it's easy to see how this could take lots of power and time.

Texture Mapping: Realism Made Easy

Texture mapping is an excellent way to add extra realism to a scene. You can think of texture mapping as applying wallpaper or a sticker to an object;

FIGURE 2-3

Shading gives our castle a 3-D effect.

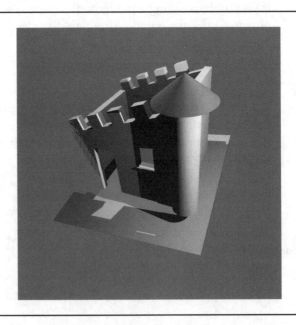

it lays an image onto an object in a scene. Through texture mapping, you can add minute, precise details, which can bring your VRML world's complexity a step closer to the real world. Without texture mapping, adding tiny details—such as the nap of a carpet or the dusting of pollen on the inside of a lily—is taxing to your CPU. By using texture mapping, however, you can greatly increase a scene's realism without actually having to hand-create each detail.

Because texture mapping eliminates the need for special-purpose drawing software, it's widely employed in computer graphics hardware and graphics software interfaces. Although texture mapping usually has a minimal effect on a program's complexity, some browsers don't process it quickly. Check your browser to see if it optimizes texture mapping; then check your graphics hardware manual to make certain your computer can texture map.

You can add texture mapping to any VRML shape and you can add any image you like to create a texture. You must specify the following when texture mapping shapes:

- The texture image to be mapped onto the shape

- How the texture should be adjusted (rotated, translated, or scaled) to fit the shape's dimension

- Whether the texture should repeat infinitely over the shape or whether it should occur a single time

- What parts of the texture correspond to what parts of the shape

Here are the Texture nodes' definitions:

- **ImageTexture**   defines a texture map and parameters for that map

- **MovieTexture**   defines an animated movie texture map and parameters for controlling the movie and the map

- **PixelTexture**   defines a 2-D image-based texture map as an explicit array of pixel values and parameters controlling tiling repetition of the texture

- **TextureTransform**   defines a 2-D transformation applied to texture coordinates

- **TextureCoordinate**   defines a set of 2-D coordinates to use to map textures to the vertices of subsequent PointSet, IndexedLineSet, or IndexedFaceSet objects

VRML primitives (Cube, Sphere, Cylinder, and Cone) have a simple syntax and they're easy to texture map. Here's the simplest form of the Texture2 node:

```
Separator {
    Texture2 { filename "mayaimag.jpg" }
    Sphere { }
}
```

In this chapter, we've covered information about 3-D graphics that will help you create more exciting and realistic VRML worlds. By using VRML's graphic nodes to their full potential, you'll be able to make scenes replete with more sensual stimulation and richly satisfying detail. Some of the new nodes in Moving Worlds VRML 2.0—especially the Sensor and Script nodes—have wonderful potential to create complex worlds.

Remember, though, your worlds will only be experienced if they can be loaded; if your images are too big to load, their worlds won't be investigated. The increased interactivity in VRML worlds doesn't complement the increased interchange of the Web, which is experiencing serious traffic problems. Try to keep files, as well as the images within them, as small as you can. Testing your worlds on a range of browsers is always a good idea, too. And try to experience your world through different eyes, particularly the ones that using a 14.4 modem and a 486 computer might create.

The world of VRML 3-D graphics is constantly changing—now new browsers are pushing new corners of envelopes and renegade developers are concocting fresh brilliant paradigms for movement and 3-D interaction. If you'd like to stay abreast of VRML's hot graphic trends, check out these Web sites that cover the bleeding edge:

The VRML Foundry:

```
http://www.mcp.com/general/foundry/
```

WAXWeb:

```
http://bug.village.virginia.edu/
```

Aereal BOOM! is a site that links to a plethora of VRML worlds:

```
http://www.aereal.com/boom/
```

Arc Gallery is an extensive collection of VRML goodies:

```
http://www.construct.net/worlds/
```

building

VRML

World

chapter 3

The Basics of
VRML Files

B EFORE you attack the task of creating wondrous VRML worlds, it's helpful to know a bit about how VRML files are constructed. Even though authoring tools will allow you to skim over many of the more technical aspects of file creation, understanding how files are constructed and how they operate will help you troubleshoot problems that may sometimes occur, and will make you aware of VRML's full power.

Don't Let the Jargon Get You Down

Before diving into this chapter, some words of warning: It isn't easy to explain VRML in a linear, disconnected fashion, so some of the definitions and groupings you encounter in the upcoming pages may seem slightly disjointed. Although some visual aids are included for elucidation, the best way to figure out how this highly interconnected language operates is simply to watch it in action, perhaps with the specification in hand. Reading through our explanations of how VRML files function, as well as the descriptions of how the files' contents create VRML worlds, is an initial step toward understanding VRML's technical side. After reading through the details of this chapter, it's safe to predict that your second step may entail finding a usable authoring tool, which allows you basically to ignore VRML's inner workings.

The VRML 2.0 Specification Hype

VRML is developing quickly. When you look at VRML worlds in their present form, you may wonder what the hype is because they're often lethargic, jagged, and cartoonlike. Even the release of the greatly expanded VRML 2.0 specification attests to something that's both frustrating and intriguing: The most exciting part about VRML is not what has been created so far, but its vast potential for the future. To procure a deeper understanding of this language, browse through the VRML Moving Worlds' specification at:

http://vrml.sgi.com/moving-worlds/spec/

Because this is currently the newest version of VRML, this specification will be referred to throughout the chapter. The default file formats included at the beginning of each node definition are taken from this resource, as are many of the graphics.

For any questions specifically pertaining to VRML 2.0 design, refer to this URL:

http://webspace.sgi.com/moving-worlds/Design.html

Now About Those Files . . .

A VRML file serves as a textual description of a VRML world; it contains the information about how shapes should be drawn, where they should be placed, what color they are, and much more. The file extension for VRML files is ".wrl" (for world); all VRML files carry this extension. The text inside VRML files can be created with any word processor or text editor. It can also be written with authoring applications that generate this text automatically. Authoring applications include Caligari Pioneer, Virtus Walkthrough Pro and 3-D Website Builder, and Paragraph's Home Space Builder—all of which are profiled later in this book. VRML files can also be written by a utility that translates other graphics file formats into VRML format.

VRML files are sometimes referred to simply as "worlds." All VRML worlds are defined through the objects, properties, and groups they contain. These fundamental "building blocks" are called nodes; all VRML files must contain at least one node. A *scene graph* is the entire list of a VRML file's nodes, so all VRML documents can be called scene graphs, as well.

In this chapter, the intricacies of these .wrl files will be discussed, beginning by examining their composition, and then by covering VRML nodes and their components. The changes from VRML 1.0 to VRML 2.0 will also be chronicled and how this evolution has affected the language will be considered.

Some of the hot new additions to Moving Worlds (the name of SGI's proposal for VRML 2.0, which was accepted as the standard) include:

- Sound nodes, which allow you to add 3-D sounds to VRML files

- Scripting nodes, which are the key to VRML 2.0's long-awaited interactivity

- Nodes like Fog node and Background node, which imbue your world's environment with a whole new level of realism

- Prototyping (explained in detail later in this chapter), which allows you to define nodes just the way you want them

These fresh new nodes are a crucial part of VRML's second version because they propel its worlds from static, noninteractive scene graphics into more complex worlds, which include behaviors and interactivity.

What Your Browser Needs to Know: VRML's MIME Type

Before you go wild downloading VRML files, you should know your Web browser can only recognize the information in VRML files if it's configured to accept VRML's MIME type. MIME specifies content type for browsers, so they know what kind of information they're receiving. *MIME types* consist of a set of two words, separated by a slash. The MIME type information is something typically only seen by your Web browser.

The MIME type for VRML files is defined as follows:

```
x-world/x-vrml
```

X-world is the MIME primary type for 3-D world descriptions, and *x-vrml* is the MIME subtype for VRML documents. You can transmit other 3-D world descriptions, like SGI's Open Inventor ASCII format, (iv) or the Geometry Center's Object-Oriented Geometry Language (oogl) by using different MIME subtypes.

The official MIME type is eventually expected to change to *model/vrml*.
When this change occurs, servers should present files as being of type
x-world/x-vrml. Browsers should be able to recognize both *x-world/x-vrml*
and *model/vrml*.

What Makes a VRML File?

In an abstract realm, VRML's file format simply describes objects. These
objects can theoretically contain data such as MIDI files, JPEG images, or
3-D geometry. This extensibility is a useful perk because it allows VRML to
stretch beyond its own format.

Because the language defines a set of objects, it shouldn't be a surprise it
is technically classified as an object-oriented language, like Java or C++.
Although these languages may differ in their complexity, they all employ
uniform, reusable objects as their basic units, hence, the definition.

VRML enables a set of objects, called *nodes,* which can be used to perform
multimedia, build interactive worlds, and create 3-D graphics. These nodes
all store their data in "fields" and "events."

VRML Sample File

Before examining the nodes that make up VRML files, here's a sample
VRML file, taken from the VRML 2.0 second draft specification at the VAG
Web site (http://vag.vrml.org). If you're not familiar with VRML files, take
a look at this code to gain a little familiarity. This particular file creates a
simple scene, which defines a view of a red sphere and a blue box, lit by a
directional light:

```
#VRML Draft #2 V2.0 utf8
Transform {
  children [

    DirectionalLight {          # First child
        direction 0 0 -1        # Light illuminating the scene
    }

    Transform {                 # Second child - a red sphere
      translation 3 0 1
      children [
        Shape {
          geometry Sphere { radius 2.3 }
```

```
      appearance Appearance
        material Material { diffuseColor 1 0 0 }    # Red
      }
    ]
  }
```

The VRML File Header

This is the simplest VRML file:

```
#VRML V2.0 utf8
```

This file header tells the browser the file is

- A VRML file

- A utf8 file (VRML 1.0 files were ASCII files—utf8 was adopted for the 2.0 specification because it lets VRML display international characters)

- In conformance with the VRML 2.0 specification

For a VRML browser to accept a VRML file, it must be preceded by this line, which tells the browser what kind of content and format to expect from the file. A VRML file isn't valid without this header, which must be included to define the file as a VRML document.

In this header, the utf8 identifier allows international characters to be displayed in VRML using the UTF-8 encoding of the ISO 10646 standard (of which Unicode is an alternate form).

Comments in VRML Files

A line that begins with the pound sign (#) is recognized by the browser as a comment line, and is, therefore, ignored. The browser disregards any characters that follow the pound sign until the next new line or carriage return. (One exception to this rule does exist: # is sometimes part of the string within double-quoted SFString and MFString fields.)

tip *Comments let you put extra information into VRML files without affecting the way your world appears. Their purpose is to make it easier for humans to read VRML files. Comments can include a wide range of helpful information, including:*

- *Who created the file*

- *What it contains*

- *When it was created*

- *Where it was created*

- *Why it was created*

- *Notes describing what is drawn by the files' parts*

Comments are especially helpful for the absent-minded because they can help you remember what's in a file and what a file does. This ability to make notes comes in handy when you start creating files en masse, then leave them untouched for a few months. Comments also can be helpful when working in a group and files must pass among multiple authors, none of whom will think—or code—exactly alike.

All comments begin with pound signs and end at the close of a line. Here's an example of a comment line:

```
# created 1996 by the nefarious hoyden
# this scene contains ritual castle number 30127
```

caution   *It's possible a VRML document server will strip comments and extra white space from a VRML file before transmitting it. Whenever commas, blanks, tabs, new lines, and carriage returns appear outside string fields, they're regarded as white space characters. For that reason, if you need to ensure information, such as author information or copyrights, remains intact in your file, use WorldInfo nodes to store this vital information.*

Nodes: The True Building Blocks of VRML

Nodes are frequently called VRML's building blocks. *Building blocks* are the set of objects defined by VRML to make 3-D graphics. Nodes are those elements that describe shapes and their properties in VRML worlds—basically, a form of drawing instructions. When your browser reads a VRML file, it follows the instructions conveyed by nodes to create the intended VRML world.

Three main types of nodes exist:

- Property
- Shape
- Group

The data these nodes contain is stored in fields. Nodes and their fields define what kind of shapes are drawn, and where, what those shapes' colors are, and whatever else is involved in rendering the world described within a VRML file. Because everything in a VRML scene graph is a node object, nodes' design specifications must be extremely flexible.

The Structure of a Node

Nodes contain these characteristics:

- The node's type name, which is something like Sphere, Box, DirectionalLight, or Sound.
- Parameters, called *fields,* that distinguish the node from other nodes of the same type.
- A set of associated events it can send and receive.

This is the node syntax:

```
DEF objectname objecttype { fields children}
```

The only required parts of this syntax are the object type and the curly braces.

Fields

Fields are the properties within a node that establish its unique characteristics. Nodes aren't required to have any fields, although some nodes have dozens of fields. When a node lacks fields, it's without any sort of descriptive content.

Each node specification defines what each field's type, name, and default value should be, and every value with a field—size, color, position, etc.—is defined by its corresponding field value. If a field's value isn't specified in a VRML file, a default value is used, which is why fields can usually be omitted from nodes and not cause a problem. It's not important to specify fields within a node in a particular order.

Two kinds of fields exist: fields that are private, unchangeable definitions of a node state's initial value, and *exposedFields*, which similarly define a node's initial value, but are public and modifiable.

Fields also have two classes, Single-Value and Multiple-Value. Single-value fields, which begin with SF, only have one value. This value can be a single number, an image, or a *vector* (three or four numbers). Multiple-value fields (indicated by MF) can contain multiple data items, which are normally surrounded by square brackets and separated by white space.

For more information on specific types of single- and multiple-value fields, refer to this link:

```
http://webspace.sgi.com/moving-worlds/spec/part1/fieldsRef.html
```

Events

Nodes can be altered by receiving events. Most nodes are equipped to handle incoming events, called *eventIn* events. By receiving these *eventIn* commands, a node changes its state. For example, a node's color can be changed from an incoming *set_* events, such as *set_color*. When a node changes, it may also reflect its altered status by sending out a number of *_changed* events, which are classified as *eventOut*. Through eventOut, nodes can send messages to destination nodes, alerting them that things have changed in nodeland. *Color_changed, position_changed*, and *on_changed* are all examples of events that spread the news about a node's changed status.

Routes—The Pathmakers

A *route* connects the node that's generating the events and the node that's receiving the events. Routes aren't nodes—they're simply the syntactic construct that tells an event which way to travel between nodes. Because routes are responsible for creating paths between nodes, they're a crucial component to making nodes function. Routes can appear inside a node where fields appear or they can be placed at the top level of a .wrl file or prototype implementation.

This is the syntax used to route events from the instigating node to the receiving node:

```
ROUTE NodeName.eventOutName_changed TO NodeName.set_eventInName
```

When nodes respond to the receipt of an event by generating an additional event, this is called an *event cascade*. All events involved in an event cascade carry the same time stamp as the original event.

The Parent-Child Relationship

As an object-oriented language, VRML uses the parent-child metaphor in its structure. Grouping nodes are employed to create hierarchical transformation graphs in VRML; all grouping nodes you'll encounter have a *children* field that contains a list of the nodes that are the group's transformation descendants. There's a coordinate space defined for children by each grouping node. Because transformations accumulate down a scene graph, the children's' coordinate space is relative to that of its parents.

Children nodes are restricted to these node types:

Anchor	NavigationInfo	SpotLight
Background	NormalInterpolator	SphereSensor
Billboard	OrientationInterpolator	Switch
Collision	PlaneSensor	TimeSensor
ColorInterpolator	PointLight	TouchSensor
CoordinateInterpolator	PositionInterpolator	Transform
CylinderSensor	ProximitySensor	Viewpoint
DirectionalLight	ScalarInterpolator	VisibilitySensor
Fog	Script	WorldInfo
Group	Shape	
LOD	Sound	

Nodes: Barren or Fecund

Several different classes of nodes exist, but the majority of nodes fall into two node categories: grouping nodes or leaf nodes. *Grouping* nodes allow you to gather a collection of nodes together and treat the collection as a single object. This technique is essential when you're trying to build complex worlds or to keep large files in manageable shape. Grouping nodes also make it possible to place groups within other groups.

Leaf nodes are barren. Unlike the fertile grouping nodes, leaf nodes cannot have children. They exist in one or more coordinate systems and they are defined by the groups to which they belong. The following nodes are considered leaf nodes:

- Lights
- Shapes
- Sounds
- Scripts
- Sensors
- Viewpoints
- Interpolators
- Nodes that give information to the browser

Bindable Children Nodes

When a node is *bound* (or it is a *bindable* node), it's dependent on values specified in another node. You can identify binding behaviors to act on faces, vertices, or parts of geometry. VRML 2.0 has four bindable children nodes. These four nodes cannot interoperate—they all have a unique behavior, meaning the user can only be simultaneously experiencing one of each type:

- Background
- Fog
- Viewpoint
- NavigationInfo

Instancing

Instancing occurs when you use the same shape multiple times within a VRML file. Because instancing allows you to reuse any node you've named, regardless of its complexity or size, it can save you lots of time in creating VRML worlds. The instances that appear are all identical; they usually only differ in their orientation. Other systems may call this technique *aliasing* or *multiple references*. The named node in instancing is referred to as the *original* node, while each of the copies is termed an *instance*.

tip *To instance, you employ the USE and DEF keywords: DEF gives names to nodes (or groups of nodes). It's the name you indicate with DEF to which you refer when instancing. These names can be supplied to USE, which allows you to create multiple instances of a node or group. The naming ability that's provided through the DEF construct gives USE its naming ability. When you give several nodes the same name, then whatever DEF is last encountered during the parsing process is used. If you want to refer to a node type in another file, use EXTERNPROTO/PROTO because DEF/USE is limited to a single file. Remember, the USE name must exactly match the DEF name, otherwise the browser won't know where to go.*

Because new node instances created through this process are carbon copies of their originals, instancing can be an efficient and interesting technique to apply in VRML world creation. Lots of objects exist that merit reuse, and employing USE judiciously leads to powerful, but compact, VRML files. (See Figure 3-1.)

In the previous example, you can see how the DEF and USE constructs can be misused. For more information on how DEF and USE are employed, surf over to the home of this graphic and read the information on scene graphs:

```
http://HTTP.CS.Berkeley.EDU/~daishi/vrml/vrml.html
```

FIGURE 3-1

In this graphic, figure (a) shows an illegal USE contained within the DEF it references; figure (b) shows an illegal USE pointing to an undeclared DEF.

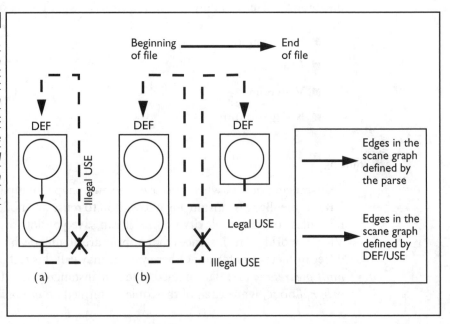

An Example of Instancing

When the following scene is rendered, it results in three spheres being drawn. The spheres are both named "Joe." Note that the second (smaller) sphere is drawn twice on either side of the first (larger) sphere:

```
#VRML Draft #2 V2.0 utf8
Transform {
  children [

    DEF Joe Sphere { }
    Transform {
      translation 2 0 0
      children [
        DEF Joe Sphere { radius .2 }
      ]
    }

    Transform {
      translation -2 0 0
      children [
        # radius .2 sphere will be used here; most recent one defined
        USE Joe ]
    }

  ]
}
```

Prototyping

Prototyping makes it possible to extend your world to include nodes that don't technically exist. When you prototype, you can define a new node in terms of other pre-defined nodes. All of the VRML 1.0 extension mechanisms (such as fields[] and isA) are superseded by prototypes. Through EXTERNPROTO you can specify how you want your objects (or worlds or behaviors) to be used within other objects (or worlds or behaviors). Prototyping also permits application-specific policies to be imposed on a general scene structure. Because prototyping lets you define a world structure once, and then reuse it, it conserves bandwidth. Prototyping also packages behavior and/or geometry more conveniently.

Remember, a prototype only declares a new *kind* of node. If you want to create a new *instance* of a node and insert it into a scene graph, you must instantiate a prototype instance.

Here are the syntaxes used to declare a prototype's interface. These syntaxes can contain any number of field/eventIn/eventOut declarations, in any order:

```
PROTO name [ field    fieldType name defaultValue
             eventIn   fieldType name
             eventOut fieldType name
         ] { implementation }
EXTERNPROTO name [ field    fieldType name
                   eventIn   fieldType name
                   eventOut fieldType name
               ] URL(s)
```

Bounding Boxes

VRML 2.0 has several nodes that include a bounding box field. Bounding boxes help you to navigate more efficiently through VRML worlds: a *bounding box* is an empty box that shows what an object's dimensions will be when it's completely loaded. With the help of bounding boxes, it's often possible to begin navigating through a world before it's had time to load fully because you can see the rough cubes formed by bounding boxes around the objects, which have yet to materialize. VRML calculates the bounding box for each defined shape it encounters on-the-fly. The bounding box field is used by grouping nodes to help the browser to determine a group's approximate size.

The default size for bounding boxes is -1, -1, -1; when the browser encounters these numbers, it knows it must either compute the actual size or assume the most conservative case. *BboxSize* field values must be greater than or equal to 0.0 but, beyond this rule, the results are undefined. You can have a *bboxSize* value of 0, 0, 0, which represents an infinitely small box or a point in space. It's conceivable the bounding box may change when the children of any specific node are changed.

To specify a maximal bounding box for the objects inside a grouping node, use the *bboxCenter* and *bboxSize* fields. These fields act as hints and they can assist certain operations, such as deciding whether or not to draw a group. In cases where the specified bounding box is smaller than the group's true bounding box, the results are undefined.

When you create bounding boxes, it's imperative to consider future effects because the bounding box must be sufficiently large to contain whatever effects or objects a group's children require. Future movement from animating children contained in these boxes must be accommodated, as well. Bounding boxes shouldn't contain any transformations that are performed by the group itself—rather, a bounding box is ideally the union of the group's children's bounding boxes.

The Way of the Node: How Nodes Are Processed

Most VRML browsers or renderers undertake a series of steps when they encounter a VRML file. In the following sections, you'll see the five components of the node processing sequence:

- Parsing
- Traversing
- Rendering
- Translating
- Picking

Parsing

Parsing is a browser's initial action upon loading a VRML file. In parsing, the VRML viewer looks at each node and determines whether the node has any children. If children exist, they're studied, as are the children of the children (this process can go on to the great-great-great-great grandchild level, if this many child nodes exist). Child nodes are always processed before parent nodes wherever nodes are grouped together.

When the VRML viewer completes all its parsing tasks, it generates a class tree delineating your document's structure.

Traversing

Traversing is a virtual reminder that children carry lifelong instructions from their parents; during this stage, a child's state is passed onto each successive child, and then onto the group's parents. In traversing, the browser also creates a rendering display list that is used in the next step of the process. This list describes exactly how the scene will be drawn and indicates what functions will be used in the drawing.

Rendering

Rendering is the first graphical indication that something is happening with your VRML file; in this state, the VRML browser draws the objects that are specified in the rendering display list.

World Transforming

By this point, you're able to move through the world. You can walk through the world, change its orientation by rotating it on its axis, or move the scene from side to side (or up, down, forward, backward, etc.—at least with most browsers).

Picking

Picking is the final step in the node processing sequence. The world is completely intact at this point; you can click on 3-D objects, as well as wander through the scene, exploring everything in its fully loaded glory. Links to other VRML worlds can be activated or you can click on hyperlinks to the Internet at large.

An Overview of Node Types

Understanding what specific node types accomplish is the most powerful way to create convincing VRML worlds. Although the fields that VRML nodes contain can be ordered in any way you like, the nodes themselves cannot. When the nodes are out of order in a VRML file, the world it creates will not appear as intended. A table may appear upside down or you can end up putting a lawn in the wrong place. Although chance elements may take your oeuvre into interesting realms, learning to order your nodes accurately ensures that your world's reality only trips in the direction of your choice.

Node Changes in VRML 2.0

Two major changes exist in the node structure of VRML 2.0:

- The Transformation and Separator nodes are combined. In the new specification, a Transform defines a coordinate system that's relative to its parent.

- Shape properties (shapeHints, material, texture) no longer exist. They've been transformed into an integral part of the shape.

These two implementations improve VRML 2.0's performance and lower its memory requirements. The new Shape and Appearance modes simplify the VRML design process by removing nodes, such as Separator and MatrixTransform, and by redefining nodes like Transform.

New Node Types in VRML 2.0

Each of the following nodes will be covered in depth in their appropriate categories. Some nodes were eliminated from Moving Worlds VRML 2.0; they will be covered in the following section.

- Grouping Nodes
- Browser Information
- Lights and Lighting
- Sound
- Shapes
- Geometry
- Appearance
- Geometric Sensors
- Special Nodes

Nodes Changed in Moving Worlds VRML 2.0

Here's a list of node changes in the new specification:

- ASCIIText—replaced with Text
- Info—replaced with WorldInfo
- OrthographicCamera—shifted to browser UI responsibility (that is, browsers may provide an orthographic view of a world as an option)
- PerspectiveCamera—replaced with Viewpoint
- Separator—use Transform instead

- Transformation nodes—incorporated into Transform

- MatrixTransform

- Transform

- Translation

- Rotation

- Scale

Important New "Common Nodes"

Some of the most important new nodes have been lumped together under the classification *Common* nodes. Here are some of these common nodes, including those that affect lighting, sound, and informational qualities.

AudioClip

```
AudioClip {
    exposedField    SFString  description        " "
    exposedField    SFBool    loop               FALSE
    exposedField    SFFloat   pitch              1.0
    exposedField    SFTime    startTime          0
    exposedField    SFTime    stopTime           0
    exposedField    MFString  url                []
    eventOut        SFTime    duration_changed
    eventOut        SFBool    isActive
}
```

The *AudioClip* node is important. The audio data it contains can be referenced by other nodes (like the Sound node) when an audio source is required. This is one of the nodes that will propel VRML toward Mark Pesce's vision of a more sensual cyberspace, because the inclusion of sound in VRML worlds will make them significantly more convincing.

The AudioClip node contains a *description* field that's a textual description of the audio source. Browsers can display this description field in addition to (or in place of) playing the sound. All browsers will support the *wavefile* format; they are also encouraged to support MIDI files.

The Moving Worlds specification contains lots of interesting information on the AudioClip mode, including how timing can be used with it and how its pitch can be affected. Investigate the AudioClip's power as described in the spec:

```
http://vrml.sgi.com/moving-worlds/spec/part1/nodesRef.html#AudioClip
```

Shape Nodes

```
Shape {
    field SFNode appearance
    field SFNode geometry
}
```

The only reason for the existence of a *Shape* node is to contain information about geometry and appearance. The introduction of the Shape node means it's much easier to share geometry and appearances, so it's a useful inclusion in the new specification. The Shape node contains only two fields: the *geometry field,* which must contain a geometry node (Sphere, IndexedFaceSet, etc.) and the *appearance field,* which can contain one or more appearance properties (Material, ImageTexture, etc.).

Sound

```
Sound {
    exposedField SFVec3f   direction     0 0 1
    exposedField SFFloat   intensity     1
    exposedField SFVec3f   location      0 0 0
    exposedField SFFloat   maxBack       10
    exposedField SFFloat   maxFront      10
    exposedField SFFloat   minBack       1
    exposedField SFFloat   minFront      1
    exposedField SFFloat   priority      0
    exposedField SFNode    source        NULL
    field        SFBool    spatialize    TRUE
}
```

The ability to control how sound is shaped in your VRML reality, which is what the *Sound* node allows you to do, is a rich—and new—opportunity. VRML 1.0's capacities in this realm were truly limited; the only way to play sound was to link through your browser to a sound file.

VRML 2.0's Sound node is responsible for describing how sound is positioned and spatially presented within a VRML scene. You can locate your sound at a certain point or cause it to emit noise in a specific pattern (like an ellipsoid, which can point in a specific direction and make the viewer aware of the sound's location). The Sound node brings the power to imbue a scene with ambient background noise, as well. It can describe an ambient sound that will fade away at a specified distance from the sound node.

It's the *source* field that specifies what sound source the Sound node uses. The source field can specify either a MovieTexture node or an AudioClip. When no source is specified, then no audio is emitted from the Sound node.

Many fun ways exist to manipulate sound within your world. Try using *intensity*, which adjusts each sound source's volume and *priority*, which indicates which sounds are most important for the browser to play.

Lighting Nodes

Shape nodes are generally illuminated by the sum of all the lights in the VRML world, including both direct and ambient sources. There are three types of *Lighting* nodes: DirectionalLight, PointLight, and SpotLight. All three types of light source nodes contain *intensity*, *color*, and *ambientIntensity* fields. See Chapter 2 for more information on how to use the powers of these Lighting nodes or refer to the "Concepts" section of the VRML 2.0 specification, under "Lighting Model" at the following URL:

```
http://vrml.sgi.com/moving-worlds/spec/part1/concepts.html#Lighting
```

Script Node

```
Script{
    exposedField MFString url             []
    field        SFBool    directOutput   FALSE
    field        SFBool    mustEvaluate   FALSE
    # And any number of:
    eventIn      eventTypeName eventName
    field        fieldTypeName fieldName initialValue
    eventOut     eventTypeName eventName
}
```

The Script node is one of the most important new additions to VRML 2.0. Through the *Script* node, you can program the events you want your viewer to experience within a world. These events are comparatively sophisticated—you can program your world to require the viewer to drink a magic potion and perform a chanting ritual before a script reveals itself. This level of complexity is made feasible by the Script node's ability to receive, send, and process events to and from other nodes.

Much of the buzz surrounding VRML 2.0's inclusion of the Script node has to do with Java and JavaScript and their potential to bring impressive interactivity to VRML 2.0. Browsers aren't required to support any specific language, however, and, despite the hype, other languages exist besides Java and JavaScript, which can be used for VRML 2.0 scripting. For example, SGI's Cosmo player uses one called VRMLScript, which is very effective. For more information on the Script Node capacities, refer to Chapter 2 or to this URL:

```
http://vrml.sgi.com/moving-worlds/spec/part1/concepts.html#Scripting
```

WorldInfo

```
WorldInfo {
  field MFString info   []
  field SFString title  ""
}
```

WorldInfo is another new node, one that contains information about the world. The contents of WorldInfo have no impact upon how a world behaves or is represented. Instead, its data is used solely for documentation purposes.

In the *title* field, the world's name or title can be stored. Browsers can display the information contained in this field in the window browser or another location. Data besides the world's title can be thrown into the *info* field; it's useful to store crucial information about copyright, authorship, and public use in this field because *info* field data won't be lost, where a comment could be lost.

Appearance Nodes

Appearance nodes are a new—and welcome—addition to the VRML 2.0 specification. By bundling properties into an Appearance node, sharing between files becomes easier, file size more manageable, run-time improved, and instancing streamlined. Through the grace of Appearances, it's easy to create a single surface, such as a type of wood, which you can apply to many different objects and surfaces within a world.

VRML 2.0 contains the following Appearance nodes:

- Appearance
- FontStyle
- ImageTexture
- Material
- MovieTexture
- PixelTexture
- TextureTransform

Appearance Node

```
Appearance {
  exposedField SFNode material        NULL
```

```
   exposedField SFNode texture          NULL
   exposedField SFNode textureTransform NULL
}
```

The Appearance node is where the visual properties of geometry are specified through definition of the Texture and Material nodes. It's possible for each field in this node to have a NULL value. Non-NULL fields must contain a node of the appropriate type, though. If the material field is specified, it must contain a material node. The scene's lighting will be off and the unlit object color is (0,0,0) when the material field is unspecified or NULL.

If the texture field is specified, it must contain a type of Texture node (PixelTexture, ImageTexture, or MovieTexture). When the Texture node is NULL or unspecified, there's no texture applied to the object referencing the appearance. The TextureTransform node must be used if the TextureTransform field is specified. The TextureTransform field doesn't have an effect when the texture field is NULL or unspecified, or if the TextureTransform is NULL or unspecified.

FontStyle

```
FontStyle {
   field SFString family      "SERIF"
   field SFBool   horizontal  TRUE
   field MFString justify     "BEGIN"
   field SFString language    ""
   field SFBool   leftToRight TRUE
   field SFFloat  size        1.0
   field SFFloat  spacing     1.0
   field SFString style       "PLAIN"
   field SFBool   topToBottom TRUE
}
```

Use the *FontStyle* node to define the font family, size, and style of text font. You can also employ this node to control the direction of text strings, as well as specific language techniques used for non-English text.

ImageTexture

```
ImageTexture {
   exposedField MFString url     []
   field        SFBool   repeatS TRUE
   field        SFBool   repeatT TRUE
}
```

By specifying an image file, as well as general parameters for mapping to geometry, the ImageTexture node defines a texture map.

Material

```
Material {
    exposedField SFFloat ambientIntensity  0.2
    exposedField SFColor diffuseColor       0.8 0.8 0.8
    exposedField SFColor emissiveColor      0 0 0
    exposedField SFFloat shininess          0.2
    exposedField SFColor specularColor      0 0 0
    exposedField SFFloat transparency       0
}
```

The *Material* node defines what the surface material properties will be for all subsequent shapes. The material node can specify meaningful details of how your surface should look—use it to specify color, reflectivity, or whether or not an object emits light. Materials with multiple values are interpreted differently by materials with multiple values. Several fields exist within the Material node, which you can employ (or discard) to affect your scene's visible characteristics. All of these fields range from 0.0 to 1.0 and exist to determine how light will be reflected off an object. By controlling light reflectivity, these fields create objects' colors.

MovieTexture

```
MovieTexture {
    exposedField SFBool    loop              FALSE
    exposedField SFFloat   speed             1
    exposedField SFTime    startTime         0
    exposedField SFTime    stopTime          0
    exposedField MFString  url               []
    field        SFBool    repeatS           TRUE
    field        SFBool    repeatT           TRUE
    eventOut     SFFloat   duration_changed
    eventOut     SFBool    isActive
}
```

With the *MovieTexture* node, you can define a time-dependent texture map contained in a movie file, as well as the parameters to control the texture mapping and the movie. The texture maps defined in MovieTexture are structured in a 2-D coordinate system (s, t). This system ranges from 0.0 to 1.0 in both directions. (See Figure 3-2.)

The MovieTexture node can be specified by the Sound node's source field, in which case it must refer to a movie format that supports sound.

MovieTexture is a time-dependent mode, which, like TimeSensor and AudioClip, activates and deactivates at specified times.

A duration_changed eventOut is sent when a movie is loaded; *duration_changed* indicates, in seconds, how long the movie is. Scripts can read this eventOut value to see how long the movie will play. When a value of -1 exists, this means the movie hasn't been loaded or the value is unavailable.

The movie's speed is indicated by the *speed exposedField*. You can play movies backward by using a negative speed exposedField, although this technique may not work for big movie files or streaming movies.

MovieTextures can be referenced by the texture field of Appearance nodes (as movie textures) and also by the source field of a Sound node.

PixelTexture

```
PixelTexture {
    exposedField SFImage   image      0 0 0
    field        SFBool    repeatS    TRUE
    field        SFBool    repeatT    TRUE
}
```

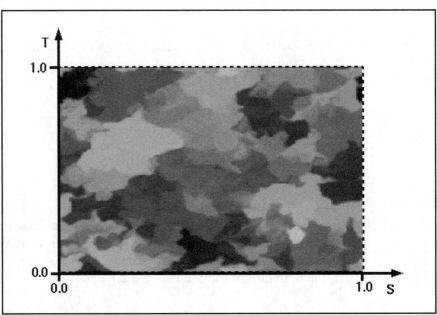

FIGURE 3-2
This graphic is an example of a texture map.

The *PixelTexture* node is used to define a 2-D image-based texture map. The PixelTexture node creates this definition through an explicit array of pixel values and parameters, which control the tiling repetition of the texture onto a geometry.

TextureTransform

```
TextureTransform {
exposedField SFVec2f center       0 0
   exposedField SFFloat rotation     0
   exposedField SFVec2f scale        1 1
   exposedField SFVec2f translation 0 0
}
```

TextureTransform defines a 2-D transformation, which is applied to texture coordinates. The TextureTransform node affects how textures are applied to the surface of a geometry. It's impossible to combine or accumulate TextureTransforms.

Sensor Nodes

Sensor nodes generate events in VRML worlds. Sensor nodes are an exciting addition to VRML 2.0, which make creating dynamic events possible. Through the ProximitySensor, VisibilitySensor, TouchSensor, CylinderSensor, PlaneSensor, SphereSensor, and the Collision group, you can create events based on user actions. The TimeSensor nodes make events transpire as time passes.

Sensor nodes have the powerful capability to be dependent on each other's actions, so by setting off one sensor node, another can be activated. After a sensor (or a script) generates an initial event, then the event is propagated along routes to other nodes. These nodes may generate events of their own, an action called an *event cascade.* When events unfurl as the result of an event cascade, they're all classified as having the same timestamp and are considered instantaneous occurrences. It's even possible for some sensors to generate multiple events simultaneously, which makes a different event cascade initiated for each event.

Because sensor nodes are children nodes in the hierarchy, they can be parented by grouping nodes. Some of the sensor nodes are *pointing device sensors,* meaning they're activated by pointing the mouse or by browser action.

Pointing Device Sensors

When the viewer points to geometry that's influenced by a specific pointing device sensor, pointing device sensors spring into action. All geometry that's descended from the sensor's parent group is influenced by pointing device sensors (except with the Anchor node, which is its own parent group).

These are the nodes classified as pointing device sensors:

- Anchor

- CylinderSensor

- PlaneSensor

- SphereSensor

- TouchSensor

DRAG SENSORS *Drag* sensors are a subset of pointing device sensors. The three drag sensors are:

- CylinderSensor

- PlaneSensor

- SphereSensor

With these drag sensors, the pointer motions cause events to be generated according to the "virtual shape" of the sensor. It's possible to construct a simple dragger by sending the output of the sensor to a Transform whose child is the object being grabbed. Here's an example:

```
Group {
      children [
          DEF S SphereSensor { autoOffset TRUE }
          DEF T Transform {
              children Shape { geometry Box {} }
          }
      ]
      ROUTE S.rotation_changed TO T.set_rotation
  }
```

Grabbing the box with the pointer will make it spin.

CylinderSensor

```
CylinderSensor {
  exposedField SFBool      autoOffset TRUE
  exposedField SFFloat     diskAngle  0.262
  exposedField SFBool      enabled    TRUE
```

```
   exposedField SFFloat    maxAngle     -1
   exposedField SFFloat    minAngle     0
   exposedField SFFloat    offset       0
   eventOut     SFBool     isActive
   eventOut     SFRotation rotation_changed
   eventOut     SFVec3f    trackPoint_changed
}
```

You can generate events through the *CylinderSensor* if a mouse (or other pointing device) is activated while it's over any descendant geometry nodes of its parent group and then moved while it's activated. When the sensor's geometry registers the pointing device is active, an isActiveTRUE event is sent.

PlaneSensor

```
PlaneSensor {
   exposedField SFBool  autoOffset          TRUE
   exposedField SFBool  enabled             TRUE
   exposedField SFVec2f maxPosition         -1 -1
   exposedField SFVec2f minPosition         0 0
   exposedField SFVec3f offset              0 0 0
   eventOut     SFBool  isActive
   eventOut     SFVec3f trackPoint_changed
   eventOut     SFVec3f translation_changed
}
```

The claim to fame of the *PlaneSensor* is it maps the motion of your mouse (or other pointing device) and translates this mapping into two dimensions (the XY plane of its local space). The PlaneSensor determines whether or not a hit occurs through the descendant geometry of its parent node.

The PlaneSensor is enabled and disabled through the *enabled* exposure field. When the enabled exposed field is TRUE, the sensor reacts appropriately to user events. If the enabled exposed field is FALSE, however, the sensor won't track user input or send output events. Should enabled receive a FALSE event when isActive is TRUE, the sensor becomes both disabled and deactivated; it outputs an isActive FALSE event. The sensor is enabled and ready for user activation when enabled receives a TRUE event.

ProximitySensor

```
ProximitySensor {
   exposedField SFVec3f    center      0 0 0
   exposedField SFVec3f    size        0 0 0
   exposedField SFBool     enabled     TRUE
   eventOut     SFBool     isActive
```

```
    eventOut     SFVec3f    position_changed
    eventOut     SFRotation orientation_changed
    eventOut     SFTime     enterTime
    eventOut     SFTime     exitTime
}
```

The job of the ProximitySensor is to generate events according to how the participant moves within a specified invisible region in the VRML space, designated by a box. Entering, exiting, and general moving are actions that can set off the proximity sensor's events. If you want to enable or disable the ProximitySensor, send it an enabled event with a TRUE or FALSE value. When the ProximitySensor is disabled, it doesn't send output events.

As the viewer enters and exits a scene's rectangular box (defined by its size and center fields), the ProximitySensor generates *isActive*TRUE/FALSE events. The browser keeps track of when the viewer enters the proximity region by timestamping the *isActive* events with the exact time the region was entered. The *size* field specifies a vector that defines the bounding box's dimensions, while the *center* field specifies where the center point of the proximity region falls in object space.

A variety of actions can cause the proximity sensor to register user movement—entering and exiting, browser navigation, Viewpoint position or orientation changes, or ProximitySensor coordinate system changes. When these movements are registered, the *orientation_changed* and *position_changed* events send events. It's possible that each ProximitySensor may be receiving and sending simultaneous events because each behaves independently.

SphereSensor

```
SphereSensor {
    exposedField SFBool     autoOffset          TRUE
    exposedField SFBool     enabled             TRUE
    exposedField SFRotation offset              0 1 0 0
    eventOut     SFBool     isActive
    eventOut     SFRotation rotation_changed
    eventOut     SFVec3f    trackPoint_changed
}
```

The *SphereSensor* is used to map the motion of your mouse (or other pointing device) into spherical rotation about the center of its local space. The rotation it produces has the sensation of a rolling ball. To determine if a hit occurs, the SphereSensor uses the descendant geometry of its parent node.

TimeSensor

```
TimeSensor {
    exposedField SFTime   cycleInterval 1
    exposedField SFBool   enabled        TRUE
    exposedField SFBool   loop           FALSE
    exposedField SFTime   startTime      0
    exposedField SFTime   stopTime       0
    eventOut     SFTime   cycleTime
    eventOut     SFFloat  fraction_changed
    eventOut     SFBool   isActive
    eventOut     SFTime   time
}
```

Through the use of *TimeSensors*, the browser can affect a scene's passage of time because TimeSensors generate events as time passes in a scene. The times TimeSensors create typically mimic "real" time—if you think a time system that chronicles the zero hour as 00:00:00 UCT January 1, 1970 can be tagged as "real." Specialized authoring applications and browsers that allow you to experiment with different speeds of time do exist, in case you become inspired to tweak with our conception of chronology.

TimeSensors are useful for making things happen at a regular interval or for making single occurrence events transpire, like the ringing of an alarm clock. TimeSensor's discrete eventOuts include *isActive* and *cycleTime*. TimeSensor's other outputs, *fraction_changed* and *time*, both generate continuous events. Like MovieTexture and AudioClip, TimeSensor is a time-dependent node, which activates and deactivates itself at specified times.

tip   *It's impossible to generate events from the "past"—if you process an event with timestamp 't' you may only succeed in generating events. Events "in the past" cannot be generated; processing an event with timestamp 't' may only result in generating events with timestamps greater than or equal to 't'.*

TouchSensor

```
TouchSensor {
    exposedField SFBool   enabled TRUE
    eventOut     SFVec3f  hitNormal_changed
    eventOut     SFVec3f  hitPoint_changed
    eventOut     SFVec2f  hitTexCoord_changed
    eventOut     SFBool   isActive
    eventOut     SFBool   isOver
```

```
    eventOut      SFTime   touchTime
}
```

The *TouchSensor* is one of the nodes that makes VRML help make cyberspace a more sensual place, as its cocreator Mark Pesce intended. TouchSensor's eventOut field *touchTime* is generated when all three of the following conditions are met:

■ The pointing device was over the geometry when it was initially activated (isActive isTRUE)

■ The pointing device is deactivated (*isActive* FALSE event is also generated)

■ The pointing device is currently over the geometry (*isOver* is TRUE)

VisibilitySensor

```
VisibilitySensor {
    exposedField SFVec3f center   0 0 0
    exposedField SFBool  enabled  TRUE
    exposedField SFVec3f size     0 0 0
    eventOut      SFTime   enterTime
    eventOut      SFTime   exitTime
    eventOut      SFBool   isActive
}
```

The *VisibilitySensor* has the power to detect visibility changes of a rectangular box as you navigate through the world. It's possible to employ the VisibilitySensor to tell when the viewer is seeing a certain object or region in the scene or to set off animation or behavior that would attract the user (or even improve performance).

Anchor

Although the *Anchor* node is fundamentally a grouping node, it also acts as a pointing device sensor when it's trying to figure out which sensor or anchor to activate. In the file that follows, you'll see how the Anchor node works its sensory magic—a click on Shape1 is handled by SensorA and SensorB, a click on Shape2 is handled by SensorC and AnchorA, and a click on Shape3 is handled by SensorD:

```
Group {
    children [
        DEF Shape1  Shape        { ... }
```

```
DEF SensorA TouchSensor { ... }
DEF SensorB PlaneSensor { ... }
DEF AnchorA Anchor {
    url "..."
    children [
        DEF Shape2  Shape { ... }
        DEF SensorC TouchSensor { ... }
        Group {
            children [
                DEF Shape3  Shape { ... }
                DEF SensorD TouchSensor { ... }
            ]
        }

    ]

}
    ]
}
```

Grouping Nodes

Use *grouping* nodes when you need to create hierarchical transformation graphs. All grouping nodes have a children field containing a list of the nodes that are the transformation descendants of the group. A coordinate space is defined for children in each grouping node. Because transformations accumulate down the scene graph hierarchy, the coordinate space is relative to the coordinate space of the parent node.

The grouping nodes are:

- Anchor

- Billboard

- Collision

- Group

- Transform

Anchor

```
Anchor {
    eventIn      MFNode    addChildren
    eventIn      MFNode    removeChildren
    exposedField MFNode    children       []
    exposedField SFString  description    ""
```

```
  exposedField MFString  parameter        []
  exposedField MFString  url              []
  field         SFVec3f   bboxCenter       0 0 0
  field         SFVec3f   bboxSize         -1 -1 -1
}
```

When you click on some geometry contained by the Anchor's children, the Anchor grouping node instructs the intended URL to be fetched over the network. If the URL leads to a valid VRML world, then that world will replace the world to which the Anchor belongs. If the URL links to a non-VRML data type, however, the browser must decide how to handle the data. The browser will typically pass it onto the necessary viewer.

To display a prompt as an alternative to the URL in the *url* field, you can employ the *description* field. To include extra information that you want the VRML or HTML browser to interpret, use the *parameter* exposedField. With browsers that allow the specification of a link's "target," use this *parameter* field:

```
Anchor {
  parameter [ "target=name_of_frame" ]
  . . .
}
```

Using an Anchor to bind a world's initial viewpoint is sometimes useful. To perform this function, you specify a URL ending with "#Viewpoint-Name," where "ViewpointName" is the name of a viewpoint defined in the file. Here's an example:

```
Anchor {
  url "http://www.school.edu/vrml/someScene.wrl#OverView"
  children  Shape { geometry Box {} }
}
```

This code includes an Anchor that loads the "someScene.wrl" file, while binding the initial viewpoint to "OverView."

Billboard

```
Billboard {
  eventIn       MFNode    addChildren
  eventIn       MFNode    removeChildren
  exposedField SFVec3f   axisOfRotation   0 1 0
  exposedField MFNode    children         []
  field         SFVec3f   bboxCenter       0 0 0
  field         SFVec3f   bboxSize         -1 -1 -1
}
```

The Billboard node works its angle by modifying its coordinate system to turn the local Z-axis so the billboard points at the viewer.

Collision

```
Collision {
    eventIn        MFNode    addChildren
    eventIn        MFNode    removeChildren
    exposedField   MFNode    children          []
    exposedField   SFBool    collide           TRUE
    field          SFVec3f   bboxCenter        0 0 0
    field          SFVec3f   bboxSize          -1 -1 -1
    field          SFNode    proxy             NULL
    eventOut       SFTime    collideTime
}
```

Collision is one of the hottest, most important new additions brought with VRML 2.0. With the Collision node, the browser can detect geometric collisions between an avatar and a scene's geometry. By default, every object scene contains is "collidable," although not all nodes are. When the browser anticipates a collision, it prevents the avatar from crashing into the geometry.

Because blowing through objects is always entertaining, you have the option of turning off the Collision node. The *Collision* node is a grouping node that can turn off collision detection for its descendants, send events that signal when a collision has transpired, and specify alternate objects that can be used for collision detection. Collision node's browsers take responsibility for defining the navigation behavior when collisions occur. When Collision nodes aren't specified, browsers detect collision with all objects during navigation. The Collision node's collide field enables and disables collision detection.

Group

```
Group {
    eventIn        MFNode    addChildren
    eventIn        MFNode    removeChildren
    exposedField   MFNode    children          []
    field          SFVec3f   bboxCenter        0 0 0
    field          SFVec3f   bboxSize          -1 -1 -1
}
```

Look at the following Transform node definition—Group nodes are equivalent to Transform nodes, but lack the transformation fields.

Transform

```
eventIn       MFNode       addChildren
  eventIn       MFNode       removeChildren
  exposedField SFVec3f       center          0 0 0
  exposedField MFNode        children        []
  exposedField SFRotation    rotation        0 0 1 0
  exposedField SFVec3f       scale           1 1 1
  exposedField SFRotation    scaleOrientation 0 0 1 0
  exposedField SFVec3f       translation     0 0 0
  field        SFVec3f       bboxCenter      0 0 0
  field        SFVec3f       bboxSize        -1 -1 -1
}
```

A *Transform node* is a grouping node that defines a coordinate system for its children, relative to the coordinate systems of its parents. In VRML 1.0, the model of transformations was a complicated one because transformations were permitted as children of group nodes and were, therefore, accumulated across the children. This model was already problematic, but coupled with VRML 2.0's addition of behaviors, it would have been a disaster. For that reason, each group node can only have one coordinate transformation. Through the additions of the old VRML 1.0 Transform nodes (seen in the following code), the new Transform node allows scaling of either coordinates or texture coordinates, arbitrary translation, and rotation:

```
Transform {
    field SFVec3f    translation        0 0 0
    field SFRotation rotation           0 0 1 0
    field SFVec3f    scaleFactor        1 1 1
    field SFRotation scaleOrientation   0 0 1 0
    field SFVec3f    center             0 0 0
    field SFVec2f    textureTranslation 0 0
    field SFFloat    textureRotation    0
    field SFVec2f    textureScaleFactor 1 1
    field SFVec2f    textureCenter      0 0
}
```

Geometry Nodes

For Geometry nodes to appear to the viewer, they must be contained by a Shape node and they can only appear in the geometry field of a Shape node. Geometry nodes can't be children of group nodes because they aren't leaf nodes. Geometry nodes, therefore, must be contained by Shape nodes. The Shape node contains one Geometry node in its geometry field. This node is required to be one of the following node types:

- Box

- Cone

- Cylinder

- ElevationGrid

- Extrusion

- IndexedFaceSet

- IndexedLineSet

- PointSet

- Sphere

- Text

Some Geometry nodes exist that contain Color, Coordinate, Normal, and TextureCoordinate as Geometry Property nodes. In these cases, Geometry Property nodes are separated as individual nodes, making instancing and sharing possible between the different Geometry nodes. The parent nodes of the Geometry node determine the local coordinate system specifying all geometry.

Box Node

```
Box {
   field     SFVec3f size  2 2 2
}
```

A *Box* node is used to specify a rectangular parallel-piped box in the local coordinate system that's aligned with the coordinate axes and centered at 0,0,0 in the local coordinate system. A Box node's default measurement is 2 units in each dimension, from -1 to +1. The size field of the Box node, which must be greater than 0.0, indicates where the box should fall on the X, Y, and Z axes. Because the Box geometry is considered solid, it only requires outside faces. (See Figure 3-3.)

Cone

```
Cone {
   field     SFFloat     bottomRadius 1
   field     SFFloat     height       2
   field     SFBool      side         TRUE
   field     SFBool      bottom       TRUE
}
```

FIGURE 3-3

This figure demonstrates the Box node's dimensions.

■

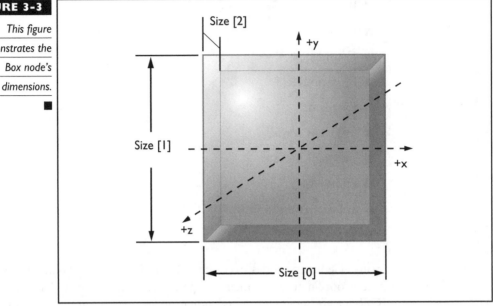

The *Cone* node specifies a simple cone whose central axis is aligned with the Y axis. The radius of the Cone's base is specified by the *bottomRadius* field, while the Cone's height (from the center of the base to the apex) is specified by the *height* field. The Cone's default is a radius of 1.0 at the bottom and a height at 2.0, with its apex at y=1 and bottom at y=-1. Both *bottomRadius* and *height* must be greater than 0.0. Because the Cone geometry is solid, it requires outside-only faces. (See Figure 3-4.)

Cylinder

```
Cylinder {
    field    SFBool     bottom   TRUE
    field    SFFloat    height   2
    field    SFFloat    radius   1
    field    SFBool     side     TRUE
    field    SFBool     top      TRUE
}
```

The *Cylinder* node represents a simple capped cylinder that's centered around the Y- axis, with a default of -1 to +1 in all three dimensions and a center at (0, 0, 0). The cylinder has three parts: the sides, the top (Y+ height), and the bottom (Y= -height). (See Figure 3-5.)

FIGURE 3-4

FIGURE 3-4

This image shows the cone's dimensions.

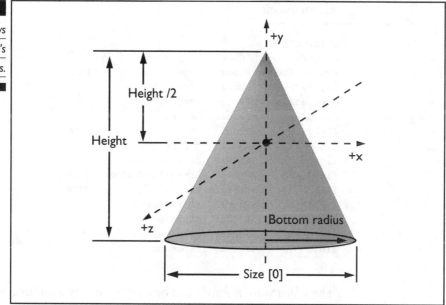

FIGURE 3-5

This image shows a cylinder's dimensions.

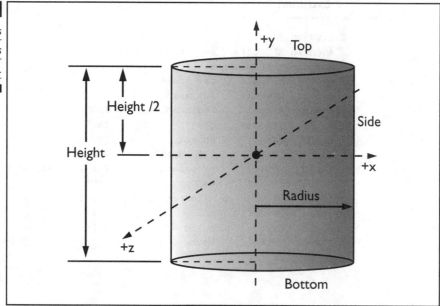

ElevationGrid

```
ElevationGrid {
    eventIn       MFFloat  set_height
    exposedField SFNode   color            NULL
    exposedField SFNode   normal           NULL
    exposedField SFNode   texCoord         NULL
    field         MFFloat  height           []
    field         SFBool   ccw              TRUE
    field         SFBool   colorPerVertex   TRUE
    field         SFFloat  creaseAngle      0
    field         SFBool   normalPerVertex  TRUE
    field         SFBool   solid            TRUE
    field         SFInt32  xDimension       0
    field         SFFloat  xSpacing         0.0
    field         SFInt32  zDimension       0
    field         SFFloat  zSpacing         0.0
}
```

The *ElevationGrid* node can be used to specify a uniform rectangular grid of varying height in the XZ plane. A scalar array of height values describe the geometry by specifying the height of a rectangular surface above each point of the grid.

Extrusion

```
Extrusion {
    eventIn MFVec2f    set_crossSection
    eventIn MFRotation set_orientation
    eventIn MFVec2f    set_scale
    eventIn MFVec3f    set_spine
    field   SFBool     beginCap      TRUE
    field   SFBool     ccw           TRUE
    field   SFBool     convex        TRUE
    field   SFFloat    creaseAngle   0
    field   MFVec2f    crossSection  [ 1 1, 1 -1, -1 -1, -1 1, 1 1 ]
    field   SFBool     endCap        TRUE
    field   MFRotation orientation   0 0 1 0
    field   MFVec2f    scale         1 1
    field   SFBool     solid         TRUE
    field   MFVec3f    spine         [ 0 0 0, 0 1 0 ]
}
```

The *Extrusion* node is used to specify geometric shapes that are based on a 2-D cross section and extruded along a 3-D spine. You can view a wide variety of shapes by scaling and rotating the cross section at each spine point.

IndexedFaceSet

```
IndexedFaceSet {
eventIn         MFInt32 set_colorIndex
   eventIn         MFInt32 set_coordIndex
   eventIn         MFInt32 set_normalIndex
   eventIn         MFInt32 set_texCoordIndex
   exposedField SFNode   color            NULL
   exposedField SFNode   coord            NULL
   exposedField SFNode   normal           NULL
   exposedField SFNode   texCoord         NULL
   field        SFBool   ccw              TRUE
   field        MFInt32  colorIndex       []
   field        SFBool   colorPerVertex   TRUE
   field        SFBool   convex           TRUE
   field        MFInt32  coordIndex       []
   field        SFFloat  creaseAngle      0
   field        MFInt32  normalIndex      []
   field        SFBool   normalPerVertex  TRUE
   field        SFBool   solid            TRUE
   field        MFInt32  texCoordIndex    []
}
```

The *IndexedFaceSet* node is used to create polygons after a set of points has been defined through vertices listed in the *coord* field. The IndexedFace-Set node is always used in conjunction with a Coordinate node and is useful in defining complex shapes.

IndexedLineSet

```
IndexedLineSet {
   eventIn         MFInt32 set_colorIndex
   eventIn         MFInt32 set_coordIndex
   exposedField SFNode   color            NULL
   exposedField SFNode   coord            NULL
   field        MFInt32  colorIndex       []
   field        SFBool   colorPerVertex   TRUE
   field        MFInt32  coordIndex       []
}
```

The *IndexedLineSet* node constructs polylines from 3-D points specified in the *coord* field. By doing so, it represents a 3-D geometry. The lines in this mode aren't texture-mapped, or lit, or collided with during collision detection.

PointSet

```
PointSet {
    exposedField  SFNode  color    NULL
    exposedField  SFNode  coord    NULL
}
```

This node represents a set of 3-D points that, in the local coordinate system, feature associated colors at each point.

Sphere

```
Sphere {
    field SFFloat radius  1
}
```

The *Sphere* node defines a sphere that's centered at (0, 0, 0). The sphere's radius field is responsible for specifying its radius and it must be greater or equal to 0.0.

When you apply a texture to a sphere, the texture covers the entire surface and wraps over the sphere in a counterclockwise fashion, starting from the back. At the point where the Y-Z plane intersects the sphere (located at the back of the shape), the texture has a seam. (See Figure 3-6.)

You can affect the sphere's texture through the TextureTransform node. Because the Sphere geometry is considered solid, it requires only outside faces.

Text

```
Text {
    exposedField  MFString string    []
    exposedField  SFNode   fontStyle NULL
    exposedField  MFFloat  length    []
    exposedField  SFFloat  maxExtent 0.0
}
```

By using the *Text* node, you can take the printed word into 2-D. The Text node can specify a string of flat, two-sided text to be positioned in the X-Y plane, meaning it's easy to make words, letters, poetry, or subliminal messaging appear in your worlds. The values that determine how the text

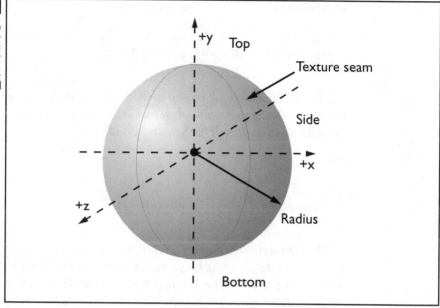

will appear are defined in the fontStyle field. Text strings are stored in visual order; they may contain multiple text strings, which are specified with the UTF-8 encoding. No collision detection exists with the Text node.

Geometric Properties

The following nodes are all properties of the Geometry mode.

COLOR

```
Color {
  exposedField MFColor color  []
}
```

The *Color* node is used to define a set of RGB colors, which are to be used in the fields of another node. The only time you'll employ color nodes is to specify multiple colors for a single piece of geometry. Examples of this function include making an object have different colors on different faces. If a geometry has both a Material node and a Color node specified, the colors ideally replace the material's diffuse material. Colors don't win out over textures, however—when a Texture node and a Color node are both specified, the Color node is simply ignored.

COORDINATE

```
Coordinate {
  exposedField MFVec3f point   []
}
```

The *Coordinate* node is used to define the set of 3-D coordinates you want to use in the *coord* field of vertex-based geometry nodes (including IndexedLineSet, IndexedFaceSet, and PointSet).

NORMAL

```
Normal {
  exposedField MFVec3f vector   []
}
```

The *Normal* node defines a set of 3-D surface normal vectors used by the geometry nodes, such as ElevationGrid and IndexedFaceSet, which follow it in the scene graph. The Normal node's definitions are used in the *vector* fields of these geometry nodes. The Normal node operates under a shroud of invisibility: its results are invisible during rendering. The job of the Normal node is simply to replace the rendering state's current normals and prepare them for the next round of nodes to use. Unless normals are unit length, they produce undefined results.

TEXTURECOORDINATE

```
TextureCoordinate {
  exposedField MFVec2f point   []
}
```

Like the Normal node, the *TextureCoordinate* node specifies elements for use with ElevationGrid and IndexedFaceSet, the vertex-based geometry nodes. Its 2-D texture coordinates what the TextureCoordinate node specifies; the geometry nodes use these coordinates to map from textures to the vertices. By identifying a location in the texture map, texture coordinates also identify what the color value should be.

Special Nodes

Only a few nodes don't fit easily within node classifications:

- Inline
- LOD
- Switch

Inline

```
Inline {
  exposedField MFString url        []
  field        SFVec3f  bboxCenter 0 0 0
  field        SFVec3f  bboxSize   -1 -1 -1
}
```

The URLs of the *Inline* node refer to a valid VRML file containing a list of children nodes at its top level. If the URL refers to a non-VRML file or if the file has nonchildren nodes at its top level, then the results are undefined. In the case of multiple URLs being specified, the browser can appease the viewer by displaying a lower preference file while it attempts to procure the preferred file. This substitution can also occur if the desired file is unavailable.

LOD

```
LOD {
  exposedField MFNode   level      []
  field        SFVec3f  center     0 0 0
  field        MFFloat  range      []
}
```

The *Level Of Detail* (LOD) node specifies how much detail or complexity a given object should have. The LOD node also tosses browsers some hints about which version of an object should be chosen based on how much distance separates the viewer and the object. For this ability alone, the LOD node has a powerful impact over the VRML viewing experience because it can effectively tailor worlds according to the viewer's location. By setting the LOD ranges so the transitions between the levels of detail are smooth, you can ensure your viewer has as seamless a ride as possible.

Browsers have the right to disregard or adjust LOD as necessary. For that reason, it's a good idea not to overwhelm the browser with a surplus of LOD information. Restrict yourself to only specifying ranges where the detail is merited and nest LOD nodes both with and without ranges.

Switch

```
Switch {
  exposedField   MFNode  choice       []
  exposedField   SFInt32 whichChoice  -1
}
```

Using the *Switch* grouping node lets you traverse zero or one of the nodes specified in the *choice* field. The Switch grouping node is handy when you're manipulating VRML scenes with scripts or programs because this group node can traverse one, none, or all of its children.

Background

```
Background {
    eventIn       SFBool    set_bind
    exposedField  MFFloat   groundAngle   []
    exposedfield  MFColor   groundColor   []
    exposedField  MFString  backUrl       []
    exposedField  MFString  bottomUrl     []
    exposedField  MFString  frontUrl      []
    exposedField  MFString  leftUrl       []
    exposedField  MFString  rightUrl      []
    exposedField  MFString  topUrl        []
    exposedField  MFFloat   skyAngle      []
    exposedField  MFColor   skyColor      [ 0 0 0 ]
    eventOut      SFBool    isBound
}
```

With the *Background* node, you can specify a single color backdrop, which simulates sky, ground, and background texture all at once. As bindable children nodes, Background nodes are affected by the accumulated rotation of their parents.

If a Background is active while a Fog node is also active, the background won't show any fog. If you want the background to reflect fog, you must set the Background values to match the fog (by making ground colors fade to foggy colors in the distance, etc.). The Background node is found during the first reading of the world that becomes automatically bound and, therefore is used when the world is loaded.

Fog

```
Fog {
    exposedField SFColor  color            1 1 1
    exposedField SFString fogType          "LINEAR"
    exposedField SFFloat  visibilityRange  0
    eventIn      SFBool   set_bind
    eventOut     SFBool   isBound
}
```

Ah, finally a chance to add some clandestine intrigue to VRML worlds—the Fog node. By using the *Fog* node, you can simulate a mysterious fog creeping into your scenes. This effect is achieved by blending objects with the color specified by the *color* field, which is based on the distance between objects and the viewer. Fog can wholly obscure objects through its *visibilityRange*.

note   *If you want to disable the Fog node, a* visibilityRange *of 0.0 or less will do so.*

For the most impressive visual result, make the Background node the same color as the Fog node. If you want objects to do a smooth fade from your world, experiment with the *visibilityLimit* field of the NavigationInfo mode.

Viewpoint

```
Viewpoint {
    eventIn       SFBool      set_bind
    exposedField  SFFloat     fieldOfView    0.785398
    exposedField  SFBool      jump           TRUE
    exposedField  SFRotation  orientation    0 0 1  0
    exposedField  SFVec3f     position       0 0 10
    field         SFString    description    ""
    eventOut      SFTime      bindTime
    eventOut      SFBool      isBound
}
```

With the *Viewpoint* node, you can define a specific viewing location for your scene. The Viewpoint node has replaced VRML 1.0's PerspectiveCamera node.

If you want your viewers to have a particular viewing experience in your VRML world, you can bind the user to a Viewpoint and then animate the Viewpoint (or the transformations above it). Even if the Viewpoint or its parent transformations are being animated, the browser permits navigation of the viewer's vantage, according to the Viewpoint's coordinate system.

NavigationInfo

```
NavigationInfo {
    eventIn       SFBool      set_bind
    exposedField  MFFloat     avatarSize     [ 0.25, 1.6, 0.75 ]
    exposedField  SFBool      headlight      TRUE
```

```
exposedField SFFloat   speed              1.0
exposedField MFString  type               "WALK"
exposedField SFFloat   visibilityLimit    0.0
eventOut     SFBool    isBound
}
```

Information that describes physical characteristics of the viewing model, as well as of the viewer, is contained by the *NavigationInfo* node. The current NavigationInfo is a perennially dependent child—whenever the current Viewpoint changes, the current NavigationInfo must be reparented to it. Likewise, whenever the current NavigationInfo is altered, it's required that the new NavigationInfo is reparented to the current Viewpoint.

Interpolator Nodes

By using an *Interpolator* node, you can define a piecewise linear function, *f(t)*, on the interval *(-infinity, infinity)*. Interpolator nodes are designed for linear keyframe animation; they come in six types:

- ColorInterpolator
- CoordinateInterpolator
- NormalInterpolator
- OrientationInterpolator
- PositionInterpolator
- ScalarInterpolator

All of the Interpolator nodes have a common set of fields and semantics:

```
exposedField MFFloat      key             [...]
    exposedField MF<type>    keyValue         [...]
    eventIn      SFFloat     set_fraction
    eventOut     [S|M]F<type> value_changed
```

Summary

Although this chapter contains far too much detailed information for normal brains to remember, we hope reading through these definitions and explanations guides you in your quest to create stellar VRML. If this mass of syntax has disconcerted you, remember VRML authoring tools make it possible to ignore completely the gory syntactical details. So rest assured—no need exists to memorize chunks of exact node definitions—unless you *want* to.

Many interesting changes have occurred between earlier specifications of VRML and today's version, the 2.0 Moving Worlds specification. Although we've covered some of the big changes between the specifications, it wasn't possible to address them all. If you're interested in comparing the specifications, these URLs will take you to the official homes of the two documents:

VRML 1.0:

```
http://vrml.wired.com/vrml.tech/crml10-3.html
```

VRML 1.1:

```
http://vag.vrml.org/vrml1-1 .html
```

Version 2.0:

```
http://webspace.sgi.com/moving-worlds/spec/spec.main.html
```

If you're interested in keeping up with VRML development, check out the links at ZDNet's VRMLinks page:

```
http://www.zdnet.com/zdi/vrml/filters/links.html
```

building

VRML

Worlc

chapter 4

Creating Good VRML

CREATING good VRML isn't a question of dotting an "i" or crossing a "t"—the myriad creation tools available preclude most syntactical problems. It's more a matter of tweaking style, which requires deeper knowledge, good instinct, and some sleight-of-hand. It's important to remember when creating a VRML world that you're making something thousands of people with hundreds of different computer configurations may visit. Many of the same caveats that apply to creating other types of CPU- and bandwidth-intensive Web content, such as Shockwave movies, apply to VRML. In this chapter we'll look at what you should watch for, how to speed up your VRML, and how to create effective VRML worlds.

Speed Versus Reality

Because its acronym contains the words "virtual reality," it's obvious VRML's creators intended it as a method of delivering and rendering realistic worlds and objects. Unfortunately, the current state of computer technology prevents a quicksilver view of cyberspace, as you can see in the movie *Johnny Mnemonic* or even the cartoony view of reality in *Toy Story*. Consequently, most people's first exposure to VRML is disappointing: They either download a small object that's boring, pointless, and lacking in texture, or a large world that takes several minutes to download, only to find they don't have enough memory to render fully what they've been waiting for (often, for good measure, it crashes their browser, too). Balancing speed, accessibility, and realism is the key to creating good VRML.

Consider the Client Machine's CPU

Despite hardware advances since its inception, VRML still runs best on a Silicon Graphics system. It's one of the few machines that has the on-the-fly rendering capabilities necessary to make large, complex VRML worlds manageable.

In reality, however, most Internet users run Windows 95 on a 486 or Pentium CPU, while many others run the Macintosh 7.5 OS with a PowerPC 601 CPU. These processors simply don't have the capability to render complex VRML worlds quickly. It's essential to remember your audience is most likely to consist of users with such systems and design accordingly.

Unfortunately, there's no "typical" system for which you can safely design. You can never predict what will be in the guts of any system that's rendering your world file when it's published on the Internet. Even when you're on a LAN where everyone has the same general setup, the differences don't start and stop at the processor. Two seemingly identical Pentium systems can have radically different rendering rates because of differences in architecture. High-end video hardware can also make for smoother and faster VRML: A PCI video card with lots of video RAM can help you fly your way around a VRML world.

The best rule to follow is: Make the world usable on a machine that's one step down from the system on which it's developed. For instance, if the virtual world is developed on a Power Macintosh 9500 with a PowerPC 604 processor, make it tolerable on a Power Macintosh 6100 with a 601 processor. As with any type of Web publishing, it's up to the creator to judge what performance the audience can tolerate. We suggest you try out your VRML world on as many systems as possible, including some slower, more old-fashioned varieties, for a different kind of "reality check."

Consider the Client Machine's Internet Connection

If you plan to make your VRML world available via the Internet, connection speed is something that affects how intricate you can make your VRML world. The larger and more complex the world, the larger the file will be. Larger files take longer to download; Internet users are often an impatient breed and they will quickly click on another URL if yours takes too long to load. To avoid this ignominious fate, here are some points about Internet connections to bear in mind while building VRML worlds:

- Many Internet users connect from home, where they probably have only a 28.8 Kbps modem connection, at best.

■ The Internet is a collection of networks: Just because you and the client system have fast connections, doesn't mean the networks in-between are also fast. They could be slow, congested, or cover great distances. The Internet is only as fast as the slowest link between the client and the server.

■ No matter what kind of connection you or your world's users have, it will never be as fast as loading it from your local hard drive. It's a good idea to test (or at least guess) how long it takes to load using a variety of connection methods. Table 4-1 gives you a basic idea of how long it takes to download a typical VRML file. The times listed are based on straight data throughput and they assume no compression or overhead for protocols, machine load, network load, or line quality.

Keeping these points in mind will help prevent you from creating a world that's too large for your intended audience to download comfortably from your server. Nobody wants to try to drain a swimming pool through a straw!

Textures as a Bottleneck

Texture maps are both a blessing and a curse: Mapping an image over an object allows you to create a "painted-on" level of detail most computers wouldn't be able to render effectively. But where CPU cycles are saved, more bandwidth may be consumed by large, rich graphic files. As with HTML, images aren't embedded within a VRML file itself, but are loaded from the Web server via separate connections. Whereas VRML is highly compressible text, an image file is raw binary data, which is often compressed to its practical limit.

Connection Type	Transfer Rate
T1 (1.54 Mbps)	.8 seconds
ISDN (128 Kbps)	9.4 seconds
Modem (28.8 Kbps)	41.7 seconds

TABLE 4-1 *A Comparison of Amount of Time Needed to Download a Typical GNU-Zipped World File of 150K via a Typical Modem, Bonded ISDN, or a T1 Connection* ■

Follow these good guidelines when you create texture maps for Internet delivery:

- Save texture maps for when extreme detail is needed. Don't just use them "because you can." There are elements to almost all VRML worlds that are nothing more than unimportant placeholders.

- Experiment with shading, lighting, and color to see if you can find reasonable and effective alternatives to texture maps. Sometimes the proper combinations allow a viewer to get the gist of an object sans texture maps.

- Let the viewer's brain fill in the gaps. It's amazing how easily the human brain can create a *gestalt* for a scene and fill in details it thinks *should* be there, even when they're absent. For instance, a viewer may remember leaves on a tree that doesn't play an important role in your VRML scene, even if you don't have an image map for leaves surrounding the tree top.

- Stick to standard Web image file formats like GIF, JPEG, and PNG. These files are easily rendered by VRML browsers and are compressed to save bandwidth. Other file types, such as TIFF and BMP, are too bulky and often won't render in VRML browsers.

- Use 16-bit color depths or less; 16-bit color supplies 32,768 colors (hopefully, more than enough!). Dropping to 8-bit depth (256 colors) can cut file sizes in half!

- Tile small textures for wallpaper or similar background images whenever possible.

- Try to use any texture several times in the same world; it can be cached after the first use and, subsequently, will save time.

- Do not disperse images across too many machines or too many networks. Although situating images on different machines can save resources and sometimes speed downloads, network lags can disrupt the browser when it's putting a world together.

Texture maps are great ways to improve the realism of a VRML world without sacrificing CPU cycles—but they should also be used sparingly. Not only can this approach save bandwidth, it can also enhance the artistic value of your world. As with billboards, too many texture maps can create a noisy and annoying scene.

Ways to Increase the Speed of VRML Worlds

As with any type of source code, VRML can be optimized to produce faster, cleaner results. For most programming languages such as C or Perl, optimization concerns itself with memory allocation, building efficient arrays, and reducing code path lengths. VRML itself isn't concerned with any of these—it leaves all of that up to the VRML browser; thus, VRML is a language of ends rather than means.

Essentially, VRML instructs a browser on *what* to do, rather than *how* to do it. It doesn't care where the browser stores the transformation matrix of a cube in the computer's memory; it only cares that the browser makes the cube move. Excluding syntax problems, there's really no such thing as "bad" VRML code that causes a browser to crash. A VRML browser will usually crash because it contains a few bugs, which the VRML code happened to flush into the open.

Because of this, there are really only two factors you can optimize in VRML code: delivery rates and rendering speed. We'll cover ways to increase both of these in the following sections.

GZIP Your Worlds

An excellent way to decrease the file size of a VRML world for transfer is by using the Free Software Foundation's GNU Zip utility: GZIP. GZIP exists for several platforms, including UNIX, PC, and Macintosh, and many VRML browsers contain routines for unzipping GZIPped worlds automatically.

Because they're text-only, VRML world files can be compressed to an astonishing degree. For example, a 358 KB ".wrl" file ends up being about 69 KB once compressed, a 5:1 compression ratio! An incredible amount of download time can be saved by compressing files. Of course, you don't want the amount of time it takes to uncompress a file to make the total amount of time—from download to render—actually increase. So it's a good idea to test how long it takes to download and uncompress your GZIPped worlds, versus how long it takes just to download an uncompressed ".wrl" file.

You can get GZIP for Windows 95 at the Winsite FTP site:

```
ftp://ftp.winsite.com/pub/pc/win95/dskutil/
```

GZIP for the Macintosh can be found at any of the Info-Mac mirror sites, including the ever-popular Wuarchive:

```
ftp://wuarchive.wustl.edu/systems/mac/info-mac/cmp/
```

GZIP comes standard with most UNIX distributions. If yours didn't happen to include it, you can get it from the GNU archive:

```
ftp://ftp.uu.net/archive/systems/gnu/
```

Don't Create Objects That Aren't Visible

Although "don't create objects that aren't visible" sounds like an obvious waste of time, placing such objects into a VRML world also has performance repercussions. What this really means is you shouldn't create objects *inside* of other objects. For example, why would you create garbage inside a closed trash can, which will never be opened by the user? Not only will these objects never be seen, they'll still be rendered by the VRML browser. The extra time to render the garbage causes delays in viewing the scene.

Use Primitives Rather than Polygons

Many VRML browsers contain algorithms that let them render primitives much quicker than an object created from scratch with polygons. Examples of such primitives include the shape nodes: Cone, Cube, Cylinder, and Sphere.

The computational savings (both for the author's brain and the client system) are obvious when you consider that a primitive, such as a Sphere, has only one variable property: its radius. By comparison, the information necessary to create a sphere-like polyhedron would be enormous.

Use as Few Polygons as Possible

When creating any VRML world or object, use as few polygons as you possibly can. The complexity of a VRML world is a direct function of how many polygons it contains; transforming one polygon after another causes a drain on any CPU. Table 4-2 should give you an idea of the processing power necessary to transform a given number of polygons smoothly.

For the types of systems in common use today, you should keep your worlds in the range of 5,000 polygons. As a general rule, most VRML experts

CPU	# of Polygons
386 or 68030	1 - 1,000
486 or 68040	1,000 - 3,000
Pentium 60 or PowerPC 601	3,000 - 6,000
Pentium 133 or PowerPC 604	6,000 - 10,000
PentiumPro or SGI	10,000 +

TABLE 4-2   *Several CPU Types and the Number of Polygons They Can Transform Smoothly* ■

agree you should *never* let your world exceed 10,000 polygons! On most people's machines, such a world would be too choppy to be usable.

The Pros and Cons of WWWInline

WWWInline, one of the Internet-specific VRML nodes, is also one of the most powerful statements in the VRML code set. As with any power, it's something you must learn to use wisely. Much like the <IMG SRC> tag in HTML, WWWInline can be used to "draw-upon" resources from other Web servers on the Internet. With <IMG SRC>, an image is loaded using a URL pointing to an image file on a different server from the one on which the document resides, as in:

```
<IMG SRC="http://www2.outer.net/caffeine.gif">
```

This line pulls the image "caffeine.gif" from the server "www2.outer.net", no matter from what server the original HTML document is called.

WWWInline works in much the same way, except it's often used to reference another ".wrl" file from within a VRML world (although it can also be used to grab texture maps from other Web servers). A typical WWWInline call looks something like this:

```
WWWInline {
    name "http://www.outer.net/VRML/office.wrl"
    bboxSize 15 15 15
    bboxCenter 0 0 0
}
```

This bit of code includes the "office.wrl" world file from the server "www.outer.net" in the calling VRML world. The *bboxSize* field sets the height, width, and depth of the bounding box around the object residing at *bboxCenter*. These fields let the VRML browser know the size of the world before it's loaded so it can create a bounding box around the area it will occupy. The bounding box is a visual clue that lets users know data is still being retrieved to create the scene.

Figure 4-1 gives you an example of how WWWInline should work. The client with the VRML browser accesses the world file "cool.wrl" from "www.servera.com". When the browser steps through the VRML code, it comes across the WWWInline statement. This statement instructs it to include the world file "cooler.wrl" from the server "www.serverb.com" within the original world.

Problems with WWWInline

Unfortunately, the distributed file feature of WWWInline can also cause difficulties in a VRML world. The problem is not the command itself, but that various pieces of your VRML pie may be housed on a multitude of

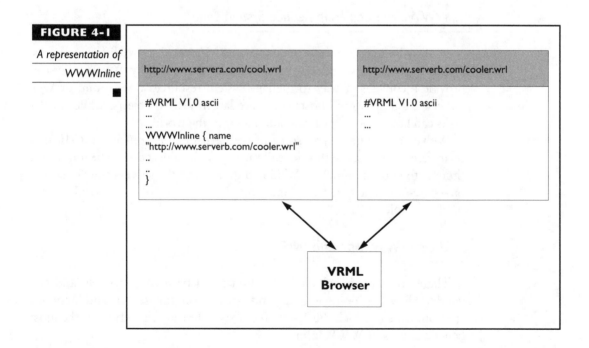

FIGURE 4-1

A representation of WWWInline

servers residing on a variety of networks. You may or may not have control over any or all of these servers. What if one of them crashes? What if one of the Internet Service Providers has a routing problem? What if you're "borrowing" someone else's ".wrl" file and he or she moves to another job and takes the file along?

The answer is the WWWInlined world affected by this will display bounding boxes where all of the worlds it can't load *should* be! If all the bits of the WWWInlined world live on a single server or on servers under your control on your network, then the chance of this occurring is reduced.

A Single Server Isn't the Solution

This doesn't mean all WWWInline documents that are part of a world should reside on a single server. Many browsers have the capability to open several simultaneous connections, meaning they can load several WWWInline documents at once. Netscape Navigator and other Web browsers perform a similar action when downloading multiple image files simultaneously. If numerous clients attempt to download the same half-dozen or so world files at the same time, this could overwhelm some Web servers.

WWWInline Can Help Reduce System Load

By distributing the objects that form a VRML world across different servers, system load on any single server can be lessened. In this way, WWWInline can provide a convenient way to manage system resources on a group of Web servers: Large, powerful hosts can serve larger VRML objects, while smaller hosts can house those parts that add flavor to the world.

We've already given you some of the caveats about putting VRML files on different servers, but this doesn't mean you shouldn't do it. The important thing is to choose your WWWInlined data—and the servers they're stored on—carefully. The speed, aesthetics, and functionality of your world depend on these choices!

Using WWWInline Effectively

There are ways in which WWWInline can be used effectively and elegantly. How it's done will depend greatly on the server and network environments in which the ".wrl" files exist. Here are three tips for the most beneficial uses of WWWInline:

1. Gathering data that may change.

2. Serving data used by many documents.

3. Providing a new LOD.

We'll look at each of these tips in depth and see how each one can help you use WWWInline beneficially.

GATHERING DATA THAT MAY CHANGE   One great way to use WWWInline is to insert dynamic objects into a world. These objects are often generated or chosen by a CGI program called by the WWWInline statement. The output can be based on user action, the output of another CGI program, or some other internal event. An example of this would be to insert a clock to display the current time in a VRML room. A meteorologist could use it to display a 3-D view of cloud cover, mapped over a model of the Earth, for a given time of day.

VRML 2.0 allows for a mixture of VRML and Java classes. As more VRML 2.0 worlds spring up, no doubt a similar application of WWWInline to client-side Java applets will occur. Netscape already has something similar to this in their VRML extensions for Live 3-D, which can produce minor animation.

SERVING DATA USED BY MANY DOCUMENTS   Objects and textures used by many World Wide Web documents—VRML or otherwise—are good candidates for WWWInline. For example, you may want to use the simulated woodgrain background on your HTML home page as a texture map for a tabletop in a VRML world; you may have several different worlds where that table would look nice. WWWInlining makes it possible for you to share images with your HTML pages and to share VRML objects between worlds, without duplicating copies.

PROVIDING A NEW LEVEL-OF-DETAIL   Combining WWWInline with the LOD group provides a powerful synergistic tool for VRML developers. They basically help imbue each other with some much-needed "smarts" when it comes to loading extra data.

LOD allows a VRML browser to load a version of an object based on the viewer's point of view: The closer a viewer's "eyepoint" moves toward an object, the richer and more intricate the object becomes. For instance, in a given VRML world you may see a point of light on a field of black. As you move closer, the light might begin to expand into a reflective blue sphere. Move closer still and you see it's actually a model of the Earth, with texture-mapped clouds and continents.

LOD keeps the VRML browser from rendering unnecessary detail until the viewer is actually close enough to see it. This is an effective way to speed up a VRML world, without ultimately sacrificing data you may eventually want to show. Mixing LOD with the WWWInline can speed things up further by not even *loading* more detailed (and usually data-intensive) objects until they're required.

Here's a "pseudo code" example of using the LOD group with the WWWInline node, based on the Earth example in the preceding passage:

```
LOD {
    range [ far, closer, near Earth orbit ]
    center x y z
    Sphere {
        radius small_size
    }
    Separator {
        diffuseColor 0 0 1
        Sphere {
            radius bigger_size
        }
    }
    WWWInline {
        name "http://www.earthpics.com/earthwaterandsky.wrl"
        bboxSize x y z
        bboxCenter x-center y-center z-center
    }
}
```

As you can see, the first two views of the Earth are Spheres whose nodes exist in this ".wrl" file. The closest and highest-resolution view of the Earth is actually loaded from another server, which happens to contain VRML models of the Earth. If that model of the Earth was really part of this file, then the file would have to be much larger. If the viewer never even got close to the Earth, then loading that much data would be a waste of time.

The rendering speed of your VRML world should be one of your primary concerns when you create it. No way exists for you to speed up friends' Internet connection, their CPU, or their VRML browser (unless you want the daunting task of writing your own). But you can lessen the burden all these factors impose by targeting certain systems and making your worlds Internet-friendly.

Avoid Building "Movie Set" Worlds

During the Shogunate era, the Japanese emperor maintained a garden at his palace, which looked best when viewed through a certain window in a certain room. Instead of being planted for strolling through, this garden was planted for viewing. When creating a VRML world, you'll want to take exactly the opposite approach. After all, VRML worlds are meant to provide a 3-D interactive environment for a user to explore, manipulate, use, and (hopefully) to find somewhat entertaining.

A modern analogy to the emperor's garden is a movie set. Remember the gunslinger looking down the dusty main strip of Dodge City in a Spaghetti Western? To the left and right of him are a saloon, a funeral home, a jailhouse, and several other buildings. These buildings look perfectly realistic from the gunslinger's point of view. If looked at sidelong, however, you would see these "buildings" are facades, propped up by wooden planks. A visitor to a VRML world constructed like this would be disappointed. He or she would actually want to go *inside* one of the buildings and walk around.

Figure 4-2 shows an example of a "movie set" world created in Autodesk's 3-D Studio. It's a look at a "cybercafe" that orbits the Earth on a space station. This is, of course, the best vantage point from which to examine it. If you were to actually move around the cafe, you would see things look a little "off." Objects would be suspended in mid-air and parts of objects wouldn't be attached. The Earth itself is also an object, the same relative size as the table, positioned close to the observation window. This means if you were to take a walk through the cafe, the Earth would shift position greatly: You would be standing next to New York on one side of the room and next to Los Angeles on the other side!

To avoid creating movie-set worlds, you must learn to think in 3-D. You'll want to create a scene that is as realistic as possible and that uses relative distances appropriately.

---

tip *Remember in VRML, it's up to the viewer to decide from which angle he or she likes your world best!*

FIGURE 4-2

A look at the orbiting cybercafe as an example of a "movie set" world

The Benefits of Functional VRML Worlds

Another way to rate a VRML world is by its functionality. VRML objects that act as "eye-candy" are interesting, but most people's idea of virtual reality is an environment that's interactive and ultimately *does* something. It can be something as simple as providing a walkthrough map of a Web server or as far-reaching as an interactive medical guide, which lets you manipulate organs and perform virtual operations. See Chapters 14 and 15 for ways to add participation and purpose to your VRML worlds.

Making Good VRML Isn't (Completely) Easy

At the beginning of this chapter, you learned VRML creation tools have made the creation of simple VRML worlds easy, and that they have made errors in VRML code unlikely. These statements are indeed true. VRML, like HTML, has become a design system where drag-and-drop user interfaces make the creation and publication of virtual worlds quick and easy. But as with the HTML creation tools, the easier and simpler you make the process of creating VRML, the more you'll be bounded by the command-set the authoring software supports.

What this means is that for many of the performance tweaks described in this chapter, the VRML developer will have to change code by hand. What you'll find is VRML tools create good, basic structure for you to work with, but they may not find the most effective solutions for your particular server environment. It's going to take experimentation, time, and attention on the developer's part to create a VRML world that's anywhere close to perfect.

With these things in mind and with the background of the VRML language itself behind us, it's time to start working with VRML creation tools. In Chapter 5, you'll learn the answer to the question: "What makes a good VRML tool?"

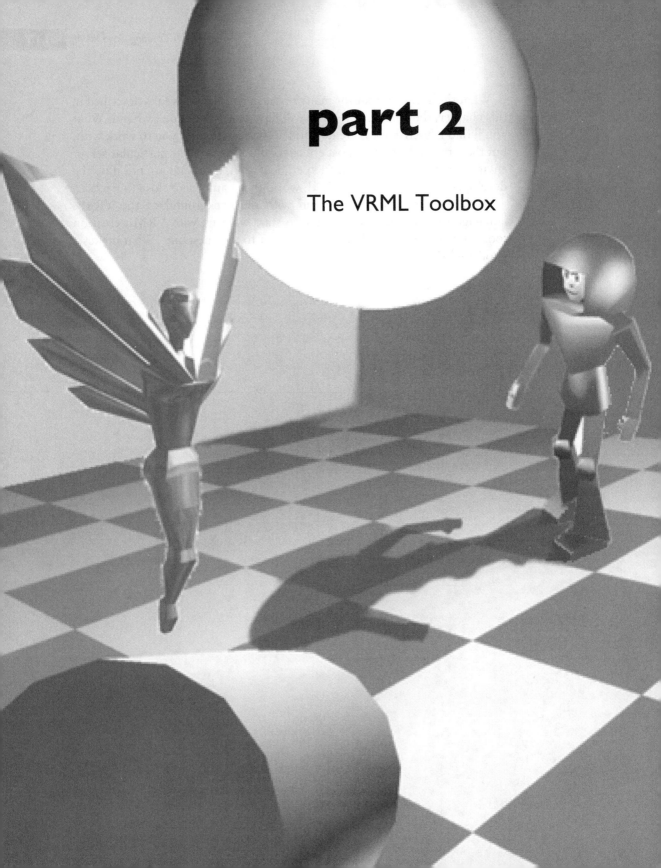

part 2

The VRML Toolbox

THIS section of the book moves into the nuts and bolts of VRML creation. Chapter 5 examines how to gauge the ease of use and functionality of VRML development tools and a few reviews of some specific tools.

Some review chapters, which look in-depth at specific products, follow. Chapter 6 examines Paragraph International's Virtual Home Space Builder. Chapter 7 explores Caligari Corporation's Pioneer. Chapter 8 continues the reviews with two Virtus products: WalkThrough Pro and 3-D Website Builder. From there, Chapter 9 covers some popular virtual reality server tools, including: WebMaster, Inc.'s VRServer, Dimension X's Liquid Reality. Chapter 9 also provides other resources to help you locate up-to-date information.

Chapter 10 looks at VRML extensible rendering packages, as well as some rendering pointers, including the five points of rendering and object creation and shaping. Chapter 10 also examines some specific VRML topics, such as animation, multimedia, and interaction. Specific shading and lighting techniques, including multipoint lighting, the four qualities of light-to-object interaction are then explored and, finally, diffusion. In closing, two rendering packages are reviewed: Strata's StudioPro and AutoDesk's MAX 3D Studio.

building

VRML

Worl

chapter 5

What to Look for in a VRML Authoring Tool

V
R M L isn't something a beginner would want to program by hand. The mathematical requirements of the language alone make writing VRML from scratch difficult.

Fortunately, the VRML creation tool market has exploded recently; at least a dozen tools are already available for nearly every major platform. These programs are lumped into two categories: "VRML-world creation tools" and "rendering packages."

The VRML creation tools are typically geared toward creating VRML worlds and no other type of multimedia. Their feature set is simple and focused on creating virtual "walkthroughs" of a building or city, which can serve as a map of a Web site or other cyberspace venue.

Rendering packages are high-end graphics and multimedia programs that can be used to create realistically rendered images. Most state-of-the-art rendering packages have been updated to incorporate World Wide Web (WWW) features, such as URLs, and to produce VRML output. But their WWW extensions represent just a small subset of what these packages can really do.

This chapter looks at the capabilities and features you would want in a VRML tool, then explains the differences between VRML creation tools and rendering packages. By the time you've finished this material, you should have a good idea of what you want from a VRML tool. When you read the upcoming chapters that review specific software packages in detail, you'll have a better idea of what's happening, which features make the most sense, and why.

ase of Use

Ease of use is the primary function you want from a VRML tool. Because VRML creation is a visual sport, any good VRML tool should have a visual interface. This graphical user interface (GUI) should also be manipulated without a large number of commands, which must be entered by hand.

In an environment where you are building—a VRML world or other graphical utility—ease-of-use typically translates into a large number of buttons and other gadgets that are helpful to view, create, mold, and otherwise manipulate 3-D objects. The typical tradeoff is between how much control you want to have and how many options and buttons you can recognize (or remember).

View Windows

Because you're working in 3-D with VRML, having access to a variety of viewpoints from which to look at your scene is advantageous. One view you'll definitely want is an orthographic "grid" view, where you can actually place and move objects on a grid with top, front, and side views.

Another view you'll want is what the world will look like when it is finally rendered. This view needn't be perfect, but the view should give you a decent idea; all the polygons don't have to be rendered or all the texture maps placed.

Toolbars

Another helpful interface item that makes a VRML tool easy to use is toolbars. A *toolbar* provides the VRML developer with the tools most commonly used in world creation. When creating VRML worlds, you'll want a toolbar that contains the basic building blocks of your world—simple polygons, "prefabricated" objects from an object library, lights, and cameras. Another toolbar you'll want is one that allows you both to move your objects about in cyberspace and to "mold" them like clay, elongating and distorting part, or all, of them. Textures available in texture libraries should be available for drag-and-drop placement into your scenes. Finally, a toolbar that contains buttons for moving about your world is also helpful because this toolbar will help you navigate and direct your efforts to the object or objects of your choice.

tip *A good GUI is a matter of taste: Some OS users even prefer the command-line to a windows environment! Browse through this book's CD or download the demos for several VRML tools and examine their interfaces before you choose one for yourself. If you don't like the GUI, chances are you won't like the package, either.*

Exportability of VRML-Compliant Files

Although you may want to export whatever you create into a VRML-compliant format, this isn't completely necessary. A number of translators exist such as AutoCAD DXF to Inventor (DxfToIv) and Inventor to VRML (IvToVRM), which convert rendering package, CAD, and other formats to VRML. But the ability to save your work *directly* into VRML is a definite plus.

You'll also want to make certain your tool can export VRML files that comply with the specification of your choice. Most packages today export VRML 1.0-compliant files, which is fine for today's VRML browser and plug-in market, many of which only support this specification. Over the coming months, however, these browsers and plug-ins will support the VRML 2.0 spec and authoring tools must keep up. Virtual Home Space Builder (VHSB) 2.0 is an example of a VRML tool that already supports VRML 2.0. Chances are good you'll want a VRML creation tool that keeps up with the latest VRML specification and, possibly, adds its own extensions.

Importing Other File Formats

VRML is becoming a preferred method for delivering 3-D files over the Internet or in an intranet environment. Many companies, however, still have much of their legacy design or multimedia work in CAD or rendering formats; CAD and rendering tools may remain the preferred workbenches for 3-D modeling for years to come. To make use of the flexibility of VRML, these companies must be able to export these files to that format. This means whatever VRML tool companies choose, it must be able to import other 3-D file formats. Strata StudioPro is an example of a rendering package that can import a number of file formats, including AutoCAD DXF, 3DMF (Apple's QuickDraw 3-D format), QuickTime VR, and even Adobe Illustrator. This is an important feature unless you can find a third-party conversion utility that can handle this function instead.

Objects and Textures

Most VRML authoring tools include a decent collection of predefined textures and objects; some of the nicer authoring tools include a CD full of extra textures and objects for your use. These textures and objects are distributed as public domain, which means you don't have to pay the distributor or author any royalties to use them in your VRML world. With such textures and objects included with a tool, you won't have to buy them separately at a higher price or spend time developing them yourself.

The more objects included with a VRML tool, the easier creating a virtual world will be for you. Instead of spending time shaping a polygon into a couch, you can choose a couch from an object library and, in the more advanced packages, drop it right into a VRML world. Virtus 3-D Website Builder comes with over 500 prefabricated objects on its CD, making this a great resource to speed a world's construction.

A good repository of textures also enlivens a VRML world with the click of a mouse. VRML tools are more likely to contain texture libraries than object libraries because VRML development companies may find varying a few textures on a theme—creating hundreds of them—easier than creating large numbers of unique objects. Virtual Home Space Builder 2.0, for example, contains over 560 textures, but no objects.

Ability to Add New Texture and Object Libraries

Practically all VRML tools allow you to add new texture and object libraries, whether they're designed specifically for VRML development or a rendering package that can export VRML formatted files. Many of the packages have their own texture and object libraries that are available; some support the importation of texture and objects from libraries for other packages. The question quickly becomes: *What* file formats can the package accept?

If you plan to make your 3-D models relatively detailed and you don't want to build most of them from scratch, you'll probably want a VRML authoring tool that accepts a variety of object library formats. When browsing the Internet, you'll find Open Inventor, AutoCAD DXF, and 3-D Studio are some of the most popular object library formats. The only package that can definitely accept all of these formats "as-is" is Silicon Graphics' WebSpace Author. Luckily, a number of translators are also available to covert these formats into other, more readily usable, forms.

tip *Texture libraries are a bit easier to migrate to VRML authoring tools because they consist only of graphic images in a particular format. Most rendering packages, such as Strata StudioPro, accept graphics of almost any kind, especially TIFF, JPEG, TARGA, and Encapsulated PostScript (EPS) files. VRML authoring tools, however, may only support a few graphics formats, such as JPEG and BMP. If this is the case, obtaining a general-purpose graphics conversion package, like DeBabelizer for the Macintosh or PaintShop Pro for Wintel PCs, is an excellent idea.*

Text as Well as Graphics

Because much of the excitement around VRML centers around its use to make 3-D objects (and animation with VRML 2.0), you may forget VRML is also capable of rendering 3-D text. Consequently, VRML creation tools that supply a wide variety of font choices via the operating system are also desirable.

Many VRML-specific tools neglect text rendering. This is expected because most of these tools are new to the market, include only basic features, and are geared more toward the "gee-whiz" aspect of VRML. Most rendering packages, on the other hand, are typically more mature products used for production-quality multimedia presentations. Because these products are more mature, they incorporated the ability to generate quality 3-D text long ago. 3-D Studio MAX can even import TrueType and PostScript fonts.

note *The rendering of 3-D text is not the same as VRML 2.0's Text node. This discussion has been about the creation of 3-D geometry from fonts. VRML's Text node, on the other hand, only allows for the creation of 2-D text with the limited number of fonts selectable in the FontStyle node.*

Multimedia Effects

One of the most disappointing aspects of VRML 1.0 has been a lack of multimedia effects. With virtual reality this dull, most people didn't want to bother. VRML could have been overshadowed by the quick animation of Shockwave and the more versatile Java. But VRML 2.0 turned out a fresh language brimming with multimedia power. Among its abilities: Sound nodes, animations, Java, and JavaScript.

To create what is now supported in the VRML 2.0 specification, you will want a VRML creation tool that supports multimedia. Most VRML-specific authoring tools support these directly, while some rendering packages may not because they prefer to stick to their own formats for now. A tool that provides a library of public domain animation, Java applets, and sounds is preferable. 3-D Studio MAX offers a plug-in that allows you to develop some multimedia aspects of VRML 2.0.

WWW Awareness

The power of your VRML world on the Internet depends greatly on how well it interacts with the rest of the Web. The goal of many VRML worlds is to provide an environment to navigate the Web itself; therefore, using a tool that allows you to include elements directly from the Web is desirable.

Most VRML-specific authoring tools, such as Virtual Home Space Builder, include the ability to add WWWAnchors and WWWInline nodes (just Anchor and Inline under VRML 2.0). Rendering packages often only have limited Web features, though, and they may only allow URL address linking. Strata StudioPro is an example of rendering software subject to this limitation.

VRML Power Features

Level-of-detail control is another VRML feature that would be nice to have in a VRML package. *Level-of-detail control* allows you to define a level of detail for views of an object based on the viewer's distance. Most VRML tools, unfortunately, don't implement this feature. Finally, the ability to implement VRML 2.0 sensors (as discussed in the specification) is another feature that adds power to VRML worlds but, again, most VRML tools don't implement this feature now. As more products mature and adopt the VRML 2.0 spec, no doubt even more of them will be seen with LOD and sensor editors.

VRML Creation Tools vs. Rendering Software

So far in this chapter you've seen what features make up a good VRML tool. Both VRML-specific creation tools and rendering software packages incorporate many of these features, but this crossover of features and capabilities can get confusing. This crossover can make the decision of which kind of package to buy difficult for new VRML developers. In this section, the differences between VRML-specific creation tools and rendering software will be discussed and we will try to help you decide which kind to select.

The Interfaces

Given VRML's visual nature, a requirement for all VRML tools is to run from a GUI. This is the only way to drag-and-drop polygons, lines, and textures easily onto a creation. For both VRML and rendering tools, two or more floating or fixed toolbars usually exist, which give ready point-and-click access to the software's features. But you'll notice some differences in the interfaces for the two types of software.

VRML Tool Interfaces: Simple But Effective

Most VRML tool interfaces offer few choices and limit themselves to a few buttons for lines and primitives (such as polygons or even complete objects, as in Figure 5-1). VRML tool interfaces also typically have a toolbar or menu to let you choose both the view of your scene and a palette of textures. This simple design may seem confining, but it squelches confusion by cutting out features a typical VRML author may never use.

Rendering Packages Interfaces Have More Items

Most people who use rendering software first notice the complexity of the interface. It's not that such packages are poorly programmed or did not go through human factors testing—the point is rendering packages can do *so much*. In any rendering package you'll see several views of an object or a scene simultaneously: Some views will have shading and lighting, some will have wireframe, some will be in perspective, and some will be orthographic (no perspective). In addition, toolbars typically exist to manipulate every aspect of a scene. Strata StudioPro, shown in Figure 5-2, is a good example.

The Power

Sheer power is where VRML and rendering tools differ most. Which kind of rendering tool you choose will depend greatly on how complex you want to make your VRML world.

FIGURE 5-1

Virtus' 3-D Website Builder has a complete collection of household objects for drag-and-drop world building.

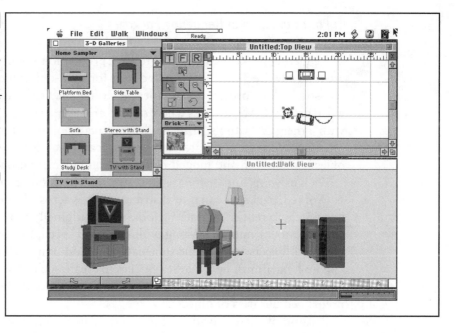

FIGURE 5-2

Strata StudioPro has buttons, menus, and views for editing objects in practically any conceivable way.

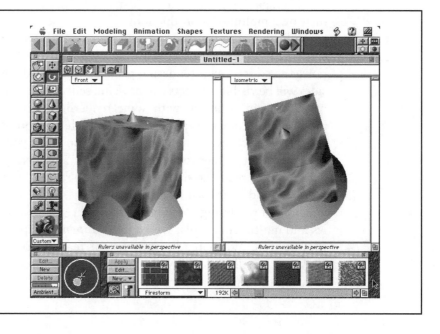

Power to Spare in Rendering Packages

Rendering packages are geared toward production-quality graphics. They are typically used in science and industry for solid-object modeling to create realistic-looking prototypes. Rendering is often the final stage of a computer-aided design (CAD) process where objects are raytraced after they are created with other CAD tools. The ability to create a three-dimensional visual representation often obviates the need to create a physical model—the virtual object can be seen and judged before a real implementation actually exists.

As hardware and software improve and as more computers become networked, packages can now distribute frames across the network for other computers to render. Rendering jobs, which originally took days, have been cut to hours or minutes. Along with increased speed, the ability to animate rendered objects has also became easier. In addition, GUI interfaces mean you no longer must be a mathematician to create such objects; now you can create them by simply dragging and dropping graphical objects, often from predefined libraries of objects.

Because of these advances, the entertainment industry has begun using rendering packages to create the special effects in works such as *Jurassic Park*, *Babylon 5*, and almost any computer game on today's market. Even small companies and individuals can take advantage of these tools to create their own multimedia productions.

With any rendering package (and a considerable amount of practice) you can create objects and scenes of amazing realism. A sphere with enough polygons created by a rendering package will actually appear smooth—no sides will be visible. Objects can have full reflectivity; light will obey the laws of physics. In addition, with some rendering software, you can plug in modules from other graphics packages, such as Photoshop, and add visual effects to objects even further. Some will also allow you to network a series of computers together to act as "slaves" for a rendering job, so portions of a scene can be rendered simultaneously. You're only limited by your system's resources and your own imagination.

Think of rendering packages in this light: as powerful computer graphics and multimedia tools, which just *happen* to export VRML compliant files as well. When reading the list of features on a typical rendering package, you'll see WWW publishing is only one of over a hundred amazing things it can do.

No Movie-quality Worlds Come from VRML Tools

VRML-specific creation tools are geared toward the quick and easy creation of VRML walkthrough worlds, rather than realistic-looking objects. The rendering capability of VRML-specific creation tools, consequently, is not typically powerful. Most VRML tools will opt for creating texture maps and primitives rather than creating polygons of any great complexity or depth. Likewise, you'll find lighting and shading aren't quite as rich for VRML tools.

This means anything built from a VRML tool probably won't be as stunning as something raytraced from a rendering package. Remember, though, the *ultimate* place your VRML world will be rendered is on someone else's VRML browser. VRML browsers often don't parse ".wrl" files or render polygons as quickly as VRML authoring tools or rendering packages. In addition, much of what a rendering package can do will not come across in the VRML 2.0 specification. Don't let your masterpiece get out of hand and become a burden for users to view. Instead, allow your masterpiece to be a joy.

The Price

Price is another area where VRML-world creation tools and rendering packages differ greatly. How much you spend will depend upon how much power you think you'll need and if VRML production is an interesting hobby for you or part of your livelihood.

Typically, VRML creation tools are *much* cheaper than the more advanced rendering packages. The average price for a VRML-world creation tool is around $100, which is the price of both Caligari's Pioneer and Virtus' 3-D Website Builder. ParaGraph International's Virtual Home Space Builder comes in at around $50.

Caligari and Virtus also have two "intermediate" products that allow you to create even more advanced walkthroughs. Caligari's Pioneer Pro and Virtus' WalkThrough Pro both list for around $495, which puts them closer to the rendering packages' price.

The major rendering packages carry a much heftier price tag—at least $1,000—which puts them out of range for many home hobbyists. Even most businesses must weigh the benefits of spending so much money for this software. Before they buy, they will ask: Will this product get more than just casual use? Can we use this product for any other purpose? Is this much power necessary?

When to Use VRML Tools or Rendering Packages

The following lists will help you decide if you should use a VRML tool or a rendering package. Consider each suggestion; then make your decision accordingly.

Use a rendering package if:

- You are experienced in 3-D design
- You need a high level of detail
- Your objects are extremely fluid or elaborate
- You plan to create other multimedia work in addition to VRML
- You are a multimedia, graphics, or game design workshop
- You will get at least a thousand dollars' use from the package

Use VRML-world authoring tools when:

- You are new to 3-D design
- Your objects don't need too much detail
- You will work only in primitives or simple objects
- You only want to create VRML, not other multimedia works
- You want to make a simple map of a Web space
- Your interest in VRML is as a hobby or entertainment
- You don't fit into any of the "rendering package" categories

Following these guidelines will prevent you from spending an inordinate amount of money on a package in which you will use only a few features.

Summary

In this chapter, you have seen what features make up a good VRML tool. These features include: ease of use, the ability to export VRML files, the ability to import other file formats, object and texture libraries, multimedia effects, and Web-awareness. You have also seen the interface, power, and price differences between the current genres of VRML tools: VRML-specific tools and rendering packages.

Armed with this information, read the upcoming chapters on some of the tools and rendering software available for authoring VRML. Then decide which tool best fits your needs.

building

VRML

World

chapter 6

Paragraph's Virtual Home Space Builder

G OOD VRML integrates 3-D graphics and user interaction over the Internet. With Virtual Home Space Builder (VHSB), Paragraph has added two new requirements to this definition: multimedia integration and ease of use. VHSB is a welcome application to the ordinary computer user who wishes to explore his or her creativity developing three-dimensional multimedia virtual spaces and publishing these creations on the Internet. VHSB takes the code bashing out of VRML development, sacrificing flexibility for creativity. VRML pros will find Home Space Builder basic, but cute. To the fresh developer of virtual worlds, it is probably the easiest to use VRML application available. A demonstration copy of the Virtual Home Space Viewer can be obtained for free at:

```
http://www.paragraph.com
```

Download a copy today and browse the examples from their in-house developers and customers to see if VHSB is the VRML development tool for you. For viewing VRML versions of the virtual spaces created by VHSB, a VRML browser or Web browser plug-in is required.

The Technical Stuff

In the sections that follow, we'll discuss all of the resource requirements necessary to use VHSB and what the program can do, including system requirements and the VRML internals the program delivers.

System Requirements

Paragraph recommends a 486 processor with 8 MB of RAM, 7 MB of hard disk space, and a SVGA 256 color monitor. As with any application, we discovered performance was severely inhibited when tested on the lowest end of the requirement food chain (486SX-66 with 8 MB of RAM running Windows 3.1). On a 100 MHz Pentium with 32 MB of RAM running Windows NT (and a full T1 Internet connection), the implementation of both the local virtual space and a VRML version was, as expected, seamless.

Windows 3.1, a mouse, a keyboard, and a CD-ROM drive are required with the commercial version, if purchased through a retail store. A "Lite" version of VHSB can be purchased and downloaded from the Paragraph Web site. The Internet version requires 4 MB of disk space; the CD version requires 2 MB of disk space. If you choose the custom or standard installation option from the CD, the installer will leave most, or all, of the image, movie, sound, and example files on the CD, thereby saving several megabytes' worth of disk space. When they're needed, the program accesses the required files from the CD instead.

A good quality monitor and a sound card are essential to experience the full effect of VHSB's multimedia capabilities. And, of course, for downloading VHSB files or viewing VRML files over the Internet, a 28.8 Kbps modem or higher speed connection to the Internet will also be needed.

VRML Considerations

VHSB allows virtual spaces to be saved in VRML format (".wrl") for direct publication to the Internet. To set up a VRML world fully from your virtual home space, consider three other things: First, to view your VRML creation or any other ".wrl" file, either a VRML browser or a VRML plug-in for your current Web browser is required. This is a major consideration because every VRML browser and plug-in currently available failed to function when tested with the low-end configuration. So it's possible to create and publish your virtual space on a low-end machine, but it will be impossible to view your creation in VRML.

Second, because the image and movie files included in VHSB's library are stored in Windows bitmap format (".bmp"), file storage quickly becomes an issue. VHSB will automatically link all objects to your virtual space in ".bmp" format when the VRML version is created. If storage space at your Internet Service Provider is an issue (and it will often impose additional costs), it may become necessary to convert your image files to a more compact format, such as JPEG or GIF.

Third, the version of VHSB reviewed here is only VRML 1.0 compliant, which doesn't permit the use of standard movie files, like MPEG or Quick-Time. Bitmap movies will work on local spaces, but will be viewable only as static images in a VRML session. This means VHSB will not support moving images or animated sequences within your virtual world.

As with all Internet publishing, consideration of the end-user's resources must be a major development concern. An intricate and flashy space may stoke the developer's ego, but when an end-user cannot load that file on a standard PC machine for lack of resources, the ability to reach any audience will be severely diminished. This wouldn't necessarily apply to a personal development project, but as VRML approaches full multimedia presentation capabilities—and potential commercial viability—widespread accessibility becomes increasingly important.

The main things to remember when designing for your audience's re-sources should include the following: computer configurations, Internet connection speeds, and technical prowess. Any of these three could inhibit a VRML developer's goals, either commercial or personal. This is true even with an application as simple as Virtual Home Space Builder!

VHSB: The Guts

The interface for VHSB consists of groups of toolbars, where each function is available through pointing and clicking on the appropriate icon. Although a bit confusing at first, after some practice, this interface becomes easier to use. VHSB marks a departure from typical VRML publishing, much like the recent emergence of other point and click Web publishing tools. Most VRML authoring tools have moved away from mastering a complicated command set; they focus instead on creating personal virtual spaces. Like easy-to-use Web publishing applications, VHSB sacrifices the flexibility of straight VRML programming for ease of operation. The most significant sacrifice is the program's inability to draw curved objects or anything else that doesn't mesh with a rigidly linear approach to the Cartesian coordinate space within the program.

Getting Started with VHSB

In the following sections VHSB's basic capabilities and its modes of operation will be reviewed. By the time you've completed this material, you should have a good idea of what this program can do and how it works.

Guest Mode and Master Mode

The interface through which the user or developer gains access to VHSB depends on the mode chosen from the main menu. The View option, shown in Figure 6-1, initiates Guest Mode and allows browsing-only of an existing virtual space via the navigational tool pad with a single 3-D view window, a Plane Walker window for an overhead view, and a camera positioning window.

The New or Edit option enables Master Mode (shown in Figure 6-2), which permits the designer to create a fresh space or to alter an existing one. Master Mode extends the functionality of the navigational tool pad by allowing the placement of images through a Chooser window. It also furnishes a Builder tool pad for the shaping of the space on the Plane Builder window and provides the ability to set the height of walls and boxes via the Height Control Tool.

Likewise, the 3-D View window's functionality is extended, granting the creator the ability to view and manipulate objects already positioned within the virtual space. And, finally, the Expert option gives the designer the flexibility of switching between Guest and Master Modes, as selected from the 3-D View window menu.

FIGURE 6-1

The VHSB

Main Screen

FIGURE 6-2

Master Mode

Screen

■

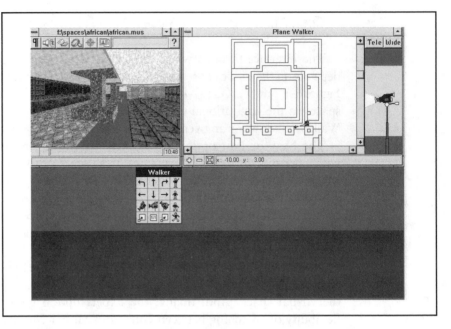

Walker Menu

The Walker menu is present in both the Guest and Master Modes. Both views share navigational functionality, though in Guest Mode several functions are removed. In both modes, the tool pad shown here

allows the user to manipulate the view in the 3-D window by raising, lowering, tilting up or down, and zooming in or out. In Master Mode, several functions are added, permitting the designer to move, alter, delete, or resize images in the 3-D view window, play sound files, enable another tool pad, or undo the most recent action. From the Walker menu, a user can also record a "walk-through" show, which could, when completed, be used to guide a Guest Mode user through the virtual space.

The Chooser Window

The Chooser window (shown below), available only in Master Mode, gives the designer access to thumbnail menus of images, movies, textures, and a selection of colors for placement on the surfaces within a virtual space. From this window, a file option may be selected: image, color, texture, or movie. Using the file browser, the creator can select a directory of objects. Thumbnails then appear in the bottom section of the Chooser window for easy selection and pasting.

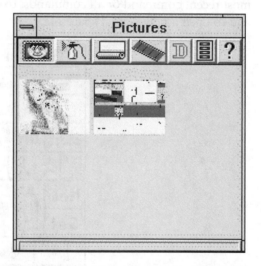

Image files are placed by dragging and dropping them on the 3-D View window; they are positioned using the Move/Resize tool on the Walker tool pad. Texture images dropped onto a surface automatically copy themselves to cover the tool pad completely. The same is true when the color chooser, which allows the selected surface to be painted with a desired hue, is enabled.

The fifth button on the Chooser window gives a creator control over appearance and placement of movie files. From this menu, frame exposure time, movie direction, and movie tiling can be controlled. VHSB includes an extensive library of objects, but one of its most versatile aspects is the ability to use any of the major image formats, including GIF, JPEG, EPS, PCX, and many others. This gives designers the opportunity to build personal libraries of objects without the time-consuming task of producing or converting images with third-party applications.

Builder Window

This tool pad is only available in Master Mode; it gives the designer the ability to plot out and build the actual virtual space on the Plane Builder window. By selecting various tools, shown in the following illustration, the builder can draw ceilings, floors, and walls on the Plane Builder window's grid or in fractional spaces between the grid lines, using the snap-to-grid options. Likewise, the creator can cut out areas to make doors and windows and to shape structures into furniture, columns, or other fixtures inside or outside the structure. Other functionality allows you to enable or disable the Camera Position window and the Wall Height window, to undo the builder's most recent command or all commands, to change Builder window settings, and to open a new virtual space file.

Plane Walker/Plane Builder Window

The Plane Walker window is provided for Guest Mode. It is an easy reference for the user to see quickly the position of the "Pinocchio" camera, which is the point of view in the 3-D window. In Master Mode, this window becomes the Plane Builder surface, where the developer actually lays out the virtual space's walls, surfaces, and objects other than images or similar multimedia add-ons.

Both versions of this window provide buttons for zooming in or out on the Plane window, or for resetting the window to a full view of the space.

In Master Mode, a grid is added, which aids in the placing of walls and objects. This grid can be set to snap to the actual grid lines or in fractions of space between the lines from the Builder tool pad, or the grid can be turned off completely. Another feature available to both Master and Guest Mode is the ability to pick up the camera and move it to a desired location. This is especially useful during design, when a specific area of the space needs development, or if the user has a slow computer.

Camera View and Wall Height Windows

As the names imply, these two windows, shown in Figure 6-3, control the view of the user camera and the size of a wall or box. Using the Wall Height window, walls can be lowered or raised as needed; a structure that floats in space can even be created. Using this tool, a designer can set ceilings and floors, create boxes to slice into furniture or other objects, and set the limits of the Remove Box tool to cut down walls and boxes to their desired shapes.

The overall potential height of walls or boxes can be set in the Builder Settings from the Builder tool pad previously discussed. The Camera View window allows elevation and depression of the view in the 3-D View window, functionality duplicated on the Walker tool pad.

FIGURE 6-3

Camera View and Wall Height Tools

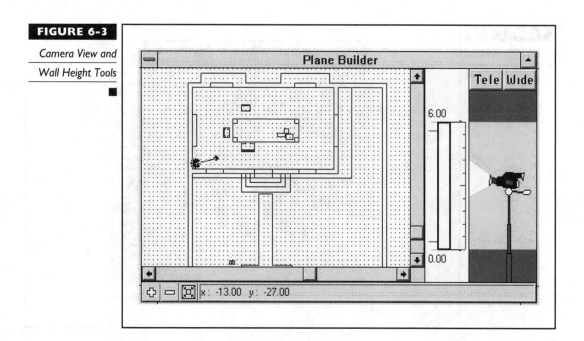

3-D View Window

This window, shown in Figure 6-4, displays the virtual view of the home space as the user or developer navigates through the underlying data. Although it has functionality in the form of menus, this window is basically for display and it supplies the work area for placing and manipulating object files. The menu options across the top of the window allow for file management, such as saving the home space, and three tools for adding functionality or altering the form of objects.

Clicking the magnifying glass icon opens an image utility screen, which displays the selected object and gives the developer the options for altering brightness, contrast, and gamma correction for the image. Likewise, the designer can zoom in or out from the picture and save the changed image to the same file or a separate file. The "gunsight" icon zooms the 3-D window view to include a full screen shot of the selected image.

Clicking on the last icon, the Picture Attachment Editor, makes it possible for the builder to add functions to the selected object. Not only can the object be linked to another home space or VRML file, but it can also be joined with URLs and sound files, and it can even activate some other functionality with VHSB—such as exiting the program or starting a walk-through show.

FIGURE 6-4

3-D View Window

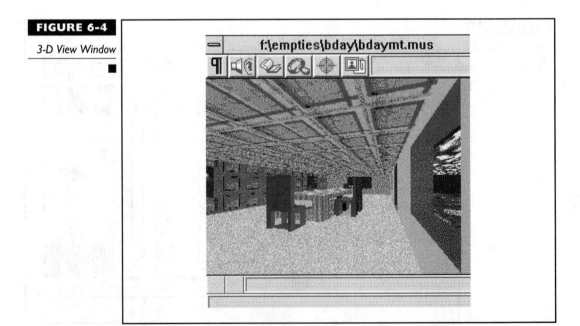

Libraries

Paragraph includes a standard library of images, textures, colors, sounds, and movies. All of these may be used and stored directly on the CD or saved to a hard disk. In addition, an extensive collection exists of both fully developed examples and *empties,* which are bare-bones creations for further elaboration by the developer.

The developer also may build libraries of objects to be used with personal spaces from a personal collection or by obtaining them through a third-party source, such as clip art programs or the Internet. With the variety of image file formats that VHSB supports, the possibilities are endless.

Building a VRML Virtual Space in Seven Easy Steps

Follow these easy steps to build a VRML virtual space:

1. Draw a box.

   a. Using the Builder tool pad, select the Draw Box function.

   b. Select the Wall Height window; then raise the bottom lath and lower the top lath. This will leave room for the ceiling and floor later.

   c. Select the Plane Walker window and draw a box of any size.

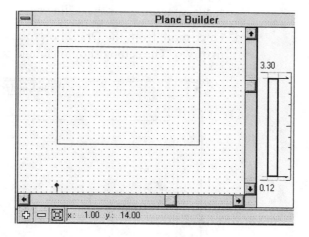

2. Cut out the box.

   a. Select the Snap-to-Grid option of 1/2 on the Builder tool pad.

   b. Select the Remove Box tool.

c. Using the Plane Walker window, cut away 1/2 a grid distance around the inside of the box.

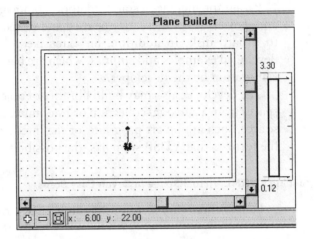

3. Create the ceiling and floor.

   a. From the Wall Height window, set a wall height equal to the space remaining for a floor.

   b. Select the Draw Box tool; then draw a box. This should cause the "floor" to change color, indicating the floor was made.

   c. Again from the Wall Height window, set the height equal to the space remaining for the ceiling.

   d. Once more from the Draw Box tool, draw a third box over the first two. The ceiling should change colors now.

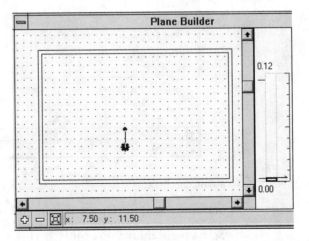

4. Set interior walls.

   a. Resize the Wall Height indicator to the correct setting.

   b. Select the Draw Walls tool; then place interior walls.

5. Cut out doors and windows.

   a. Using the Wall Height tool again, set the proper height for a door or window.

   b. Select the Remove Box tool; then cut away your doors and windows from interior and exterior walls.

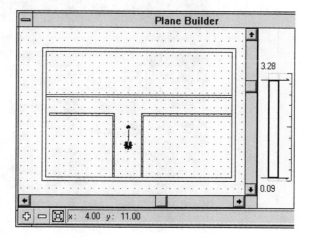

6. Decorate your creation.

   From the Chooser Window, load a texture, image, or movie library. Then drag and drop them onto the 3-D View window wherever needed. These images can be resized, deleted, or moved later as desired.

7. Publish to VRML.

   a. Save the Virtual Space as a Virtual Reality Modeling Language file (.wrl).

   b. Select Copy All from the 3-D Space Window Menu; then copy all object files from their libraries to the directory where the .wrl file resides.

   c. Launch a VRML capable browser and load the local file (see Figure 6-5)!

Load an image,

texture, or movie

library and start

pasting!

■

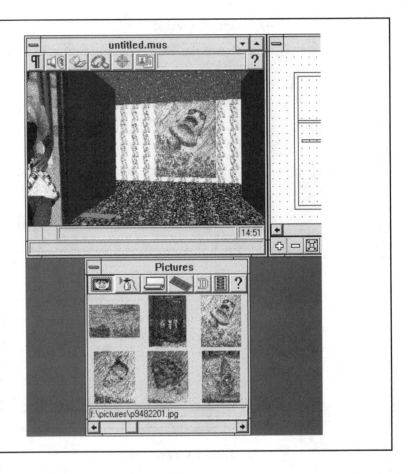

Virtual Space Finishing Touches

Once the framework is laid, the space needs detail—those personalizing touches that make the space unique. Home Space Builder is quite flexible in its support for the file formats it can use here. Virtually any image format can be linked to the space, and VHSB will display it inline wherever desired. And the same image formats can be used as textures to cover a surface in a certain pattern. With the movie file resources provided, moving images may be added.

As stated previously, VHSB does not support all standard digital movie formats but, instead, uses a collection of static images, which it displays in a certain order—much like a piece of movie film. The movie files VHSB uses are currently not supported in VRML, so they are limited to local display only in the VHSB file. Images and objects also may be linked to other functions, which enhances the capabilities of the virtual space and provides integrated Internet capabilities. Links to URLs, sound files, and other functionality with VHSB—such as linking to another virtual space—are supported. And, finally, the actual objects that fill out the space, such as furniture and other fixtures, can be created using the existing tools available on the Builder toolpad.

Colors

A painting tool, which provides an easy-to-use palette of colors for covering surfaces, is included in the Chooser window. By selecting the Paint button on the Chooser window, the developer calls up the palette. The desired color is then selected, and dropped on a surface. The color will not cover up images or other attachments already in place. By imaginative use of this function, the developer can create the illusion of light and shadow, breaking up monotonous lines that fade into each other. An example of this would be a white wall and ceiling. By making one wall slightly darker or of a different shade of white, the developer prevents "losing" the wall and ceiling in the same color.

Image and Texture Tools

Placing images and textures is achieved through the Chooser window. Once an option is selected, a directory of images must then be loaded by using the Select Directory tool on the Chooser window. This loads thumbnails of the images, which may then be dragged and dropped onto the virtual space's surfaces. Texture images will automatically copy to cover the entire surface, while static images may be moved into whatever positions are desired.

VHSB implements several tools to place, resize, alter, and move image files displayed on virtual space surfaces. Likewise, these same functions apply to texture files, which are simply images automatically duplicated to cover any surface. From the Walker toolpad in Master Mode, four function buttons are related to these tasks.

The functionality of these buttons is duplicated from the menu options at the top of the 3-D view window. The first button, the View Object tool, zooms in on an image selected in the 3-D view window when activated. This tool allows the user or developer to check out details of the picture as it is displayed within the space.

The second button is the Picture True Image tool. When this function is enabled, a selected picture is opened into a separate VHSB Image window.

Only the image is displayed and several tools are supplied to alter its appearance, as desired by the developer, or to zoom in or out for a better view by either the creator or the user. Alteration options available include: Contrast, Brightness, and Gamma Factor adjustments. The altered image may be saved either over the original or to a new file from the VHSB Image window; then the image can be repasted inline in the virtual space.

The third image function from the Walker tool pad is the Move/Resize tool. This gives designers the ability to reposition an image on a virtual space surface, or to adjust the size of the image. Once the tool is enabled, dragging and dropping is available for the selected image. By placing the cursor on the upper right hand corner of the picture, the developer can drag the edge of the image larger or reduce the image to a desired size.

The fourth tool, the Delete function, allows easy removal of unwanted pictures directly from the 3-D view window.

Movie Files

Loading movie files for use works the same way as images and textures: Select the Choose Movie button on the Chooser window; then load a directory of movies with the Select Directory button. Desired movies may then be dragged and dropped onto a desired surface to be altered or moved as needed.

Movie files are loaded, placed, and manipulated using the same tools as image files, with one exception. The Movie Detail button on the Chooser window provides a tool to alter the appearance and behavior of any displayed movie. Activating this button pops up a Movie Detail window with options for movie display either in radio buttons or entry blanks. The options are as follows: Frame Direction (Forward, Reverse, or Ping-Pong), Paste as a single image or wallpaper, Frame Exposure Time in number of frames per second and options to provide a transparent background and stop mode. Stop mode allows the movie to be activated when the user selects it (usually by clicking with the mouse). If the wallpaper option is checked, the width, height, and offsets may also be altered as needed.

The movie library provided by VHSB is sparse, but interesting. Given the limits to the file formats supported by Home Space Builder, the developer would need adequate time and the appropriate third-party applications to produce additional movie files. Although the movies files provided are limited in number, they are varied in their methods of display.

Links

Images, movies, and other objects within a virtual space may be given added functionality in the form of links. With these links, an object may be instructed to jump the user to another virtual space, end the VHSB application, play a sound file, load another document or program, or open a World Wide Web Uniform Resource Locator (URL). This adds an element of interactivity to the 3-D space's capabilities. A commercial space could display an open book on a pedestal, which, when clicked, could pull up that company's product information. Or (as in one of the better examples provided by Paragraph) a CD store virtual space could deliver images of recording artists, supply informational dialogue about these artists, and furnish sound bites of the artist's works—all at the click of a mouse.

Objects may obtain this kind of capability through the Picture Attachment Editor tool located at the top of the 3-D view window. Once enabled, a window pops up where the developer provides linking information to the Editor. This could include the path to a picture, a home space, a sound file, a document to be launched, or a URL to load on the user's local browser. "Note space" is also provided in this Editor window, which will be displayed at the top of the 3-D view window for the user's information. These links will transfer directly to a VRML file, although links to local programs or documents may be invalid on an end user's machine.

Other Objects

Furniture and other fixtures are not provided in a library format with VHSB, thus, these items must be created by hand. Although this is a tedious and time-consuming process, the tools needed are provided by the Builder window. Here is an example of the steps needed to create a couch:

1. Set the Snap-to-Grid tool to 1/10.

2. Zoom in to maximum zoom.

3. Set the Wall Height indicator's upper lathe down to an acceptable level.

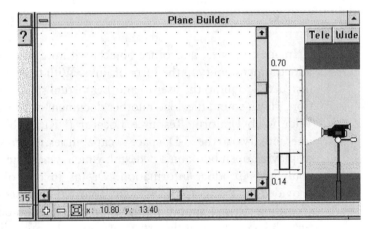

4. Select the Draw Box button and draw a box the size of a couch. (The box should appear in the 3-D view window.)

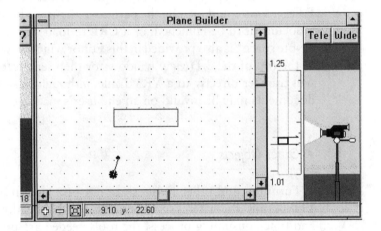

5. Set the lower lathe of the Wall Height indicator up to the level of the cushions.

6. Select the Remove Box button and cut out the space for the cushions.

7. Reset the Wall Height indicator to the appropriate range; then draw the individual cushions on the couch.

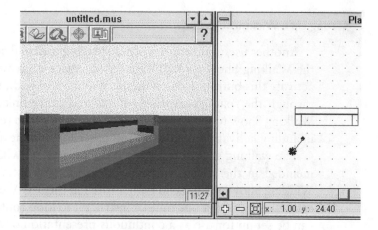

8. Select the Texture Chooser button on the Chooser window.

9. Choose an appropriate texture and decorate!

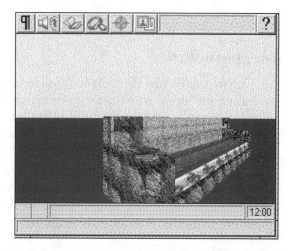

Although this example is simple, consider a normal table with its various intricacies. To create a real interpretation of a table, it would take many steps to lay out the shape correctly, cut away space for the legs, and properly color or texture its surfaces—especially if shading and lighting are also incorporated. The real joy of creating a personal space, however, is building everyday objects in a virtual world.

Setting Up a Walkthrough Show

Another useful function when displaying a virtual space to an end user is the Walking Show tool. Once a virtual space is created, the developer can activate this button (located on the Walker tool pad), then begin navigating through the space, activating sounds and other links along the way. The Walking Show tool records these actions; it will then replay them to the user, including activation of sounds and other links at the appropriate times.

The walking show presentation is saved as a ".wlk" file, and it must be included in the virtual space package for end user activation. From the Walking Show mode menu item located in the 3-D View File menu, the user can select to view it one time or instruct it to loop continuously. The display can be set up for use as a continuous presentation or as a one-time show.

n o t e   *This option is not available for Home Space Builder files converted to VRML.*

Converting Files to VRML

Converting Virtual Home Space Builder files to VRML is as easy as saving a file in any other format. First, from the File menu within VHSB, the developer chooses the Save 3-D Space option, and selects the Virtual Reality Modeling Language file (*.wrl) option from the file browser menu. This saves the working file in ".wrl" format. Second, the creator must copy all the object files used in the virtual space to the same directory as the VRML file. Using the Copy All option from the File menu performs this task in a single step. All these files should be uploaded to the developer's Web server.

Other things to consider include the following:

- The location of the main file (".mus" or ".wrl")

- The locations of the object files

- The format of the object files

Distributing VHSB/VRML Creations

Virtual Home Space Builder can save a working file in one of two file formats: the VHSB format (".mus") and VRML format (".wrl"). Both can be distributed on the Internet from a Web page or an FTP site. The VHSB viewer can be copied freely and included with the .mus file for distribution. Likewise, Netscape's Live3D plug-in is freely available for viewing VRML versions of the virtual space.

Including Object Files

If saved as a ".mus" file, the working file and its entire library of objects—including all images, movies, textures, sounds, and any walking show files—must be included either in the same directory or in separate directories, assuming the correct path to these objects is provided from the working file. Most VHSB files are distributed in an archived format, that is, PKZip, GNU Zip, etc. Not only does this save space on the distributor's hard drive, it is less taxing for the end user, who will have to download a VHSB creation to view it.

If set up on a Web page for VRML, all object files must be located on the Web server with appropriate paths set. Home Space Builder will set these paths when the file is saved as a VRML file. If these files are created locally and then uploaded to a Web server, however, the paths will either have to match the target site or be reconfigured to match after they've been uploaded.

Object File Formats

Considering the impact on end users and the amount of disk space the developer has to work with, all image, texture, and movie files should either be converted into a compact format, such as JPEG or GIF, or compressed with an archive program. VHSB files themselves, including all object files and the Virtual Home Space Viewer file, should be archived as well. This minimizes the user's download time and saves the developer disk storage fees from his Internet Service Provider.

Building a Virtual Community

It's easy to create a virtual community using VHSB and then to publish this community to the Web via VRML. Multiple spaces can be created in the same file, or multiple files can be linked using the program's built-in linking tools. Paragraph links to virtual spaces and communities created by VHSB users and developers at this URL:

```
http://vrml.paragraph.com/
```

The ease of the application's functionality and its many features make it useful for individuals or nonprofit organizations to consider when creating their virtual spaces. Publishing these communities to the World Wide Web could bring awareness of community and political issues through the power of the virtual world.

The emergence of Internet commerce as a viable option for businesses will also engender sponsored VRML sites. Collaborations on the scale of virtual malls are a tangible possibility. Every functionality that can be applied to a Web page can be duplicated on—or activated from—a VRML file. The possibilities for VRML/Web commerce abound. Virtual Home Space Builder gives business users an opportunity to create sites and functions easily, without the hassle of learning an unfamiliar language or the expense of outsourcing the work. In short, it's a great place to start working with virtual worlds.

VHSB and the Future of VRML

Virtual Home Space Builder, although very basic, marks a new direction in bringing a consumer-oriented VRML product to the public. Regardless of a developer's intentions when creating virtual worlds, VHSB provides a quick way to produce such spaces so the public can easily download or browse them online.

Paragraph recently announced its new version of Virtual Home Space Builder will be made available to current users of VHSB 1.0. This version claims to be the first VRML 2.0-compliant development tool and the easiest to use. Users who own VHSB 1.0 will be able to update to the new version for free. VRML 2.0, the new standard for transmitting 3-D VR worlds over the Internet, was finalized in early August 1996. Paragraph slated the release of VHSB 2.0 for the same time.

With the advent of easy to use VRML authoring tools, the future of virtual world development is an open book. Businesses, nonprofit organizations, and individuals are exploring the uses of the Internet and virtual reality in ways never before conceived. Developers are linking their spaces, building virtual townships on the outlands of the Internet, pitching their philosophies and products, or just letting go with their creative energy. Virtual Home Space Builder can do a lot to help developers overcome their fears about virtual reality and VRML.

CD-ROM

cd-rom   *The CD included with this book contains some of the authors' strange and wonderful experiments with VHSB, in both VHSB and VRML format. Feel free to use them as starting points for your own virtual home space!*

building

VRML

World

chapter 7

Caligari's Pioneer

THE tools needed to build a realistic 3-D space and to publish that space to VRML and the World Wide Web are often expensive and require a fairly high level of technical expertise. In addition, some of the lower-end packages already covered in this book are limited in many key areas, such as object creation. Caligari has taken the lead in VRML authoring tools, one of which is Pioneer. Caligari Pioneer allows VRML developers to create a host of 3-D images, shade and detail them, and publish them to the World Wide Web, all with a group of easy to master tools and functions. For a solid VRML development solution, Caligari Pioneer is worth a test drive.

A demo can be obtained from the following URL:

```
http://www.caligari.com
```

Technical Requirements

Currently, Pioneer is available for the Windows 32-bit platform and runs equally as well on Windows 95, NT, or Windows 3.11 with Win32s. The minimum hardware requirements are as follows:

- **Processor:** IBM compatible fast 486DX or greater (Optimal: Pentium processor)
- **RAM:** 8MB (Optimal: 16MB)
- **Hard Disk:** 15MB

■ **Internet Connection:** 14.4K modem. (Optimal: 28.8K modem).

When testing Caligari Pioneer on the lowest-end required configuration (a 486 with 8MB of RAM, running Windows 3.1), the application was nearly unusable after adding only a few objects and textures.

As with any 3-D rendering and manipulation tool, RAM and processor speed are the keys to quick, clean creation. On the low-end configuration, multiple objects and textures caused the interface to slow down considerably, making any further action difficult and frustrating. Even at the suggested optimal configuration (Pentium 133, 16MB of RAM, Windows 95), complex scenes were somewhat hard to manipulate after adding a few fairly complex objects.

On a higher than optimal system (Windows NT, Pentium 166, 64MB of RAM), Pioneer's interface is usable, even with extremely complex scenes, multiple objects, lighting options, and the like.

As with any application intended for professional use, developers are well advised to obtain the full demo version to test compatibility and usability with the systems on-hand. This will save headaches and lost productivity later, as another solution is sought. Pioneer is not as demanding of hardware as some of its high-end 3-D rendering package cousins, but the very nature of 3-D objects and world creation demands a certain level of system requirement, which, if ignored, will only cause frustration and delays later.

Pioneer: The Guts

Pioneer has a full host of one-button tool features, and pop-up tool boxes to make the job of object and world creation that much simpler. The function name is displayed as the mouse pointer is moved over the various tool buttons; most buttons have multiple functions that can be selected by right-clicking on the button itself. The interface comes in two flavors: Browse mode or World Building mode. Browse mode functions as a VRML browser, allowing you either to load the VRML world in progress locally or to load another VRML file from the Internet. From Browse mode, users can also switch to World Building mode, enabling manipulation of the 3-D space, switch the view of the selected space from shaded to wireframe (as shown in Figure 7-1), change the perspective of the view 360 degrees, and even publish the selected space to a World Wide Web directory on the Internet.

FIGURE 7-1

The Wireframe view is useful for repositioning objects without taxing the memory of the system. ∎

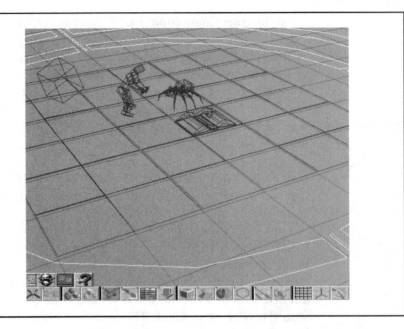

Interface

Pioneer's interface is not exactly intuitive to the newcomer, but after a few sessions with the application, the tools, icons, and functions become clear as to how they interact. Many functions are duplicated in several tool boxes, like the light and camera placement functions, and this, although seemingly a waste of space on the outset, proves useful by preventing a search for the needed tool at every turn.

In the following sections, the functions are divided into three main categories (General Editing, Environment View Functions, and Object Controls) and a brief description of the purpose of the tool or tool box is provided.

General Editing

General editing features are simply tools that appear in almost any application or are specific to this application's functionality, but do not contribute to the actual creation of objects and the space. These tools include

- **Undo/Redo** The Undo button places the object back to the state just before some edit was performed. Thus, if the face of a square was warped too far, the undo button would put the face back to where it was before it was warped. The Undo function will undo each object edit in turn until the last edit is reached; then it becomes the Redo button, which will scroll back up the various edits performed on an object. The button itself is multifunctional, allowing you to change between Undo and Redo as needed.

■ **Erase/Copy** Erase removes a selected object from the space. If the wrong object is erased from the world in progress, the Undo button can be used to replace the object in the space. The second function, Copy, makes a duplicate of the selected object, whether it's a polygon, light point, or another object.

■ **Add Hyperlinks/3-D Sound** This tool button allows you to attach a URL hyperlink to an object within the virtual space. If the URL is to another VRML site, the .wrl file automatically loads into Pioneer. If the link goes to an HTML document, the system's default Web browser loads the URL. The second function of this button, Add/Remove 3-D sound, allows you to attach or remove sound files to an object.

■ **World Browsing Mode** This button simply switches Pioneer back to Browsing mode, which allows you to view the space as a user and, if needed, publish the space.

■ **Close All Panels** This administrative function closes all tool panels that are open within the work space.

■ **Help on Tool** Although not available for all tools used in Pioneer, the Help on tool function allows you to view various options and features of enabled tools. When you click on the Help on tool button, the icon changes to a question mark speared by a pointer. Then, when a specific function is selected, Pioneer launches a short tutorial on the various uses and strategies for the enabled tool.

Environment View Functions

The view of the space is affected by many variables, all placed and controlled by you. Some of these variables, such as lighting hues, camera placement, and perspective, are critical to the success of the overall VRML piece. Pioneer has a host of functions geared toward full management of the environment within the 3-D world.

■ **Perspective View/View From Object** This tool button allows you to toggle between the overall view of the space (Perspective) to a view from a selected object, including light points and cameras within the space. Viewing the space from a specific object is useful because you can see how nearby objects affect the shading and lighting of the selected object and you can also catch any areas of objects that are not fully detailed.

■ **New Perspective View** This button is a multifunction tool which, when enabled, pops up a small window with a selected view of the space. From within this window, the designer can further manipulate objects, lights, cameras, perspective view, and the four orthogonal views: Right, Left, Top, and Front. An example of the Top View Prospective is given in Figure 7-2.

These options allow you to get a better sense of placement and distance of objects within the space and to make adjustments as necessary.

■ **Look At** The Look At tool causes an object to rotate so its axis is facing the center of another object's space. This allows you to touch up any missed spots with textures or colors or easily reposition the object within the space.

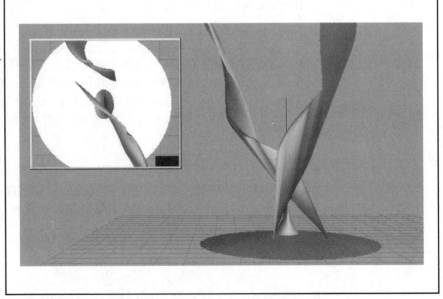

FIGURE 7-2

The Top View Perspective gives you a good idea of the spacing between multiple objects within the space.

■

■ **Camera/Light Placement** Light points and cameras do not have their own tool box, but adding them to the space is accomplished through the Primitives tool box (detailed later). The view of the environment depends on both, however, so details on each are included here. Once added, both light points and cameras can be moved, like any other object, to a desired location along the X, Y, and Z axes. Lights have an additional control panel, which is detailed next.

■ **Light Control Panel** Anytime a light point is placed or selected, a light control panel appears, as shown in the following. This control panel allows you to set and manipulate both the intensity and the hue of the light selected. Intensity can be set from low to high by sliding the slide bar up or down, depending on the whim and need of the designer. The color control cube adjusts the hue of the light as the designer moves a point across the various shades within the control cube. This allows for multiple lights with varied characteristics to create a mood for the VRML piece.

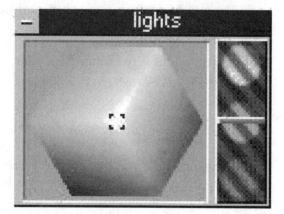

Object Controls

The real meat of any three-dimensional space are its objects, and Pioneer provides a host of features that allow designers to place, move, manipulate, alter, and otherwise create the perfect objects for the virtual world. Rendering options are plentiful and detailed for a package geared toward the PC user, but they are welcome because most VRML authoring tools so geared are lacking in the object department.

OBJECT CREATION AND RENDERING CONTROLS   The first step to set up the 3-D space is creating, detailing, and placing objects. Pioneer allows many options for basic polygons and other tools to alter or combine these primitives to create specific and detailed objects.

- **Primitives Panel**   Through the Primitives Panel, a selection of normal three-dimensional objects is available for placement within the space. The following objects are available: Plane (for covering the "floor" or for use as a free-standing plane), Cube, Cylinder, Sphere, Torus, and Cone. Also, from this tool box, you can place lines of 3-D text, add light points or cameras, and add what's called infinite light. This places a light point of high intensity in the center of the space, adding another lighting option to the mix. The attributes of this light can be controlled as any other light through the light control panel, which appears when the infinite light is added or selected.

Primitives within the tool box have certain attributes that can be altered prior to placement. Geometric characteristics, such as the radius for the Torus, and other variables, such as font and size of text strings, are all alterable by right-clicking on the object tool button and selecting the appropriate variables to change. This adds some management of the initial appearance of objects, saving you time when specific alterations are needed later.

- **Solid Render Display Tool Box**   This tool box is really a combination of tools, primarily managerial in nature, but it also supports functions that control the rendering of all objects within the space, affects the attributes of lights and cameras, as well as several other options. Each button has multiple functions and must be right-clicked with the mouse to view all the options. The following attributes can be manipulated with these buttons and affect all objects within the space:

  - **Lights**   White Lights only, Colored Lights, or No Lights.

  - **Texture Resolution**   Affects the appearance of textures within the space by affecting the image's resolution.

  - **Rendering Options**   *Faceted*: gives objects a "blocky" look; *Smooth*: smoothes over the faces of objects, such as the circle and Torus, making them look more round.

- **Use Textures Toggle**   This toggle enables or disables the use of image maps for texturing objects.

- **Show Lights/Camera Toggle**   These switches enable or disable the ability to see the placement of lights or cameras within the space. This switch does not remove the ability to place these objects, but only removes their icons from sight in the space.

- **Other Switches**   Other functions available from this tool box increase the frame rate of the space, while navigating through (preventing "jumpy" interfaces), enabling, or disabling a background image for the space around the virtual world and control for the level of detail for the rendered world.

OBJECT MANAGEMENT FUNCTIONS   Once created, objects must be moved, altered, their lighting adjusted, and generally fit into the 3-D space. The following tools enable options to do all that and more.

- **Move Object**   To move objects, three to six buttons must be enabled to the interface. First, the Object tool pointer must be selected. This will normally auto-select once an object in the space is singled out. Next, the Object Move button must be set to Move Object Scale or Rotate. Last, the axes buttons in the lower-left corner must be set to the appropriate axes (X, Y, Z, or a combination of the three). For example, if you want simply to slide a sphere away from a cube, from right to left within the space, the X axis button would be enabled and the Y and Z axes buttons would be disabled. If you plan to move an object along the Z axis (up or down), only the Z axis button is enabled, and the selected object is moved up or down while you hold down the right mouse button. X and Y axes moves are enabled using the left mouse button.

  Objects may be reduced or enlarged using the Object Scale tool button on the Move Object function. Axes are enabled or disabled appropriately, then the object is grabbed with the mouse pointer by holding down the right and/or left mouse button (depending on if the Z axis will be altered). This control over axes provides valuable flexibility for developers, who can use it to control both their point of view and how an object is rendered, making this one of the nicest features of the program.

  The third function of the Move Object tool bar is the Rotate option. As the name implies, this allows the designer to spin the object around its local axes, again controlled by enabling and disabling the axes buttons. For example, a rectangle may be flipped from right to left if only the X axis is enabled, or forward and backward with the Y axis enabled. With all three axes enabled, the rectangle may be rotated around the various axes to your heart's content.

- **Polygon Drawing Tool**   The Polygon tool creates a 2-D polygon, either in a preset format, with the number of sides determined by you (a square), or freehand, which automatically connects points as they are placed within the space and fills in the interior when all lines are joined. When you use the automatic polygon drawing tool, the polygon can be expanded or compressed as needed. Later, tools such as the Sweep or Tip tools (detailed later) can be applied to create a 3-D object from a 2-D polygon.

- **Glue Objects**   With this tool button, several objects within a space may be bound together as one object and, later, unbound, as needed. This enables you either to move objects together, while maintaining the ratios of distance, or to marry many complex polygons into a real world object, such as an automobile or human figure.

- **Pointer/Navigation Selection**   The Pointer button allows you either to select the navigation method through the working space (Fly, Walk, Encircle a selected object, or Move to a selected object) or to enable the tool pointer, with which objects within the space are individually selected. The Pointer button must be selected before moving or otherwise altering any object within the space. The tool pointer usually enables itself automatically when an object manipulation tool, such as the Move Object function, is selected.

- **Object List**   The Object list is a useful feature, especially if the space is cluttered with a multitude of objects or if a single complex object contains many simple polygons. This button, when enabled, displays a table that lists all objects within the space. Each object can be selected, both in the list and simultaneously in the virtual world, by clicking its entry in the list. This table denotes cameras and lights, as well.

tip   *When an object is selected from the Object list, a second screen pops up, which details the individual attributes of that object. If the selected object is a light, the Light Control panel pops up.*

OBJECT MANIPULATION AND DETAILING TOOLS   Once the objects are created and placed, they must be customized, combined, textured, and otherwise detailed. Pioneer has a limited texture library, which can be customized and expanded according to your needs. Other detailing functions, such as object mutating, subtracting, and others, allow the object to be shaped in any way desired.

- ■ **Material Library**   The Material Library button, when clicked, pops up several screens. The main tool box is the actual basic library of textures, of which there are ten. Four other tool boxes also appear: Material Color (same as Light Control panel), Material (which displays the selected texture or color, if no texture is selected), Shader Attributes, and Shader/maps (see below). The last two tools control a variety of shading functions and give the texture a variety of looks, from shininess to transparency.

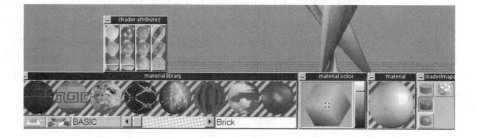

- ■ **Shader Attributes control screen**   This screen is divided into four sections: Ambient Glow, Shininess, Roughness, and Transparency. The level of each is controlled by sliding the tool bar up or down, depending on what you desire. For example, if the Transparency slide bar is pushed all the way to the top, the texture and the object become transparent, with just a hint of color or texture applied.

- ■ **Shader/maps control box**   This box allows you to select the consistency of the color or texture: Smooth, Auto-Facet (which mirrors the object's setting), or Faceted (which facets the texture to its own faces, regardless of the object's setting). The Smooth option curves the intersections of polygons, while the Faced option simply shows the polygons, but shades the faces of the object. The

Auto-Facet option smoothes polygons used to make up the object, which meet at less than a 30 degree angle.

A fourth selection enables the use of texture maps instead of colors. Textures may be altered with the previous tools and saved as a separate texture for later use. Currently, Caligari Pioneer can import both JPEG image files and material libraries from Caligari's TrueSpace 3-D object modeling application.

- **Edit Face**   The Edit Face tool button spans three separate functions, which can be used in conjunction or separately. The actual button itself executes a second window, which allows the user to select and manipulate a single face of an object. As shown in the following, after placing a simple square, the Edit Face button is selected, then the Point Move function is enabled on the Point Navigation Control Panel. After selecting the appropriate face, this entire square can be moved over and the other attached "walls" of the cube follow. Now a whole new object exists, ready to be detailed. The other two buttons on the Point Navigation Control Panel are the Point Rotate, which rotates the selected face while maintaining point integrity of the face, and the Point Scale, which increases or decreases the size of the face while maintaining the proportions of the points on the face.

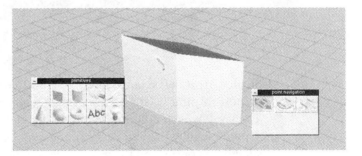

The second tool button performs many more complex operations.

- **Sweep Function**   The Sweep function extrudes a 3-D polygon from a 2-D polygon. This tool can be used on a polygon drawn with the Draw Polygon tool or on a face of an existing 3-D object. Thus, with the Draw Polygon function, you could create a simple 2-D circle (see Figure 7-3), which, when the Sweep function is activated, would then create a 3-D cylinder, as shown in Figure 7-4.

FIGURE 7-3

An example of a simple 2-D circle

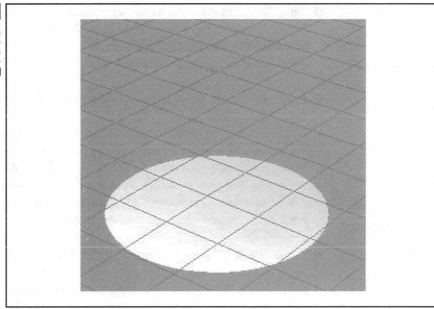

FIGURE 7-4

Using the draw polygon tool, a cylinder can be extruded from a simple circle, using the Sweep function.

■ **Tip** The Tip tool uses the vertices of a 2-D polygon to create a pointed tip, like the pyramid in Figure 7-5. Similar to the Sweep function, this can be applied to either a stand-alone 2-D polygon or a face on a 3-D object within the space.

■ **Paint** By far the most tame and easy to understand tool, the Paint function has four sibling control panels, exactly like the ones used to edit textures. The main control panel alters the color across the spectrum and sets the intensity of the color. The Shader Attributes panel, previously described in detail, controls the Ambient Glow, Shininess, Roughness, and Transparency of the color to be applied. The selected color is previewed in the Material control panel, and rendering options are set in the Shader Maps control box.

■ **Lathe** By far, the most complex tool is the Lathe function. While Pioneer's low cost is attractive to designers looking for low-price solutions, it should not be said that the product lacks high-end modeling functions that the Lathe tool provides. This tool is used to make goblets, bowls, and spindles for table and chair legs—objects created in the real world by craftsman using wood lathes—although this tool can even produce nautilus-type objects like the one in Figures 7-6 and 7-7.

FIGURE 7-5	
Using the Tip tool, a square, drawn with the Draw Polygon tool, is changed into a pyramid. ■	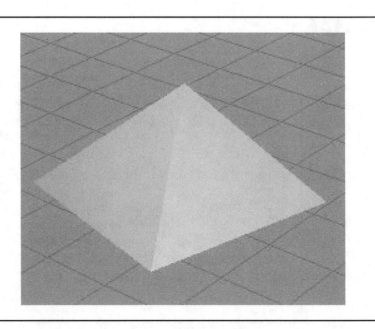

FIGURE 7-6

The Lathe function creates a nautilus object from a circle drawn with the Draw Polygon tool.

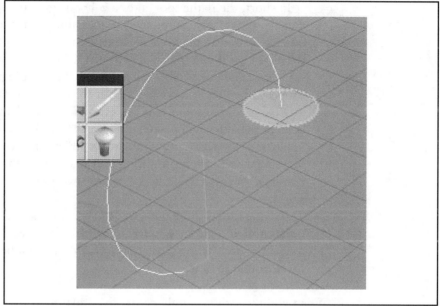

FIGURE 7-7

The nautilus object can be resized or manipulated like any other object.

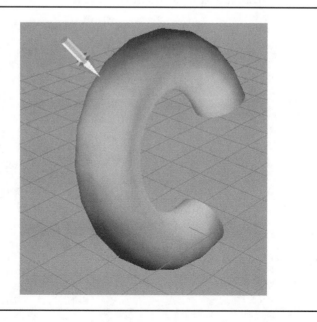

In short, the Lathe tool takes a 2-D polygon and spins it around an axis, filling in the volume as it goes along. Take a penny and quickly spin it on the table like a top; the blurry sphere you see is what you get if you took the penny and "lathed" it around an axis set in its center. Actually, you need only half of the penny for a proper lathe (but you couldn't get it to spin on the table). Lathing a 2-D polygon that looks like the letter "P" around an axis set on the stem of the letter will make an object that looks like a candied apple or a maraca. Lathing the letter "B" along its stem will look like two wheels of cheese sitting on top of each other. To make a nautilus, you give the lathe a "twist," sweeping the object in a spiral.

The Lathe tool is quite powerful but it's not especially for the faint of heart; if you have a good knowledge of geometry, 3-D object modeling, or a strong sense of the random, you'll be equipped to make good use of it.

When you're ready to apply color, five separate tools can perform this function. The simple Paint tool applies the selected color to a single face of an object; the Paint Object tool applies a coat of paint to the entire object. Existing colors or materials can be painted over using the Paint Over tool (the icon looks like a paint roller), and, using the Paint Vertices tool, a single-color gradient is applied to the vertices of a polygon, which radiates from a particular point (see the following).

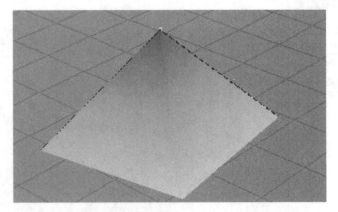

Once done, the Inspect button pulls in the painted areas for closer observation and editing.

How to Make a Complex World in Six Easy Steps

When a new user first approaches Caligari's Pioneer, he or she may be a little put off by the number of functions and the complexity of the operations. Pioneer was developed with PC end users and developers in mind, however, and it makes the process of 3-D world and VRML publishing much easier. One or two sessions with the application will familiarize you with its interface and functionality. After that . . . have fun! Pioneer adds a new level of creativity to 3-D and VRML development, and has made this available to the low- to mid-level computer user. After a few minutes and some unexpected results, you will be hooked, too!

To assist designers in the familiarization process, the following is a quick guide to creating a relatively complex 3-D scene, from concept to VRML publishing in 20 minutes!

The Quick, Clean Guide to VRML Publishing with Pioneer

Using Caligari Pioneer, only five basic steps are needed to create, edit, and publish a virtual world with VRML. These steps will follow later, with some examples to help familiarize you with the interface and some of Pioneer's basic functions.

Before beginning the creative process, the application must be started and the interface set to World Building Mode (lower left-hand button on the main screen).

note *You may want to close and exit all other Windows applications, especially if the project you plan is complex and you are using a system from the low-end of the requirements' food chain.*

Once Pioneer is set to World Building Mode, open a new world. This is accomplished from the File menu and the World menu item. From the World submenu, select New. At this point, a blank gray screen with a muted grid field appears, as shown in Figure 7-8.

Now you have a blank palette to begin the 3-D creation.

■ **Set Up the World** Before the creation process can take hold, you must make a few decisions. The first is the nature of the plane the world will sit on, if you need this at all. The second is the number of lights and cameras. The third, and last, is the attributes of both the lights and the home plane, such as color, intensity, etc.

FIGURE 7-8

The plain gray screen and muted grid are the starting points for VRML creation.

■

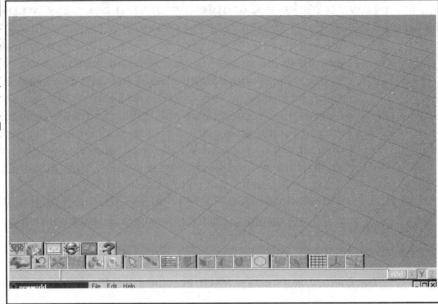

tip *These seemingly unnecessary considerations affect the overall space and should be thought out carefully. All of these may undergo changes, however, and they can be changed easily as the world evolves.*

Once you make these decisions, proceed with setting up the World:

- **Make a Plane** The world needs a field on which to sit, so first select the Regular Polygon tool button (or the Freehand button, for the daring). Set the number of sides in the Poly Modes control panel (we chose a circle) and expand the field as far as needed (see Figure 7-9).

- **Create Light Points** Lights provide visibility for the objects you want to place in the world and they create certain effects as multiple lights interact with color and shadow. Lights are created from the Primitives tool box and can be moved using the Object Movement tools. Placement is the most important aspect at the moment because the objects themselves will probably cause you to change some other attributes later.

- **Set up Cameras** Depending on the need of the project, you may need several different views within the space. Once this need is determined and outlined, cameras can be created and maneuvered

FIGURE 7-9

Setting up the space is one of the most important parts of VRML creation. Here, all light points and cameras are visible, as well as the base on which the world will sit.

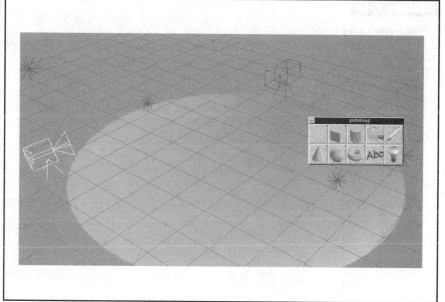

to appropriate positions. Like light points, cameras are created from the Primitives tool box and can be moved using the Object Movement tools.

- **Detailing** This can be done immediately or as the project develops, as the tools for both filtering light and coloring the home plane are available at any time. If you plan to use a texture on the plane, make certain it fits in with the overall scheme of the space.

- **Create an Object** VRML spaces are dominated, and created for, the display of 3-D objects and information. Thus, the most important step for development in Caligari Pioneer is to plan and develop objects fully to place within the space (see Figure 7-10).

- **Start Simple** When the objects of the space are planned, the creation process can start. First, a simple 3-D polygon from the Primitives tool box is placed within the space. With the Object Movement tool, the object is then positioned where needed.

- **Sizing** In most cases, the object will be of a default size, unless it is set beforehand with the Object Control screen. Using the Object Resize tool (found under the Object Movement tool button) the object can be sized appropriately.

■ **Ancillary Objects** Other dependent objects can then be created and bound to the parent object using the Glue Objects tool. Now you can move the objects as a unit, as needed.

■ **Detailing** When the objects are created, bonded, and positioned, the time for details has come. All VRML worlds need a certain level of detail to keep those Web users returning! So, time and consideration must be taken to determine the right textures, colors, and additional features that will enhance the virtual world (see Figure 7-11).

■ **Colors** Using the Paint functions, you can customize colors, shades, and object attributes, such as reflectivity and transparency, to suit the needs of the virtual piece best. Once applied, lighting options, set at the beginning of the development process, can be altered to enhance these colors further.

■ **Textures** Textures are the meat and potatoes of VRML. All the textures provide an easy to implement solution to object detailing (drag and drop). Textures should be used, but not overused, as too many conflicting textures may reduce the effectiveness of the world.

FIGURE 7-11

Once created, objects need those details that make the space striking.

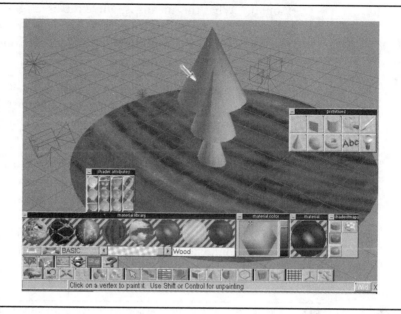

■ **Rendering Options** If the world to be laid out is a complex one, you may choose to do the initial design in wireframe, as this is the fastest rendering option available. At some point, though, you will need to render the VRML world fully and you can set the rendering option (Faceted or Smooth) for either the space as a whole (from the Rendering Options tool box in the File Menu), or for individual objects (from the Materials tool pad).

Once the details have been added, step back from your work and determine where you need finishing touches. Such items as lighting or camera adjustments, color touch-ups, and last-minute texturing are essential to cover every detail for the virtual space. Other considerations include the following items:

■ **Hyperlinks** With Pioneer's easy to implement hyperlink tools, you need a good set of links both to Web pages and VRML files, as well as to 3-D sounds—a feature supported by both Pioneer's on-board browser and VRML 2.0. Using the Intel RSX 3-D sound API, sound links to specific points within the space enable "3-D sound." What this means is, while the user's browser approaches the link, the sound gets louder; as the browser moves away, the sound recedes. The sound will also fade from one speaker to the other as the browser turns from left to right.

- **Text** From the Primitives control panel, consider adding 3-D text to the world. Such items as sign posts, signatures of the artists, and announcements of new products are eye-catching when presented in fully rendered 3-D text.

- **Publish** Finally, the goal is reached! The details have been detailed, the touch-ups touched up, and you are now ready to publish the Pioneer 3-D space to VRML. This process is as simple as saving the file. From the File menu, select Save, and the 3-D world becomes a VRML file. All objects, textures and other files, such as sounds, are stored in the same directory, as selected. They are then ready to upload to a Web directory near you!

tip *Selected objects may also be saved separately from the world itself, but they are saved as Caligari Object files (with the .COB extension). Although they can be imported to other Pioneer worlds and Caligari applications, they cannot be translated directly to VRML format with Pioneer.*

Drawbacks

Caligari Pioneer is a stable and feature-rich application, but a few problems were encountered, even on the high-end system requirement configuration. When fairly simple scenes were rendered and manipulated, the system quickly ran out of physical and virtual memory. It took about four basic objects (fully rendered and textured) for the systems on which we tested the application to start complaining about memory. The good news was the application did not lock or shut down and it was still usable, once the virtual memory error screen was cleared. One would guess Caligari needs to adjust the system requirements on the second release of Pioneer or a better memory management system should be implemented.

The only other real problem was the learning curve. For a virgin user—unversed in 3-D object creation and VRML publishing—the curve is about a week of intensive use and misuse. This drawback is not a function of Pioneer's interface or operation, however, but simply inherent with the family of 3-D object modeling applications. A user with a background with other 3-D modeling tools and a good sense of 3-D object creation should not have a problem. The Help on Tool tutorials are well laid-out and give the user a snapshot of functions and implementation related to a particular tool.

Conclusion

Caligari Pioneer is a strong package for modeling 3-D objects and worlds and for publishing these creations to the World Wide Web in VRML.

Because Caligari Pioneer is PC-based, the application is open to business development use and personal entertainment. The main strengths of Pioneer are a function-rich interface and a one-button VRML publishing capabilities. The main drawbacks are its hardware requirements and the learning curve required to get a developer up to speed. The possibilities are endless, opening up a whole new vista for in-house VRML publication.

building

VRML

World

chapter 8

Virtus WalkThrough Pro and 3-D Website Builder

N this chapter, two VRML authoring tools from the Virtus Corporation will be reviewed: 3-D Website Builder (WB) and WalkThrough Pro (WTP). Virtus Corporation has long been esteemed as a pioneer in the realm of 3-D design tools and is recognized as one of the most important companies in the VRML software business. Virtus' 3-D WB was the first cross-platform product that allowed users to create 3-D VRML worlds for the Internet with accessible drop-and-drag technology. WTP was the first commercially available VRML world builder. Both products include a VRML browser, in addition to the creation software. One drawback about both of these products is they are unable to import VRML files.

Virtus' Background

Virtus (whose logo follows) was founded by David A. Smith in 1990. Smith originated the 3-D technology, which forms the basis of the Virtus product line, in his 3-D computer adventure game, The Colony. The Colony was the first real-time, interactive 3-D game released and its exposure led Smith to work on the movie *The Abyss* with James Cameron. Smith created the movie's set on his desktop. His creation opened the floodgates of Hollywood's love affair with virtual space.

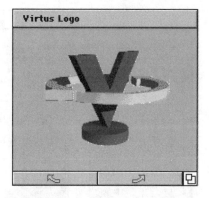

In 1990, Smith started Virtus Corporation, planning to expand The Colony into the realm of real-life use. Virtus set the groundwork for desktop VR. Exploring virtual worlds at this time typically required expensive workstations and a full regalia of add-ons (gloves, headgear, etc.). Virtus' products were the first to open VRML creation up to the Macintosh platform. In addition to their alliance with the movie industry, Virtus has other interesting connections. Tom Clancy, author of the blockbuster books, *The Hunt for Red October* and *Patriot Games*, is on Virtus' board of directors. Frederick Brooks, who founded the Virtual Reality Lab at the University of North Carolina at Chapel Hill, is also on the board. Several high-ranking Motorola executives also advise Virtus, which has strategic alliances with Simon and Schuster Interactive to boot.

The Virtus Web Site

Virtus' home page, shown in Figure 8-1, is located at:

```
http://www.virtus.com
```

Visit the Virtus Web site to check status on the two tools that are examined in this chapter. Even though they're included on the CD-ROM, you'll want to make certain you have the latest version before you install these programs. Playing with the software as you read will give you a much better idea of the concepts and capabilities being covered. Because both these tools are save-disabled versions, you won't be able to keep any of the work you do, but

FIGURE 8-1

*This page is what
you'll see upon
arriving at the
Virtus Web site.*

■

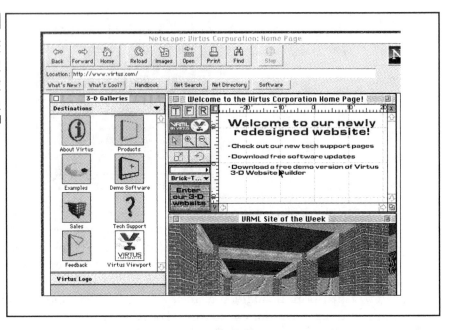

experimenting with the interface and the tools will help you decide if you want to buy the software. If you feel like giving Virtus demographic information (putting your name into a drawing for a free copy of WB in the process), go to the download section of the Virtus home page. If you're in the mood for a direct download, try this link:

```
ftp://freedom.interpath.net/pub/virtus/
```

Virtus sponsors a "Virtus VRML site of the week," which is open to any VRML site or model created with Virtus products. You can find current and past winners at this URL:

```
http://www.virtus.com/links.html
```

Winners receive "wicked cool Virtus stuff" (whatever that may be), and the chance to share their otherworldly creations with the Web community. The commentary of Virtus' judges also appears on the page, so it's a good place to figure out what good VRML is all about.

Virtus Help

Virtus offers online help to its users through a Frequently Asked Questions (FAQ) section at its Web site, which is found here:

```
http://www.virtus.com/techsupport.html
```

If your query isn't addressed in the FAQs, you can consult Virtus' spectral "Johnny Dos" character for additional support at info@virtus.com.

The 3-D Durham Bulls Ballpark: A Virtus Creation

You'll also find models and worlds created by the Virtus team at their home page. An example is the virtual version of the Durham Bulls Athletic Park (shown in Figure 8-2), which Virtus released in June 1996. The Bulls are a minor league baseball team based in Durham, North Carolina, near Virtus' HQ. Having created the model with both 3-D WB and WTP, the Virtus team decided it would be good advertising to have it posted on their site. A considerable qualitative difference exists between the baseball park model and models Virtus released a year earlier; the excellent detail and complexity of the park make it an impressive model. The Bulls were pleased with the job, commenting they thought it was the best 3-D model of a sports facility created to date.

You can check out the models at the Virtus home page or download the files from the Bulls site:

```
http://www.dbulls.com
```

Virtus' VMDL: A VRML Alternative?

Virtus has developed a language they proclaim as a VRML alternative, called the Virtus Modeling Language (VMDL). When you create worlds with either WTP or WB, you're actually creating them in VMDL, Virtus' proprietary file format for 3-D worlds.

Anything written in VMDL can only be viewed by a Virtus product, such as Virtus Player (which reads only VMDL; future versions of Virtus Voyager

FIGURE 8-2

*Here's a shot of a
virtual ballpark
created by Virtus.*

will be capable of reading both VRML and VMDL). Exporting the VMDL models you create to VRML needn't provoke any anxiety, however. Virtus knows why many people buy their products to create VRML worlds and they've made it extremely easy to do so. A brief tutorial on exporting files to VRML follows shortly.

Virtus is proud of heralding that VMDL files are a great deal smaller than VRML files. VDML files tend to be one fourth the size of their VRML counterparts. This decreased size allows them both to download and to walk faster.

In addition, VMDL models can have textures embedded in the files. This eliminates the need to keep track of multiple graphics files, which, in turn, results in a wholly self-contained model that runs with speed and efficiency, as long as you're using a Virtus browser!

If you're creating worlds with Virtus products that you're going to put on a Web site, consider putting both VMDL and VRML files on your site. (Because they use the same texture links, throw them in the same folder.) Your viewers with Virtus products will appreciate the quality and speed of the VMDL files in their native environments.

To look at VMDL models (with your requisite Virtus browser), head to this URL:

```
http://www.virtus.com/vmdl.html
```

Exporting to VRML

Because anything you create with a Virtus product will be in VMDL, you must export your VMDL files to VRML. This procedure isn't too complicated and, because it's similar for WTP and WB, the procedure for both will be covered in a brief tutorial.

Follow these steps to export your VMDL files to VRML, making them "Webified":

- Create your model with either WTP or 3-D WB (see Figure 8-3)

- Add URL anchors to objects within your world

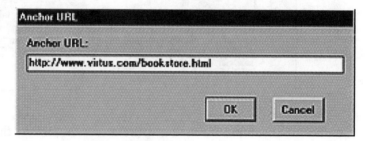

- Export the model to VRML

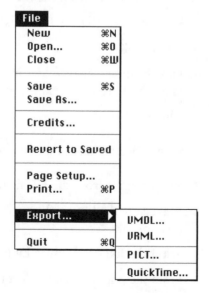

FIGURE 8-3

The 3-D WB

creation space

and tools

■

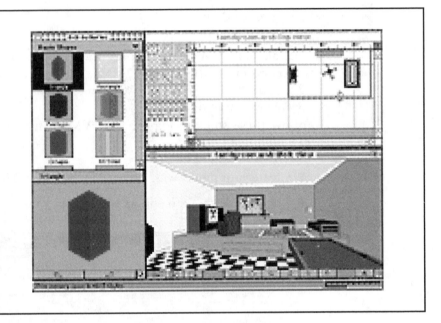

If you're exporting it without textures, follow these steps:

1. Select "Export" from the file menu; then drag to "VRML."

2. Uncheck the "Export Textures" box when its dialog box appears.

3. Select "OK."

4. Pick the directory or folder in which you want to save the file (add ".wrl" to the filename, to format it properly for VRML).

5. Choose "Save."

If you're exporting a file that contains texture links, follow these steps:

1. Select Export from the File menu and drag to "VRML."

2. Make sure the Export Textures box is checked when the dialog box appears.

3. Select the Export Texture Links radio button.

4. From the pop-up menu, select the file type for export.

5. Select OK.

6. Pick the directory or folder in which you'd like to save the file and its linked textures.

7. Choose Save.

Fetch (FTP) your .wrl file to the appropriate Web server. All textures need to be FTPed in binary mode, while the .wrl files must be transferred in text format. The textures accompanying your files must be in the same directory as your model. See Figure 8-4 for an example of a completed world.

3-D Website Builder

Virtus' 3-D WB is designed for easy and quick creation of 3-D Web sites. WB includes a subset of Virtus' more powerful creation toolset, WTP, and comes with a nifty set of preconfigured 3-D and geometric objects. WB makes it wildly easy to create VRML. All you have to do is grab an object and drop it into a window. Its brightly colored interface and simple tools make ideal software for impatient novices.

FIGURE 8-4

An example of a completed virtual world

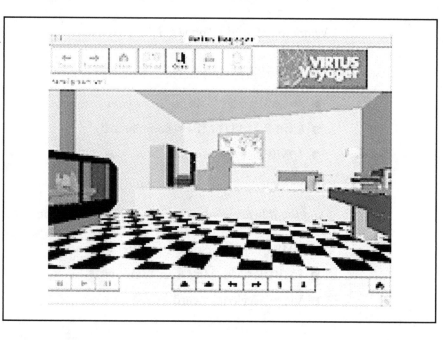

As the first cross-platform VRML development tool, WB has garnered lots of positive attention. WB's facile drag-and-drop interface, along with a library of predesigned objects, make it accessible for beginning VRML enthusiasts to create impressive VRML environments. WB isn't nearly as complex as WTP because WB was designed for fast, easy design. WB is ideal for novices because it doesn't require any programming, uses drag-and-drop features, is equipped with over 1,200 predesigned 3-D objects, and it doesn't demand much technical knowledge from its users. VRML professionals seeking to create highly complex worlds would probably be more rewarded by WTP's more sophisticated features.

WB is ideal for beginning VRML enthusiasts, however, as well as for people without a background or interest in the technical side of VRML creation.

WB was released in March 1996 and, currently, version 1.1 has a street price of $99 for a CD-ROM supporting Windows 95, Windows 3.1, Macintosh, and Power Macintosh.

WB System Requirements

If your machine doesn't have a CD-ROM, you can still use WB. Just call Virtus' customer service at (800) 847-8871 and ask for 3.5 HD disks. Here are Virtus' system requirements for running WB.

Windows 95 and Windows 3.1

The following configuration is required:

- 80486-based PC (Pentium or later recommended)
- 8MB RAM (16MB+ recommended)
- 10MB disk space
- CD-ROM

And the following system configuration is recommended:

- 80486-based personal computer or Pentium
- 8MB+ RAM—Microsoft Windows 3.1+
- Video accelerator card

Macintosh, Power Macintosh

The following configuration is required:

- Apple Macintosh Powerbook, Centris, Quadra or Power Macintosh
- 8MB RAM (16MB+ recommended)
- System 6.0.5 or later
- 10MB disk space
- CD-ROM

And the following is recommended:

- 16MB+ RAM
- System 7.5.2 or later

WB's Impressive Features

Some of WB's best qualities are:

- Multiplatform—Virtus has long been a supporter of the Macintosh contingent. WB's CD-ROM installs the software for Macintosh, Power Macintosh, Windows 3.1, and Windows 95.
- Easy to use with its drag-and-drop interface, WB is a user-friendly tool. "Visual learners" will find its orientation sympathetic, while hardened techies will appreciate its speed and capacity.
- Excellent price, and considering all WB can do, $99 is a reasonable price.
- The message bar is a handy tool, which appears at the bottom of the WB screen. When you pass the mouse pointer over components of the WB environment, the message bar tells you what the components can do.
- Records animations and you can export QuickTime movies, as well as FLC and AVI file formats. WB also exports to static BMP or PICT.

- WB is licensed for both personal and commercial use. Unlike some other VRML creation tools, Virtus places no restrictions on using its product for commercial gain.

- Offers a stellar 1,244 gallery objects/templates. (ParaGraph International's Virtual Home Space Builder only has 82.)

- Features a useful memory indicator. The indicator, which lives to the right of the message bar, has a colored bar that grows and shrinks according to your memory usage. When the available memory is below 75 percent, the bar goes blue; when it's above 75 percent, it's red.

A Glance at WB's Windows

WB features three different types of windows, shown in Figure 8-5.

Gallery Window

The Gallery window shows you the offering of 3-D library objects you can add to your Web site. If you want to change galleries, click the title button near the top of the window and select another gallery name. At the bottom of the Gallery window, you'll find a handy preview area where you can rotate each item and contemplate whether or not it's worthy of inclusion in your site.

Design View Window

Drop gallery items into the Design View window to create worlds. Three views are available in this window: Top, Front, and Right (touch the T, F, and R buttons in the tool pad to select them).

Walk View Window

In the Walk View window, you can view and interact with your 3-D virtual environment. Whatever gallery objects you put into the Design View are shown in 3-D glory in the Walk View. Use the navigation buttons or the mouse cursor to navigate in, through, or around these objects.

FIGURE 8-5

All three windows
are represented in
this picture: the
Gallery window is
in the upper left,
Design View is in
the upper right,
and Walk View is
below Design View.

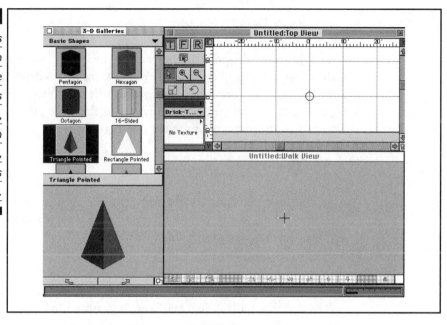

The Design Concepts Behind WB

Three important design concepts are represented in 3-D Website Builder: containment, placement depth, and auto connection.

Containment

Containment indicates that every object in WB knows what object contains it, as well as which objects it contains. Containment is efficient because all objects within a container will move as a unit, retaining their orientation to each other. Objects are either fully contained or not contained at all. For that reason, it's impossible to have overlapping objects in WB, although objects may join at a common surface. If you happen to overlap your 3-D objects, they'll probably look twisted when you render them in the Walk View. This isn't really a limitation of the program, simply something for you to remember during your creation process.

Placement Depth

Dragging and dropping an object into the Design View makes it automatically drop to 0 feet in the inactive dimension. If you drop an object into the Front View at 20 feet, when you go into the Top View, the object will still be at 0 feet. To change this height, stay in the Top View and use the Select Object Tool to manually raise the object to 20 feet.

Auto Connection

Auto connection makes the adjacent surfaces of objects share surface attributes. Sharing any surface attribute or surface feature between adjacent surfaces is possible through this feature.

WB's Tools

The WB tool pad, shown here, resides within the Design View. In the tool pad, you'll find buttons that enable you to change the Design View, as well as tools with which you can edit objects and their surfaces.

When you click on an object in WB, one of three types of "handles" (small square boxes) appears around it. The type of handle associated with an object indicates if or how an object can be manipulated. To perform the manipulation, click-and-drag the handles in the desired direction.

Black handles appear around objects whose shapes can be manipulated in any direction. White handles appear around objects open only to depth manipulation. Gray handles are shown around objects that are grouped together. Before gray-handled objects can be altered, they must be un-grouped (which, like grouping, is accomplished through the Group command under the Edit menu).

The following list briefly examines each of the tools, starting from the top and working down, left to right.

Design View Selector Button

T is the Top View, *F* is the Front View, and *R* is the Right View. Clicking these buttons changes the Design View.

Surface Editor Tool

This tool opens to the Surface Editor, with which you can alter an object's selected surface (surfaces are an object's side or face).

Select Object Tool

Click on the Select Object tool to select entire objects for editing. The selected object will show handles at its vertices.

Magnify Tool

The Magnify tool increases the Design View's apparent scale. The Design View's apparent scale will double if you click once on the Magnify tool, then point to an area.

Zoom-out Tool

The Zoom-out tool decreases the Design View's apparent scale. The Design View's apparent scale will decrease by a factor of two if you point to an area, then click once.

Resize Object Tool

With the Resize Object tool, you can scale an object about a specified anchor point or about its center. You can resize objects either uniformly along all three axes or nonuniformly along one axis.

Rotate Object Tool

Use this tool to rotate an object. It works in any view and allows rotation on multiple axes.

Color Bar

The color bar lets you assign colors to objects; it also allows you to create new colors for objects.

Texture Button

By depressing the texture button, you'll see the panoply of Texture Palettes available for your use.

Texture Bar

This tool lets you apply textures to objects. WB includes a library of predefined textures, with options for adding more, as needed.

WB Tips

These tips will help you use WB:

- If you're using a Macintosh and you are having problems with crashes, turn off the date/time control panel with your extensions manager. This conflict is a glitch Virtus promises to fix soon.

- If you're using Windows 95 and you are experiencing mysterious crashes, it could be caused by a problem with your video driver. Virtus suggests you address this problem by calling your manufacturer to make certain you have the most current version.

- Note: Textures aren't read uniformly by VRML browsers and models containing them may cause crashes.

WalkThrough Pro

WTP is a more complex version of 3-D WB (its two instruction manuals contain over 250 pages of information, as opposed to WB's 76). WTP is aimed at people interested in professional VRML creation; its more powerful features reflect this. WTP's interface shows this, too. A big contrast exists between WB's brightly colored, cheerful interface, which looks almost childlike, and WTP's more somber appearance, which features a panoply of drawing and editing tools. In addition to its much larger set of creation and editing tools, WTP enables greater control over your worlds; for example, you can "lock" objects, making them inaccessible for others to edit. WTP also has a more refined selection of drawing and design tools and it has an entire series of "Editors" that WB lacks. With WTP, you can effect highly precise movement and editing. The Tape Measure tool, for example, permits you to carefully measure distances between two points while sophisticated tools, such as the Depth Control Gauge and highly precise rulers, provide exacting control.

As with WB, with WTP, you can interact with the models you create, as well as have instant access to designs as you're creating them. The minute you build a WTP object, it appears in the rendered 3-D environment. To travel through the model scene, you move the mouse (the arrow keys also allow you to navigate, unlike in WB).

Also unlike in WB, there aren't navigation buttons in the Walk View that let you maneuver through the scene. WTP also lacks WB's message bar at the bottom of the interface, which tells you exactly where you are or what you're doing, although you can turn on the balloon help for illumination at that level. These two omissions are representative of WTP not being as user friendly as WB.

WTP has an impressive level of interactivity and it is widely regarded as one of the most advanced VRML creation tools available. For this reason, it's often used by professionals, including directors, filmmakers, architects, and set designers, and by VRML addicts.

Although WTP once cost $595, it now retails for around the bargain price of $195. The version reviewed in this chapter is 2.5.2; version 2.6 is on the way and it will be 32-bit. To get the best idea about WTP's look, feel, and capabilities, download a demo version at Virtus' site.

WTP System Requirements

Virtus' recommendations for success with WTP are:

Macintosh and Power Macintosh

The following configuration is required:

- A color Apple Macintosh (LC, Mac II, PowerBook, Power Mac, Quadra or Centris)
- 8MB RAM
- System 6.0.5 or later

And the following configuration is recommended:

- Macintosh Power Mac, PowerBook 170 or 180c, Quadra or Centris with 13" or larger monitor
- 8MB+ RAM
- System 7.5.2 or later

PC/Windows

The following configuration is required:

- 80386-based (or later) personal computer
- 8MB RAM—Microsoft Windows 3.1+
- VGA or SVGA display adapter

And the following configuration is recommended:

- 80486-based personal computer or Pentium
- 8MB+ RAM - Microsoft Windows 3.1+
- VGA or Super VGA display adapter

Virtus Rules

The "Virtus Rules of Drawing" are proffered by Virtus with the promise they will make you work more efficiently.

1. Don't overlap 3-D objects so one object is contained in another.

2. No nonconvex objects are allowed. If you want to create nonconvex objects, connect two or more convex objects. (*Convex* objects have surfaces or boundaries that bulge or curve outwards—a sphere, for example.)

3. Because speed and detail are inversely proportional, be prepared to sacrifice one for the other.

4. Use transparent (clear) and translucent (like glass) objects sparingly because they drain processing power.

remember *Everything, but everything, is an object in WTP. It's impossible to draw a line because all drawn objects contain depth.*

The Virtus World

The *Virtus 3-D world* is a cube that's 65,536 base units across. If you want to change the size of the world (hey, power trips can be fun once in a while), you can change the base unit size of this cube (go to "Units," under "Preferences").

WTP's Offerings

Here's a list highlighting some of WTP's most impressive features:

- Strong graphical drawing tools and adroit editors and modifiers.

- Supports stereo viewing and most commercially available VR hardware. Supported display hardware includes Stereographics' Crystal Eyes, Vrex, Simsalabim's Cyberscope, 3DTV's StereoSpace and WirelessIR Pro, and Victormaxx's Cybermaxx.

- Over 500 prebuilt 3-D library items. Using these saves lots of time.

- Great export options. You can export files in 2-D, 3-D DXF, Illustrator 1.1, TIFF, PICT, BMP and, most important, VRML.

- Ability to create multimedia presentations. WTP lets you perform real-time walkthroughs, which you can export as QuickTime, Lotus' PICS, Video for Windows, or Animator Pro movies.

- QuickTime (QT) movies (for Macintosh users only) can be applied over entire objects, surfaces, or surface textures.

- QT movies can also be put within another QT movie. This feat is achieved by applying a QT movie as a surface feature in a model, then walking through the model, recording the path, and saving it as a QT movie.

- WTP's Snapshot option lets you grab a snapshot of a WTP model in another file format (PICT, TIFF, BMP, or Illustrator).

- All of WTP's windows (all well as the editors) can be repositioned or resized, a valuable feature shared by WB.

- WTP gives you the ability to create custom colors from the color palette, as well as control an object's opacity and inflation type (shape).

- Option to stack objects in layers and manipulate them simultaneously.

- Power to create walls that appear to have two sides. This is achieved by creating an object inside another object.

A Glance at WTP Views

WTP has two types of views: Walk View and Design View, which contain a subset of six viewing options.

Design View

The Design View is the 2-D area where you can draw objects and examine their placement. Six Design Views exist: Front, Back, Top, Bottom, Left, and Right, all of which can be used for drawing and editing. Although only one view can be active at a time, you can keep all of the Design Views open simultaneously to see your edits and objects in all the views. If you don't have at least a 17-inch monitor, however, seeing all six views may be overwhelming. Figure 8-6 shows the Design View of WTP's interface.

Walk View

The Walk View is the window in which you can navigate through the objects you draw in your Design View. You can walk through and around the objects displayed in the Walk View by using your mouse or your arrow keys. Figure 8-7 shows the Walk View of WTP's interface.

FIGURE 8-6

The WalkThrough Pro interface as seen in Design View

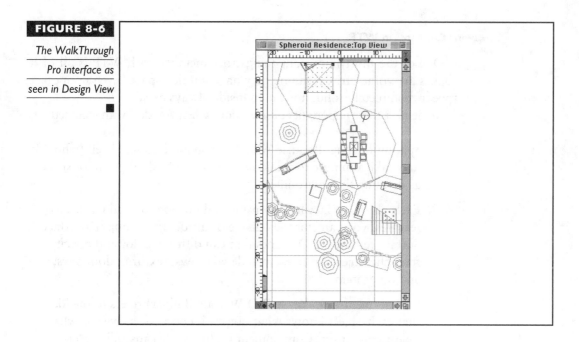

To increase the speed of your walkthrough, hide translucent and transparent objects and surfaces with the SeeIn and SeeOut preferences.

FIGURE 8-7

The WalkThrough Pro interface as seen in Walk View

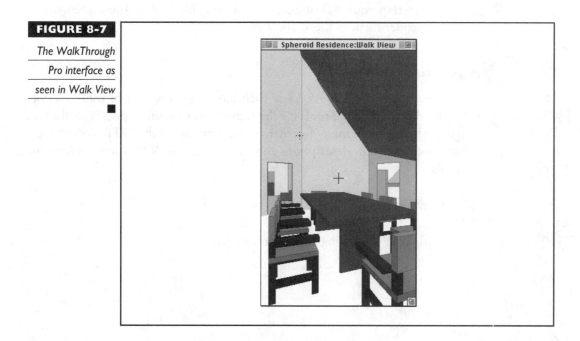

Drawing Concepts in WTP

One of the most important things to remember with WTP is all of its objects are volumetric, meaning they have interior space. Even if an object appears completely solid, it isn't; an inside always exists.

Remember three important considerations when you deal with volumetricity:

1. Space modeling. Because WTP lets you model space itself (whoa! It may take a minute to think about that one!), don't think of space as defining the environment.

2. Each object surface has an inside and outside. By adding surface features, you can edit the outside or inside of any object's surface. Surface features, 2-D shapes that can differ in color and opacity from the object surfaces, include windows, textures, doorways, and other items.

3. Containment (also key in 3-D Website Builder) refers to the idea that each object knows what objects it contains, as well as what object contains it. Containment is efficient because all objects within a container will move as a unit, retaining their orientation to each other. Objects are either fully contained or not contained at all. For this reason, it's impossible to have overlapping objects in WTP, although objects may join at a common surface. If you overlap your 3-D objects, they'll probably look twisted when you render them in the Walk View.

Highlights of the WTP Toolkit

Design View and Walk View each have their own set of tools, as does each Editor. The set of tools for the active view or Editor appears on the tool pad. Although too many fascinating components of the WTP toolbox exist to cover in detail, descriptions follow of some of WTP's most interesting tools.

Drawing Tools

With WTP's drawing tools, shown here:

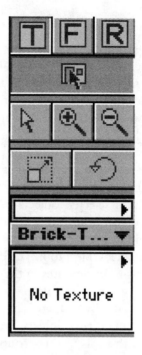

you can create 2-D polygonal outlines of basic shapes. By combining and inflating these basic shapes, you can create and render complex 3-D models in the Walk View. You can also use drawing tools in conjunction with the Surface Editor to draw surface features. Here's a listing of WTP's drawing tools:

- Create 8-sided Object tool
- Create 6-sided Object tool
- Create Square Object tool
- Create Triangular Object tool
- Create N-sided Object tool. Use this tool to create a polygonal outline with as many sides as you like (up to 32).
- Create Irregular Object tool
- Create Rectangular Object tool
- Connect Surfaces tool
- Add/Remove Handle tool
- Rotate Object tool

Design View Tools

Through the Design View tools, you create, edit, and orient objects and surfaces. One of the tools that fall under this category are the Color Lifter tool, which lets you copy a color from one object to another. This ability is ideal when you're trying to maintain a uniform color in different sections of your world. This group of tools also contains the Tape Measure tool, which indicates the distance between points (a helpful feature for constructing architectural prototypes or other worlds that demand precision).

Another advanced feature of the WTP toolkit is the Lock Object tool, which makes selected objects or surface features unavailable for editing. When an object or surface feature is locked, it's represented through a dotted polygonal outline instead of a solid outline. The Hide Object tool is nested under the Lock Object tool. The Hide Object tool permits you to hide certain objects or surface features in the Walk View or Design View (or both).

The Magnify and Zoom Out tools let you increase or decrease a drawing's size by a factor of two; the Select Object tool is used for selecting and editing objects. You can also scale and skew objects along the axis with tools in this grouping.

Walk View Tools

WTP provides you with a choice of Walk Views: Normal, Fast, Faster, and Fastest. Selecting ultimate speed means you'll get a bare-bones representation of the model. If you choose Normal, CPU-draining detail such as transparent and translucent surfaces will appear in the model. The faster you go, the less detail you'll see, as shown in Figures 8-8 through 8-10. (The Faster Walk View is not included because this world's rendering doesn't reflect a difference between Faster Walk and Fast Walk.)

The Walk View tools give you control over various elements of the Walk View. For example, when you're in Walk View mode, you can use the 3-D Object Selector to select an object for editing in the Design View. This feature is helpful for use with especially complex worlds because objects may be easier to locate in the Walk View than in the Design View.

Through the Walk View tools you can also change the background color, defining a custom color through the brightness control feature (Macintosh) or Vertical Luminosity Bar (Windows). The ability to record (and later playback) a walkthrough sequence also falls under Walk View tools, as does control over the virtual camera's zoom factor. If you want your world to be

FIGURE 8-8

Normal Walk View

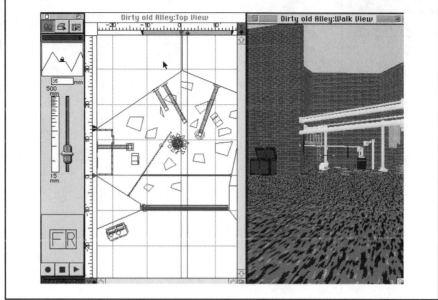

seen as through an angle lens, choose a smaller lens size; for the sense of a telephoto lens, select a larger lens size.

FIGURE 8-9

Fast Walk View

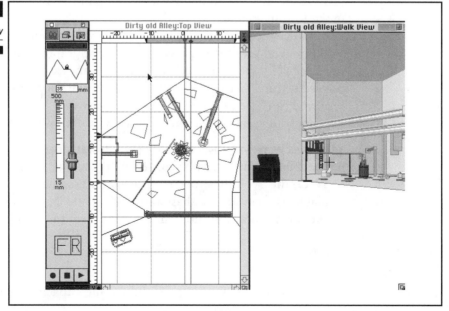

FIGURE 8-10

Fastest Walk View

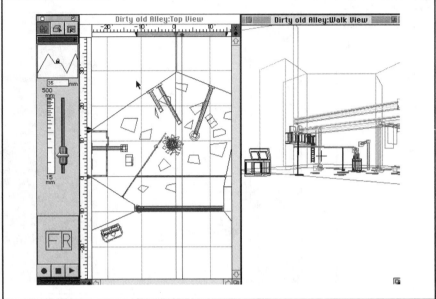

Textures

WTP comes with some excellent textures. You can add to the included textures by making your own with any paint program or by purchasing textures from commercial vendors.

It's possible to apply decals to WTP textures—a useful feature. By decaling a texture, you give the impression an outline graphic has been placed on a translucent or clear surface. The viewer can see what's underneath the decaled texture. Decals are great for objects like doors because they make it seem you can "see through" things in a real-world kind of way. Be prudent in your use of decals, however, because they can slow down your walk speed.

TEXTURES WITH VRML FILES BMP (Windows) format. To use those textures on the Internet, files must be converted to JPEG or GIF.

To do this, you must open the files in a graphics converter (plenty are available as freeware or shareware) or a paint program (such as Fractal Painter or Adobe Photoshop) and convert them to JPEG or GIF files.

Editors

Judicious use of WTP's powerful editing capacities is crucial to make outstanding WTP scenes.

LIGHTING EDITOR With the Lighting Editor, you can determine the color and intensity of light sources inside either a Virtus world or a single object. You can also add, modify, and remove light sources, as well as position directional lights.

SURFACE EDITOR You can use the Surface Editor to edit object surfaces selected in either the Design View or the Tumble Editor. Surface features (polygonal 2-D objects representing things like windows, floors, doors, etc.) can also be created through the Surface Editor.

TUMBLE EDITOR The Tumble Editor provides you with access to all an object's sides. The Tumble Editor can be accessed in both the Surface Editor and Design Views. With the Tumble Editor, you can use the Slice tool, which lets you imbue an object with more surface by removing a slice from it. The Tumble Editor also enables you to edit the color and opacity of objects or object surfaces.

Opacity Modifiers

With Opacity Modifiers, you can determine the opacity of whole objects, object surfaces, or surface features. Opacity Modifiers work in both the Surface Editor and the Tumble Editor, as well as in the Design View. Through this feature's Translucent Modifier, you can make entire parts of your world look as clear as glass or simply select objects to appear in this way. A Transparent Modifier functions in the same way.

Inflation Modifiers

Inflation Modifiers are used to affect how objects are shaped. *Inflation* refers to the process of creating a 3-D object from a 2-D polygonal outline. To determine an object's inflation, you employ the Depth Control Gauges that appear on each ruler in the Design View.

To use inflation modification with objects, you must determine their composition, and then apply the applicable inflation modifier. For example, a sphere is inflated with the Inflate Double Rounded Modifier, which inflates only objects with sides rounding to two points. Although this terminology may seem confusing at first, it really isn't as long as you don't mind calling a triangle a "Pointed Modifier."

Appearance Modifiers

Two ways exist to modify an object surface or an object's appearance: Flat Shading Modifier and Smooth Shading Modifier. The Flat Shading

Modifier is the default selected when you begin creating an object. Because the Flat Shading Modifier produces less detail than the Smooth Shading Modifier, it runs more quickly. Flat-shaded objects and object surfaces show their polygonal outline and have a rather basic appearance.

If you're trying to achieve a slick look with complex objects, you definitely want to use Smooth Shading. Smooth Shading gives a more realistic appearance by softening the rough polygonal edges of the object's outline. Using smooth shading with an object as primitive as a box doesn't accomplish much, however, so it is best employed with multifaceted objects.

Rabbit in the Moon: An Example of What You Can Do with WTP

Nancy McNelly has posted some impressive VRML files created with WTP at her Web site, Rabbit in the Moon. McNelly's site is located at:

`http://www.he.net/~nmcnelly/index.html`

McNelly's site, which focuses on Mayan glyphs and architecture, features several VRML models of Mayan architecture, including three VRML interpretations of the Bonampak murals. The events depicted in these murals occurred between 790 and 792 A.D. Figure 8-11 shows the throne being presented to the heir. Figure 8-12 shows some of WTP's editing abilities.

WTP Tips

These tips may be useful in your WTP experiences:

- Objects (like Library items) must be ungrouped before they can be edited.

- A model's texture location information isn't saved until the model itself is saved. Even if you've located a texture (or a group of textures), you still must choose "Save" under the "Edit" menu (so the application knows where to find the textures the next time the model's opened).

- Create your models from the inside out and try to make models from single objects rather than multiple objects, whenever possible.

- Although textures can make a scene look fantastically realistic, they can also make a scene look garish and unreal when overused. Underkill is better than overkill when it comes to using textures, especially because they slow rendering and can be buggy when run on non-Virtus browsers.

FIGURE 8-11

Nancy McNelly's VRML version of one of the Bonampak murals ∎

FIGURE 8-12

Some of WalkThrough Pro's editing abilities ∎

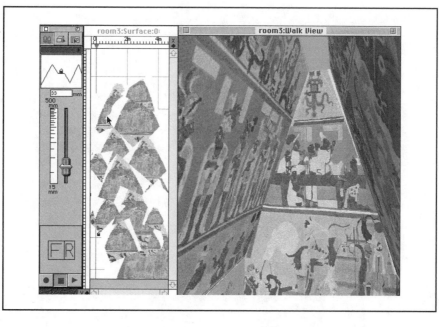

Summary

We hope you've found useful information in this chapter about 3-D WB and WTP. Both these tools are enjoyable to use. Both have good documentation, user-friendly interfaces, and a great way of putting 3-D space together. Don't take our word for it, though. Check out the CD-ROM (or head over to the Virtus home page) and try out these demos for yourself:

```
http://www.virtus.com
```

building

VRML

World

chapter 9

VR Tools

IN this chapter, you will learn about a panoply of VRML tools, from Java-based toolkits that employ VRML, to VRML translators, converters, and servers. Because the VRML 2.0 specification was finalized at press time, many tools used with VRML hadn't been updated to VRML 2.0. Tools that work with VRML 2.0 were included although, in a few cases, they were included with the expectation they were likely to become VRML 2.0-compliant by the time you read this.

Java/VRML Tools

The combination of Java and VRML is a hot one. Java makes VRML interactive. As Mark Pesce, VRML cocreator said, "VRML is, Java does." The tools evaluated in this section can assist you in bringing Java's power to your VRML creations.

Dimension X's Liquid Reality

You'll find the following slogan at the Dimension X Web site: "There's the leading edge, the bleeding edge, and then there's Dimension X." You may feel you've heard this hype before but, in the case of Dimension X, it's actually founded in plausibility (although we aren't saying this wholly pardons the cyber-hubris).

Dimension X produces a VRML toolkit called Liquid Reality, which *is* cutting edge, no question about it. Liquid Reality is a set of Java class libraries that add VRML and 3-D browsing functionality when used with a Java-friendly browser. It, therefore, supports VRML 2.0-compliant tool creation, viewers, and solutions. Liquid Reality was the first toolkit to fully support VRML 2.0; many of the "new" features in the VRML 2.0 specification (including behaviors and sounds) had existed for months in Liquid Reality before they became official in VRML 2.0.

Through Liquid Reality's world and object editor, VRML syntax is transformed into simpler syntax and direct manipulation interface, making VRML eminently more accessible to users.

Dimension X offers a native C code graphics library called Ice that can be used with Liquid Reality. You can also use Direct 3-D as the graphics library on the Windows platform, which allows you to import their preexisting graphics into the world you're building.

The Liquid Reality toolkit supports the following:

- An open Application Programming Interface (API)
- 3-D sound
- VRML 2.0 applet creation
- Java classes to build a VRML 2.0 browser
- 250 classes to support 3-D content development

Because Java is extensible, the toolkit is, too, giving you the power to dream up customized nodes. Unlike some other Java toolkits, Liquid Reality is pure Java, not a layer of Java wrapped around C or C++. The Liquid Reality class hierarchy simplifies portability, debugging, and extensibility. The decision of Dimension X to write Liquid Reality in Java reflects long-term savvy—because Java is portable to non-PC devices, Liquid Reality can be used in key developing markets, such as hand-held personal digital assistants.

Liquid Reality gives you all the necessary requirements to parse, render, and write out VRML; with the toolkit, you can also manipulate the VRML scene graph. Liquid Reality fortifies VRML 2.0 via a custom node, which accomplishes the following: When the parser meets an unidentifiable node type, it queries the HTTP that served the VRML file; then it requests a Java class to describe the unknown node. This custom node behavior exemplifies Liquid Reality's adroit manipulation of VRML nodes. Here's a concrete example of how VRML scene nodes can be accessed and manipulated to perform a NameSearchTraversal of the scene with the following code:

```
Scene scene = new Scene("test.wrl");
Node rootNode = scene.getRootNode();
Node foundNode = null;
NameSearchTraversal t = new NameSearchTraversal("foo");
rootNode.traverse(t);
if (t.foundMatch())
    foundNode = t.getFirstNode();
```

Liquid Reality is currently in its beta 1.0b5. A few components still exist of VRML 2.0 (such as MovieTexture, Text, and Background textures) that haven't been implemented.

Microsoft signed an agreement with Dimension X to incorporate a portion of Liquid Reality—the Liquid Reality Core—into the Internet Explorer Web browser for Windows 95 and Windows NT. Liquid Reality creations can be implemented as ActiveX controls; Explorer users will, therefore, be able to read, write, and view VRML through Liquid Reality. This combination exploits the power of IE 3.0's Just In Time native compiler (as any Java can).

Liquid Reality runs on Windows 95/NT 4.0, Irix, Solaris, and Linux. PowerPC and Pippin versions are in the works. For more information on Liquid Reality (including a free download, if it's still available), investigate the souped-up Dimension X home page:

```
http://www.dimensionx.com
```

Hyperwire

Hyperwire is a visual authoring tool developed to facilitate creation of 2-D and 3-D Web worlds in Java. Hyperwire was the first visual Java authoring environment that permitted the creation of fully interactive titles in 2-D and 3-D.

Hyperwire's Java-enabled structure means its titles can respond easily to real-world, real-time events, and respond to user input. Hyperwire's Java base makes it cross-platform by definition. The cross-platform capacity is a strong point because it can be used with any browser that supports Java (including Netscape Navigator and Internet Explorer). Hyperwire also supports VRML file formats, which is why it's being discussed in this chapter. Kinetix integrated their 3-D engine into Hyperwire 1.1, which also features a timer action that allows developers to synchronize a Web title's action down to the millisecond.

Hyperwire comes from Kinetix, the multimedia business unit Autodesk created in 1996. Hyperwire's unveiling occurred simultaneously with Autodesk's announcement of Kinetix's formation. Kinetix has formed Hyperwire Users Group (HUG), which it's pushing as the user group to "make Hyperwire the coolest Java development tool on the Internet."

Hyperwire has online help you can access from within the Windows help section, as well as a series of tutorials at the Kinetix Web site. It supports VRBL (Virtual Reality Behavior Language), which is Kinetix's proprietary specification for playing animations within VRML worlds.

Hyperwire Features

Hyperwire offers these key features:

- 100 percent Java output
- Tools and templates to create sprite-based applications
- Library of applets
- WYSIWYG displays of your title's interface and a graphical view of the wiring behind the title
- Buttons that allow you to create, search, and change functions
- Capacity to connect Java objects from within a 3-D world

To run Hyperwire, it's recommended you have the following setup:

- Pentium class PC or compatible system
- Microsoft Windows/Windows NT
- 16MB RAM
- 20MB free disk space
- 8-bit, 640 × 480 resolution color display

For more information on Hyperwire (including pricing details, which were unavailable at the time of writing), go to the Kinetix home page at the following URL:

```
http://www.ktx.com
```

VRML Conversion and Translation Tools

With the wide range of file formats floating around in cyberspace, at some point, it's likely you'll need a conversion tool. Many such tools exist that convert between VRML and proprietary file formats (see this chapter's summary for links that will lead you to them). In subsequent sections, you will learn about a few of the preeminent tools for performing conversions. Also included are brief descriptions of two tools that let you convert between VRML 1.0 and VRML 2.0.

Remember, all conversion programs have some limitations. For example, a program may fail to convert full hierarchies or lights or textures with certain files. Although select limitations are highlighted in this chapter, the URLs of all the conversion programs are included, so you can get the up-to-date scoop on specific programs' abilities.

InterChange

InterChange is a program from Syndesis, Inc., which performs conversions between over 50 3-D file formats; VRML is one of those formats (in its Windows and SGI Irix versions—the Amiga version doesn't support VRML). With InterChange, you can take a 3-D model you created in one program, translate it, and easily use it in another program. Big 3-D programs, such as AutoCAD, 3DStudio, and Wavefront only allow you to create in their proprietary file format; if you want to share your brilliant 3-D creations with the world, you need to take advantage of a conversion tool, such as InterChange. Although freeware/shareware programs exist that provide conversion abilities, InterChange has significantly broader conversion abilities.

InterChange's conversion is thorough; it converts an entire scene, including sub-objects and parent-child hierarchical relationships. It lets you convert in batches, so you can save time by simultaneously converting hundreds of files. You can use the "smart select" feature to highlight 3-D files only. You can also specify a text file list of filenames to convert. At this time, InterChange converts only polygonal geometry, although it hopes to support splines and NURBs patches in an upcoming release.

InterChange's translation covers attributes such as these:

- Filter color, diffuse color, specular color, and reflected color
- Coefficient values for specularity, glossiness, diffusion, and the index of refraction

■ For selected formats, InterChange also includes texture UV translation

InterChange is ideal for developing games because it provides conversion power between difficult formats, such as LightWave and 3DStudio, into ASCII. High-powered entertainment companies recognize InterChange's fortitude—it's used at Virgin Interactive, Disney Imagineering, Mindscape, Acclaim, Sony Imagesoft, and Interplay among others. InterChange has unlimited technical support by e-mail, fax, and phone, and performs sample conversions upon your request. We would have jumped at the chance to put an InterChange demo on the CD-ROM accompanying this book but, alas, no such demo exists. Syndesis does, however, sell CD-ROMs (monikered 3-D-ROMs) that demonstrate InterChange's abilities; a 3-D-ROM retails for $99.95 and has hundreds of uncompressed model conversion examples that are ready for use in your 3-D creations. If you want a 3-D-ROM, but you are short on cash, Syndesis will give you one free—if you submit 3-D models they decide to include on their next 3-D-ROM release. For more information on this deal, as well as InterChange in general, hit the Syndesis Web site:

http://www.threedee.com/

Extreme 3-D

Macromedia, Inc., one of the Web's most wildly powerful multimedia companies, made certain its 3-D modeling application, Extreme 3-D, was quickly armed with a VRML 2.0 converter. Extreme 3-D is a comprehensive cross-platform 3-D modeling tool whose VRML conversion power was welcomed by multimedia professionals. With Extreme 3-D, you can turn 2-D models into 3-D just by clicking your mouse (or your favorite ergonomic touchpad device). Extreme 3-D has lots of advanced features, including interactive texture maps and linking.

Extreme 3-D was the first cross-platform 3-D application to support VRML 2.0. The Extreme 3-D to VRML 2.0 converter, available *only* at the Macromedia site, was developed with the help of VRML cocreator Tony Parisi's company, Intervista Software. Thanks to the converter, you can model elements—such as lights, materials, geometry, and cameras—in Extreme 3-D, and then convert them into either VRML 1.0 or VRML 2.0. The converter runs under Macintosh OS 7.5.1 or higher and Windows 95/NT as a standalone executable program. Both platforms need 16MB of RAM and a minimum of 3MB free disk space to house the program files. The converter's main functions are:

- Read in Extreme 3-D 1.0 files
- Attach a URL to an object
- Add "World Info" to a scene
- Substitute an inline node or geometric primitive for an object
- Convert meshes, polygons, cameras, and lights
- Attach a texture file to an object

You can download the E3D2VRML from the Macromedia Web site:

```
http://www.macromedia.com
```

DoomToVrml2

DoomToVrml2 lets you post your Doom files on the Web. It allows you to convert the polygon and texture information in a Doom level (with extension ".wad") into a VRML 2.0 file.

DoomToVrml2 currently supports these formats:

- SGI
- Windows 95
- C source code

To exploit this worthy tool, venture to this site:

```
http://vrml.sgi.com/tools/doomtovrml2/index.html
```

VRML1to2

The Sony Corporation was one of the first to offer a VRML 1.0 to VRML 2.0 converter, which wasn't too surprising, considering the company's CyberPassage browser also supported VRML 2.0 early on. Their converter works on the following platforms:

- SUN (SunOS 5.5)
- NEWS (NEWS-OS 6.0)
- SGI (IRIX 5.3)
- Windows 95/NT

To download the converter, link here:

`http://vs.sony.co.jp/VS-E/works/util/vrml1to2E.html`

VRML1toVRML2

The VRML1toVRML2 converter comes from SGI, whose Cosmo products were also at the front line of VRML 2.0 support. To convert your VRML 1.0 file with this converter, simply type the URL of your file into a form at this Web site:

`http://vrml.sgi.com/cgi-bin/vrmlToVrml2.cgi`

To retrieve the URL's contents from across the Internet, the converter uses *getURL*. The script it uses to print the form and process the form are one and the same.

MUStoVRML

ParaGraph International's MUStoVRML 2.0 converter translates VHSB files, which have a ".mus" extension into VRML 2.0 files. Performing the translation lets you experience VHSB's multimedia features, such as sliding textures, sounds, animations, and albums in VRML 2.0. Using the converter also imbues objects with simple default behaviors.

The conversion tool is currently available for Windows 95. You can download it at ParaGraph's "free stuff" page:

`http://www.paragraph.com/vhsb/freestuff/`

ORC 3-D Translators

Several free translators can be found at the ORC Web site:

`http://www.ocnus.com/translate.html`

To translate a format into VRML at this site, you FTP your file to ftp.ocnus.com (don't forget to use binary mode for binary files). If you have files containing textures, the texture images should be sent via FTP in SGI.rgb format into the same area.

When you type in the name of the file to be translated, the script gleans its format from its extension type and undertakes the translation process. It then returns the newly formatted file to you.

The following file formats can be translated to VRML at this site:

- Alias wire files (.alias)
- AutoCAD DXF (.dxf)
- AutoDesk 3Dstudio (.3ds)
- IGES (.iges or .igs)
- Inventor (.iv)
- SoftImage (.hrc or .dsc)
- Stereolithography (.sla)
- Wavefront (.obj)

You can also access these translators via anonymous ftp from the Abaco Systems FTP site at via.net. Here's a sample dialog with a translator retrieval:

```
% ftp via.net
Name: anonymous
331 Guest login ok, send your complete e-mail address as password.
Password:
ftp> bin
ftp> get pub/abaco/ivtrans/sgi/alltoiv_v1.tar
ftp> exit
```

Although these translators are free for direct use (meaning you shouldn't post them to a bulletin board, etc.), OCR asks that you send them an e-mail at 3dsoftware@abaco.com or eduardo@via.net when you download them.

VR Servers and Other Fascinating VRML Tools

The term *VRML server* refers to an application that manages worlds on the Web in ways that extend beyond the capacities of standard Web servers. By definition, VRML servers should be able to automatically generate VRML content. More common, however, is to find VRML servers managing multiuser VRML environments, which present the data with that special VRML 3-D twist.

In this section, a few VRML servers are examined, as well as some other tools that aren't so easily classified.

V-Realm 3-D Media Server

The V-Realm 3-D Media Server, from Integrated Data Systems, Inc., is a Web server that permits real-time multiuser, multiworld interaction in 3-D. The V-Realm server isn't an HTTP Web server; it simply works in conjunction with HTTP. Currently, V-Realm's ability to offer LiveAudio chat, multiuser VRML text, and avatars is both unique and impressive with its advanced capabilities. Everyone in the V-Realm world is represented by an avatar and multiple users can view 3-D replications simultaneously, making the idea of William Gibson's "consensual hallucination" of cyberspace seem rather real.

V-Realm's capabilities for shared experiences take the interactive user experience into a whole new realm. V-Realm's technology makes it feasible to chat with friends in VRML worlds, as well as to conduct business encounters, examine 3-D objects, etc. This capability engenders limitless possibilities for shared space and viewpoint activity—coworkers can meet in virtual space to examine VRML-based business proposals, anatomy students can study virtual anatomy parts, and architects can assess ideas realized only in the virtual realm. The potential V-Realm and similar technologies bring to distance learning is also formidable.

Because V-Realm enables real-time sharing of audio, video, binary, text, and graphics files, multimedia presentations within VRML worlds are entirely viable, although the dream may be impeded or slowed for those with low-bandwidth. To share files, you attach the data type to your avatar and indicate the group or individual with whom you want to share your information. When you're attending a virtual lecture or presentation, V-Realm gives you the option to chat with select users without interrupting the speaker or other users in the room.

V-Realm's file exchanges for multiple formats make the VRML user experience much more stimulating. Watch for V-Realm's strides in the realm of immersive interactivity to be copied by many other development companies jumping onto the VRML bandwagon. Making real-time interactivity and file exchange possible from the desktop gives businesses greater freedom in training situations, as well as product presentation; the collaborative benefits are obvious. The V-Realm server's real-time chat even works via proxy servers and firewalls at both the client and server ends.

At the time of writing, V-Realm was still in beta, and only provides support for Windows NT (Intel or DEC Alpha). Its anticipated release price (in Fall 1996): $1,295 without audio, $1,695 with audio. For more information about the V-Realm 3-D Media Server, hit the V-Realm Web site:

```
http://www.ids-net.com/ids/server/srvrinfo.html
```

VRServer

With Tenet Networks' VRServer, your Web site can include 3-D walkthroughs of a site. To represent the data on the server, VRServer dynamically constructs objects such as walls, halls, rooms, etc., which represent data. Users can, therefore, walk through 3-D representations of server data.

VRServer was released in October 1995; here are some of its features:

- Functions alongside an existing server, even with different hardware
- Enables VRML walkthroughs and file system graphs
- Can be used as a basic HTTP server for standalone operation
- Provides HTML and VRML versions of all views

VRServer is currently only available for Intel and MIPS NT systems, and is in beta release. Tenet asks people who download it to act as beta testers and to contact them with problems or questions. The company anticipates the software won't become a commercial product, but its features will eventually be incorporated into another product, possibly as a commercial server plug-in. For more information on VRServer, see this URL:

```
http://www.tenet.net/html/products/vrserver.html
```

Axial Flyer Toolkit

Currently, the Axial Flyer toolkit is still a fledgling technology, but its potential is great. The toolkit consists of a VRML 2.0-compliant engine, a real-time 3-D scene manager, and a high-speed scan line renderer, which includes sample source code for creating Netscape Navigator plug-ins and ActiveX controls.

Axial was established in early 1996, specifically to develop VRML 2.0 software tools; its Flyer Toolkit release excited many VRML aficionados with its impressive speed. Before Axial hit the market, a browser didn't exist that could play games like Doom and Quake at a reasonable speed without being aided by hardware acceleration. Axial's goal to provide smooth animation of fully texture-mapped scenes on normal desktops is being achieved with their release. The toolkit's intelligent scene manager can handle any texture map without scaling; its rendering performance is impressive, as well.

For up-to-date information on Axial, head over to its home page:

```
http://www.axial.com.
```

RealVR

RealVR is a "virtual reality technology" from RealSpace, Inc. RealVR uses VRML 2.0 3-D rendering, video and audio playback, and panoramic viewing to create an integrated environment for viewing Internet VR information. RealVR includes a proprietary 3-D rendering engine with which you can draw texture-mapped 3-D polygons. RealVR is also equipped with a sprite engine for compositing and displaying image-based objects.

RealSpace's VRML 2.0 extension, called Image Worlds File Specification, lets you use panoramic images as backgrounds (see Figure 9-1). The extension also introduces two other node types, which let VRML authors describe objects through sequences of prerendered or photographic images. VRML scripts are used to provide linking information that lets world participants travel between panoramas. Image Worlds panoramas come in three flavors: cylindrical, spherical, or cubic. The following figure is an example of a cylindrical panorama.

The image warping speed brought by RealSpace's panoramic image warping engine can display full 360×180 degree panoramas; the company claims it runs 2 to 4 times more quickly than Apple's QuickTimeVR.

The RealSpace engine supports all three camera rotational degrees of freedoms (yaw, pitch, and roll) and supports a variety of panoramic images, including spherical, cylindrical, and cubic maps.

QuickTime movies can be played back in RealVR, which also supports directional audio. RealVR has a converter that takes a QuickTime VR Movie and converts it to the .IVR format. The converter is available for the Power Macintosh platform only; it can be downloaded at the RealVR Web site. Converting the files gives you a smaller file size, faster playback speed, and the ability to display object movies directly in front of panoramas. Because RealSpace was founded by Eric Chen, QuickTimeVR's inventor, the current

competition between the two technologies is intriguing. For more information about how RealVR compares to QuickTime VR, investigate this link:

```
http://www.rlspace.com/develop/ivrqtvr.htm
```

Image Worlds MIME Type

VRML files with the Image Worlds extension use the MIME type: "i-world/i-vrml". Their file extension is ".ivr".

New Image Worlds Nodes

The Image Worlds specification introduces three new nodes: Vista, ScreenIMob, and WorldIMob. Vista defines an image panorama: The viewer stands in the panorama's center to pivot the view direction. To enable jumping between Vistas, arrange Vistas and script nodes in a VRML Switch group—by switching the Vistas on and off; the user flips between them. This is the syntax for the Vista node:

```
Vista {
        field           SFString        type            "SPHERE"
        field           MFString        filename        []
        exposedField    SFVec3f         position        0 0 0
        field           SFVec2f         vFov            -1.5708 1.5708 # -90 to 90 degrees
        field           SFVec2f         hFov            0 0
        exposedField    SFVec2f         pitchRange      -1.5708 1.5708 # -90 to 90 degrees
        exposedField    SFVec2f         yawRange        0 0
        exposedField    SFVec2f         zoomRange       0 1.5708       # 0 to 90 degrees
        exposedField    SFColor         backColor       0 0 0
        field           SFString        description     ""
        field           SFString        copyright       ""
```

```
        exposedField      MFNode       children      []
        eventOut          SFVec2f      clickPt
        eventOut          SFVec2f      overPt
    }
```

The ScreenIMob node deals with an image-based object you want to display directly in the browser window rather than in 3-D space. When the user orients in a different direction, the ScreenIMob retains its location in the window. This node can be useful for examining scene objects, as well as for interface widgets. The syntax for the ScreenIMob node is

```
ScreenIMob {
    field           SFString      type            "PICT"
    field           MFString      filename        []
    field           SFString      alignment       "CENTER"
    exposedField    SFInt32       width           0
    exposedField    SFInt32       height          0
    exposedField    SFFloat       opacity         1
    exposedField    SFColor       blueScreen      []
    field           MFInt32       quantization    []
    exposedField    MFFloat       range           []
    exposedField    MFFloat       defaultView     []
    exposedField    MFTime        animRate        []
    eventOut        SFVec2f       clickPt
    eventOut        SFVec2f       overPt
    eventOut        SFBool        goodClick
    eventOut        SFBool        goodOver
}
```

WorldIMobs are much like ScreenIMobs, with one crucial distinction; they're displayed in 3-D perspective. Like ScreenIMobs, they involve concepts, such as sample ranges and quantification dimensions. The WorldIMobs syntax is:

```
WorldIMob {
    field           SFString      type            "PICT"
    field           MFString      filename        []
    exposedField    SFFloat       width           0
    exposedField    SFFloat       height          0
    exposedField    SFFloat       opacity         1
    exposedField    SFColor       blueScreen      []
    field           MFInt32       quantization    []
    exposedField    MFFloat       range           []
    exposedField    MFFloat       defaultView     []
    exposedField    MFTime        animRate        []
    eventOut        SFVec2f       clickPt
    eventOut        SFVec2f       overPt
```

```
eventOut      SFBool      goodClick
eventOut      SFBool      goodOver
}
```

RealVR and RealVR Traveler

The first product to use RealVR is the RealVR Traveler, RealVR's VR player, which functions as a plug-in to Netscape Navigator. The plug-in works on both the Windows 95/NT platform and the Macintosh PowerPC platform. Look for RealVR's incorporation into other software; Fractal Design Corporation, the makers of Ray Dream Studio/Designer, has announced support for RealVR in future releases. They plan to put a RealVR "camera" in Ray Dream to capture panoramic views of Ray Dream Designer scenes.

These are the nodes the RealVR Traveler currently supports:

Appearance	AudioClip	Box	Color
ColorInterpolator	Cone	Coordinate	CoordinateInterpolation
Cylinder	DirectionalLight	Group	ImageTexture
IndexedFaceSet	Material	MovieTexture	NavigationInfo
Normal	OrientationInterpolator	PositionInterpolator	ProximitySensor
Script	Shape	Sound	Sphere
Switch	TextureCoordinate	TimeSensor	Transform
WorldInfo			

For additional information on RealVR's range of technologies, check out its Web page:

```
http://www.rlspace.com
```

CD-ROM

cd-rom *3Dstats is a freeware program (we've included it on the CD-ROM), which analyzes Web server logfiles and creates 3-D VRML models of the server load. These models are detailed by month, day, and hour. Figure 9-2 shows an example listing of hits on a server in a single day; Figure 9-3 provides similar information, but for a month.*

Viewing the logfiles in this format is interesting because you can look at bar charts from (previously) unlikely points of view.

This is a 3Dstats VRML rendering of the hits a server received during a single day.

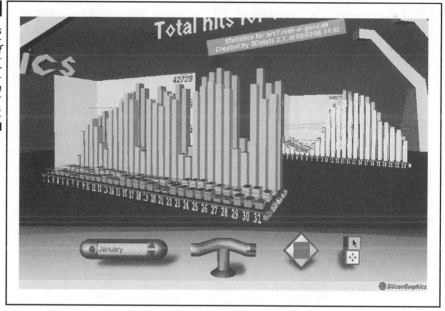

This is a 3Dstats top view of a month's logfile.

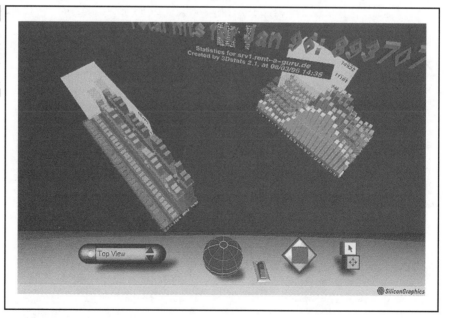

The creation of 3-Dstats was inspired by a program written by Matt Kruse, which makes a 3-D model using a POV ray tracer. The team behind 3-Dstats is based in Germany.

The 2.1 version of 3-Dstats contains many improvements over its predecessors—most importantly, it displays the VRML model much faster after loading now because it has been redesigned to use a "lightweighted" VRML model. 3-Dstats 2.1 can also create a model for an entire year's activity, including monthly models as inlines. It also features a 3-D bar chart that indicates a day's total HTTP hits, the number of documents sent out in response to requests, the number of 304s (the "Not Modified" responses caused by caching mechanisms), as well as all other responses (including server errors, "not found" responses, etc.).

Summary

Armed with the tools covered in this chapter, as well as other sections of this book, you should feel indomitable in your quest to create excellent VRML. Because VRML development occurs at a rate that's fast-paced even by Web standards, it's a good idea to surf around and investigate what's currently happening with VRML tools. Here are two excellent starting points:

```
http://www.sdsc.edu/vrml/dvcontent.html
http://www.cornishproductions.com/frames/vrmlIndex.html
```

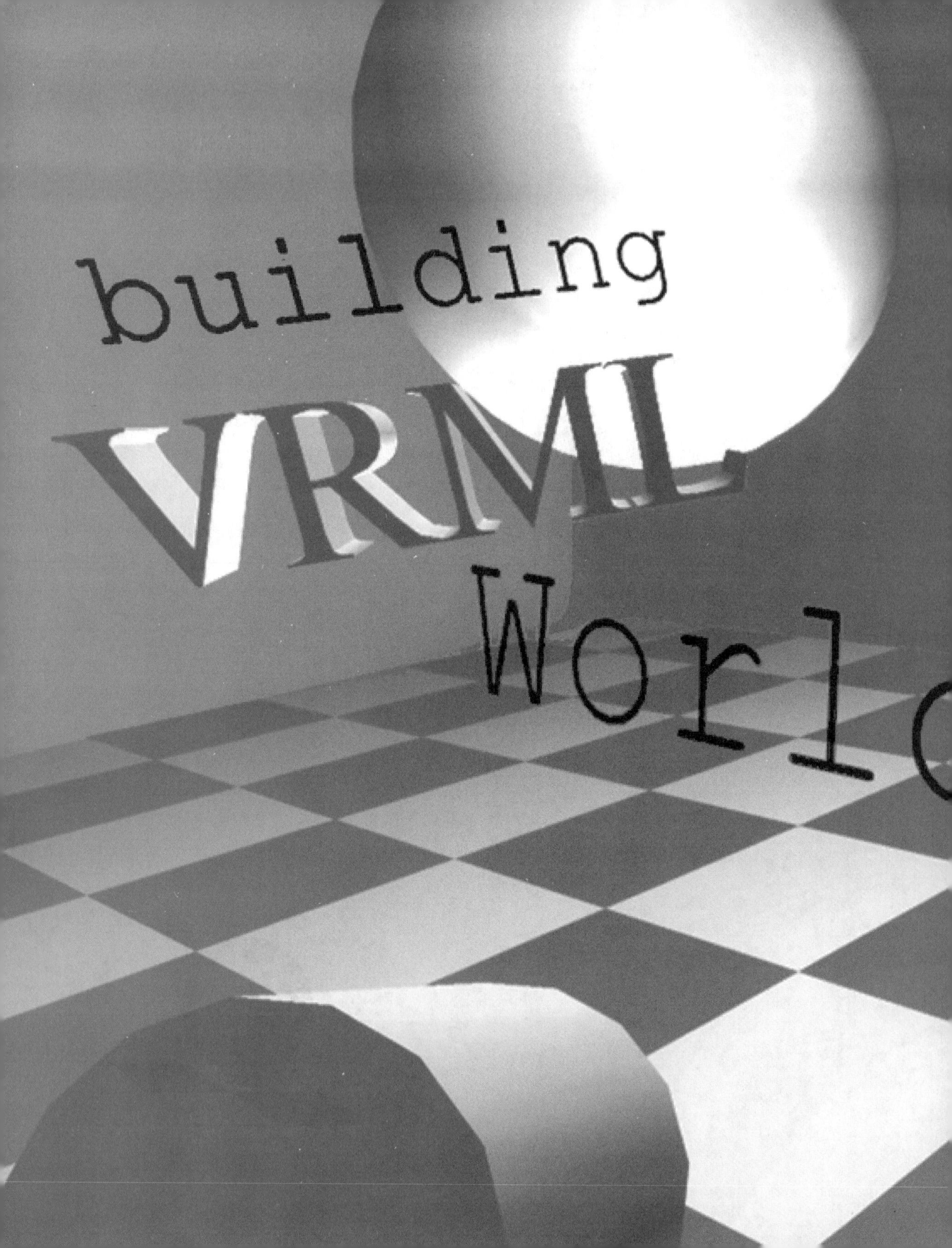
building
VRML
Worl

chapter 10

VRML Extensible Rendering Packages

Worlds

T HE Virtual Reality Modeling Language started out simply, just two and a half years ago. Eager Net surfers pointed their virgin browsers into a 3-D realm of simple polygons, glitchy interfaces and, more often than not, they had a long wait with disappointment at the end. Today, with the emergence of VRML 2.0, and integration of powerful 3-D rendering tools, virtual space is a whole new realm.

With rendering packages, a developer can add textures and shading, better position multiple light sources for the perfect effect, and generally make viewing VRML a much happier experience. Traditionally used for 3-D modeling for design, such as Computer Aided Design (CAD) work, and for generating stunning graphics in such movies as *Jurassic Park,* rendering packages continue to evolve along with the VRML development community. With the recent release of VRML plug-ins and VRML 2.0-compliant browsers, rendering packages will become even more important, as the need for high-quality VRML objects and worlds pushes the envelope of user demand and developer capability.

In this chapter, we explore two of the leading products for high-quality 3-D graphics creation and VRML world development. StudioPro Blitz, from Strata, is available for the Power Macintosh only (though a version for Windows is in the making). StudioPro Blitz is the most widely used rendering and 3-D art creation package for that platform. Kinetix 3D Studio Max is available only for Windows NT 3.51 Workstation (with a 4.0 upgrade in the works as this chapter is written). Although each is costly, both packages deliver production quality 3-D graphics and amazing virtual worlds. Kinetix 3D Studio Max is compliant with the VRML 2.0 Moving Worlds specification.

The Five Points of Rendering

Before digging into the guts of any application, developers must understand the functions and standards related to that application. For example, when comparing word processors, these programs must support a core set of functions, such as specific formatting options—like tabs and indents—and options for printing. Word processors also have a host of fairly standard, yet optional features, such as spelling checkers, thesauri, and a variety of fonts. All of these options and functions must be weighed equally before deciding which application to buy.

As with the preceding example, 3-D rendering packages have a core set of functions and some optional features that add to functionality; these may even be considered "standard" once every vendor includes them. This host of functions, taken with such essentials as user interface, file formats supported, and system requirements, must then be weighed against the needs of a VRML development team. Only then can the best package be selected.

The five core functions that every rendering package must include to be considered as a worthwhile VRML development tool are defined here. Some not-so-standard yet, somehow, essential options that make rendering 3-D objects and their display in VRML much more effective are also added. Again, the example applications were chosen, not necessarily because they represent the best choice for any organization looking for a high-quality VRML development solution, but because they are the most widely-used on their respective platforms and they appear ahead of the development curve for VRML output.

Object Creation and Shaping

This is the meat and potatoes of 3-D imaging packages: the ability to create and shape dynamic images in a virtual three-dimensional space. Simple object creation is a must, as is support for a variety of polygons and shaping options. Once created, these objects may be lit, shaded, and textured to the developer's liking. A number of types of rendering exists, which are currently used by 3-D graphics applications: algorithms, including Scanline, Phong, Raytracing, Raycasting, and Radiosity. Each is progressively more complex, both in the displayed images that result and in the processor power and time needed to produce such images.

Animation

In VRML 1.0, animation was a dream, but as the 2.0 standard is implemented, developers have already come up with browsers and plug-ins that support VRML animation. On the client side of the client/server divide, rendering packages that already support animation in other formats are porting these functions to output to VRML files.

Kinetix 3D Studio Max is currently the only high-end package that supports the VRML 2.0 file standards, but close on its heels are other players in the VRML development world. Animation porting will be a standard feature on any rendering tool within the next few months. Paragraph Software's Internet 3D Space Builder 2.0 is a low-end option for animating a virtual space.

Multimedia

Another 2.0 feature, sound integration of VRML objects and spaces, is an up-and-coming technology. The ability to attach a sound to a single object and have that sound react realistically is an exciting feature compared to static VRML 1.0 images. Most rendering packages already support sound integration for other file formats, but only 2.0-compliant rendering applications support it for VRML output. For a great example of this, get the Silicon Graphics VRML 2.0 plug-in (Cosmo) for Netscape's Navigator at:

```
http://vrml.sgi.com/cosmoplayer/download.html
```

Then, check out one of their best examples of sound integration and animation (see Figure 10-1) at:

```
http://vrml.sgi.com/worlds/vrml2/robot/robostage.wrl
```

Interaction

A third upcoming capability that will greatly increase the visibility and functionality of virtual spaces is the element of interaction. In the past, interaction with a virtual world consisted of simple URL hotlinks, which performed much like a browser, taking the user to another space or Web page. With 2.0, using scripts ported from VRML files, interaction is now a key element in even the most basic VRML world.

The Web site mentioned in the preceding section also delivers an example of a simple interaction interface. By pressing a button on the control panel,

FIGURE 10-1

Click a button on the control panel to start the robot's animation sequence.

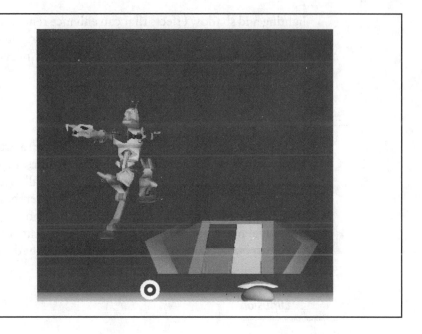

users can start the robot's animation (see Figure 10-1). Some rendering packages currently include features that enable a certain amount of interaction with an image, though, like VRML, these are generally interfaced to third-party programs. Direct interactivity in VRML files is a feature to expect in the near future.

Shading and Lighting

Every 3-D graphics development tool takes lighting into account. Color, intensity, direction, and quality of lighting are all basic considerations. Any quality 3-D development tool needs at least a rudimentary function to produce the effects of light and shadow or the effect of three-dimensionality is lost. In VRML, this functionality is critical to the success of a virtual space.

The following capabilities can enhance lighting effects for individual objects and for entire 3-D worlds, as well. This is why we look for them in 3-D authoring packages.

Multipoint Lighting

All 3-D imaging packages support multiple light sources. These should provide options such as intensity and color, which allow a variety of complex lighting and shadow effects that can enhance rendered images. Although not supported in VRML 1.0C, VRML 2.0 offers vastly improved lighting options, allows various diffusion options, and provides several new forms of directional lighting.

Four Qualities of Light to Object Interaction

The reaction of an object to light and vise versa are important details that some designers fail to consider. Such qualities as opacity, transparency, ambient glow, specularity, and roughness are all essential.

A *rendering* tool should enable designers to set these values either through some sort of light option interface or by defining these qualities in an individual object. Some packages allow a separate overlay texture, which is colorless, but exhibits a reflective sheen or a light dulling quality, depending on the desired effect.

Diffusion

Diffusion is an option within a 3-D graphics rendering package, which gives an object or scene the appearance of being filtered through smoke or fog. With VRML, this function is called *fog* and is a node in VRML 2.0.

Object Libraries

As in any development tool, object libraries are time savers when churning out generic spaces with standard images, as well as springboards to customizing any particular space. All rendering packages should include a standard set of objects, such as simple polygons, but some even include fully developed items, such as lamps, vehicles, and so on. These objects and their properties should be portable to a format supported by VRML.

Surface Texture Libraries

Texturing an object gives it a uniform surface that overlays its basic shape. Some standard textures, found in most graphic development packages, include a variety of wood grains, single-color textures, or patterned tile textures, such as what might be used to cover the floor in a virtual bathroom or hallway.

Texture Consistency

Enhanced texture properties can dramatically affect any object's appearance. Textures from a "metal class" of overlays may appear hard or soft, such as steel to gold, reflective or not, and can include a host of other apparent properties through the use of light and color. Effective textures give objects within a three-dimensional space a life of their own.

Perspective

Changes in perspective should alter the view of a 3-D space and its objects considerably. In VRML, the point of view observation window has its own light source, which affects the overall lighting of a scene.

Lighting

The general principles of lighting have already been covered, but perspective lighting deserves mention. When designing objects and spaces in a 3-D environment, additional lighting options from the perspective of the viewer must be included. These effects should not conflict with static lighting of a space or the objects displayed therein, but they do add an important note of realism to such scenes.

Physical Requirements of a Rendering Package

Rendering packages are hardware hogs. As long as this is clear, the needs of a development team can be determined and weighed against existing hardware. Most packages, including the two discussed in this chapter, are either platform-specific or even OS version-specific.

Other considerations that can influence a decision on a package are its supported file formats, both for import and export; the capabilities of the developer who will use it; and its compliance to VRML 1.0, 2.0, or both. As with any software purchase, these factors must be balanced against costs and budgets to implement the best solution.

Technical Requirements

Every rendering package has a set of requirements that must be met so the program can function properly. Rendering packages are high-end applications and require some of the most powerful and expensive computing equipment. A speedy processor, a top of the line video card and monitor, and lots of RAM are basic requirements for any such package. For VRML development, these same requirements are nonnegotiable.

But with all of this top of the line equipment and high-end graphics packages, developers must still consider the resources of their target audience. When creating a VRML commerce site aimed at the general Internet public, developers must tone down graphics and details to suit that audience's low-speed connections and mid-range hardware.

The following points further outline what to look for in a rendering package.

System Compatibility

Most rendering packages are developed either for a specific platform or a specific version of the OS running on a specific platform (usually the newest). The very latest, including those featured in this chapter, run on one or more of these machines: The Macintosh, Windows NT, or Silicon Graphics running IRIX. Whereas the first two types typically cost several hundreds of dollars, the latter typically costs several thousand.

Both RAM and video memory are essential for best results from rendering packages, as well as hard drive space. Rendering images is memory-intensive and the machines that run them shouldn't have less than 32MB of RAM and should have much more for serious 3-D scene creation. Most rendering packages require lots of hard disk space, both for swap memory and storage of images, depending on the image format and the number of images used. Count on using at least a 1Gb drive.

Export/Import Format Options

The only real export requirement for VRML development is the .wrl or world format. Image, animation, and sound files should export to types that are readable by Web browsers, such as JPEG or GIF images, AVI or GIF animation, and WAV or MID sound files.

Project Needs vs. Developer Capability

For standard, mid-level rendering packages, developers should expect to climb a significant learning curve to become proficient. Remember, the capability of the developer will be reflected in any application's output; thus,

Technical Requirements

StudioPro is in the mid-range of rendering packages as far as system needs are concerned. For its requirements (see the following list), it is a feature-rich and complete rendering package, using the power of Apple's QuickDraw 3-D and the versatility of the Macintosh platform's user interface. When tested with the minimum specifications, the interface and rendering times were quite sluggish as you'd expect. On a Power Macintosh 9500 with 64MB of RAM, the application was superb, with quick response and flawless execution. The following are the platform requirements:

- Power PC Macintosh
- 16MB RAM (32 recommended)
- Macintosh O/S version 7.1.2 or higher
- QuickDraw 3-D version 1.0.3 or higher (included)
- Hard Drive with at least 20MB free (more recommended)

Export/Import Format Options

StudioPro Blitz offers a variety of file import and export options (see the following list). Because many applications exist from which objects and textures may be developed, this is a useful feature, which should not be overlooked when you select a rendering package for VRML development.

- **Export:** DXF, PICT, EPS, TIFF, 3DMF, QuickTime, QuickTime VR-ready Panorama, QuickTime VR-ready Object.
- **Import:** DXF, IGES, Swivel 3-D, MiniCAD+, PICT, EPS, Illustrator, 3DMF, QuickTime, QuickTime VR

Project Needs vs. Developer Capability

Those developers already familiar with graphics manipulation programs and VRML will find StudioPro a powerful rendering package, which is fairly easy to master. Leveraging on the strengths of the Macintosh OS, StudioPro enables most functions, such as texture maps and object placement, through a drag-and-drop interface. This interface is intuitive and the package's functions are easy to understand and use.

the individual developer's skills and abilitie:
when choosing a development environment.

Those individuals who are already familia
lation tools and VRML will find their learnin
developers, who had a basic knowledge of su
after about a week of regular, steady interacti
time formal training on a package is avai
especially if you're trying to get someone wh(
quickly.

VRML Version Compliance

Depending on the needs of the project, ;
VRML version that best suits the site under c
2.0 is in its infancy, it will certainly breathe
ment. For sites that require any kind of longev
support is a definite requirement.

⨍trata's StudioPro

StudioPro Blitz (version 1.75+), with its arr
rendering and animation features, is an inte
high-quality 3-D computer artwork. Althoug
Macintosh platform, StudioPro boasts a wic
portability to a variety of other rendering p;
compliance.

With StudioPro, developers are able to woi
and formats. Full support for the QuickDr
StudioPro. And StudioPro's intuitive GUI int
view and edit textured scenes and see change
opened from and saved to 3DMF files, Apple's
for easy integration with other products, such
and scenes can be manipulated with the mouse
through the QuickTimeVR ready rendering
rendered scenes can be output to VRML files,
to URL addresses or AppleScripts to the VR
over 600 shapes and textures, the developer
through an easy to learn interface.

VRML Version Compliance

At present, StudioPro supports only VRML 1.0, which may not suit the needs of the organization's VRML project. VRML 2.0 support is slated for release in early 1997. Although there haven't yet been any announcements for support of the new VRML spec, we suspect Strata will soon release news of a VRML 2.0 plug-in for the current version of StudioPro.

Features

StudioPro's most attractive point is its rich collection of features, options, and customizations. Using a wide variety of object creation and rendering tools, basic shape object libraries, hundreds of textures, and lighting options, StudioPro sets the standard in 3-D rendering for similar packages in its class. All menus, options, and features are accessible from a GUI interface. Objects, lighting, and textures are drag-and-drop enabled.

The Five Points Check

Following the five required rendering capabilities previously introduced in this chapter, StudioPro rates high. Even though StudioPro is confined by its Macintosh-only nature, its many import and export options make this drawback almost nonexistent, especially in a multiplatform office environment with a plethora of graphics and multimedia applications.

Object Creation and Shaping

StudioPro supports all three main forms of rendering: wireframe, phong, and raytracing. Using the Macintosh's onboard hardware optimization features, rendering objects from simple to median complexity takes a surprisingly short time. When rendering complex images or spaces within a virtual arena, these times can increase significantly. Once a wireframe image is built, an object can be shaped, shaded, and fully rendered through the program's easy to use GUI interface.

---

 tip   *VRML developers will note that highly complex VRML sites will be huge; they not only will consume vast amounts of hard disk space, but also increase download and rendering time for end users. Unless high-powered graphics drive a VRML development site, it's best to keep your graphics relatively simple, thus smaller and less punitive, for ordinary mortals to download and view.*

Shading and Lighting

Many forms of and modifications to lighting are possible with StudioPro, enabling designers to simulate varying amounts of reflectivity on an object's surface, affect the overall shading of an object in relation to other features in the virtual space, and endow an entire object or parts of an object with varying amounts of translucency. Using the Light in Edit mode, designers can place unlimited numbers of spot, point, or directional lights, giving full control over the amount and focus of light sources within a space.

StudioPro also supports animated lights, which can pan or dance about a space randomly. What makes this useful to VRML is the ease of placing and tracking light sources, without the need for additional code. Once StudioPro supports VRML 2.0, the animation of lighting should add exciting capabilities to any virtual world.

In addition to direction and intensity, StudioPro allows various types of filters and light diffusion options, which give the designer the ability to soften or color visible light independently through each individual source. This allows you to alter or enhance the mood of a 3-D piece. Currently, no support exists for coloring or diffusing light in VRML 1.0; however, version 2.0 permits filtering light through fog, to diffuse and soften its effects.

Perspective

When fully rendered, spaces and objects in 3-D studio are realistic as the perspective changes. Shading, light, and object integrity stay constant as the user interface navigates through the space.

Texture Libraries

StudioPro includes a large collection of textures that may be copied and pasted onto rendered objects. These textures may be edited, changing their color, reflectivity, and several other parameters. Onboard or customized textures can be merged into a variety of combinations. All textures are drag-and-drop from the texture toolbar. In addition, new textures can be created using the program's built-in texture creation tools.

Object Libraries

Basic polygon shapes are included in StudioPro, though complex objects must be created from these building blocks. All objects and textures are directly exportable to the VRML .wrl format at the touch of a button.

Five Points Summary

At first glance, StudioPro appears a medium-level development tool where system resources are concerned. Upon closer examination, however, this middling rating is unwarranted. With its rich features, easy to master tools, and wide variety of options, StudioPro is an excellent choice as a VRML publishing tool. Although StudioPro is currently limited in VRML version and platform support, Macintosh users will find it intuitive and robust. Even though no support exists currently for VRML 2.0, StudioPro still creates complex 3-D images exportable to VRML 1.0, with an easy to use interface and not a lot of hardware overhead.

Kinetix 3D Studio Max

AutoDesk, the same company that built AutoCAD—the most popular design package in the industry—developed Kinetix 3D Studio Max. This application is neither for the faint of heart nor for the low end of the technology scale. Kinetix 3D Studio Max includes an intuitive user interface, powerful rendering engines, a host of texture and object libraries, and useful graphics tools. The open architecture design of Kinetix 3D Studio Max allows third-party software developers to add plug-ins at will, which gives it potential for even more functions—add-on renderers and some motion capture functions found in packages such as SoftImage—in the future. A true 32-bit Windows NT application, available for use on NT Workstation version 3.51, Kinetix 3D Studio Max is a 3-D modeling, rendering, and animation tool that ports its objects and virtual spaces to VRML 2.0 (through a recently delivered plug-in).

In addition, Kinetix 3D Studio Max is an extensible application, allowing third-party developers to add to the program's functionality and features through an extensive plug-in architecture. These enhancements meld seamlessly with the existing platform, functioning as part of the core application, with no noticeable differences in behavior or performance. This takes much of the work out of 3-D creation. Also, Kinetix 3D Studio Max's object-oriented architecture makes its built-in tools and features function similarly, resulting in the easiest to use environment of any of the 3-D modeling applications available for VRML development.

Technical Requirements

In the class of hardware-hogs, Kinetix 3D Studio Max is king. Should a development team need this kind of power, project managers should be ready to face hardware costs necessary to use such a product. But with this kind of high-end power, the price of the application and the hardware needed to support it remains small in comparison to a Silicon Graphics development platform, with nearly the same capabilities.

System Compatibility

The system needed to use Kinetix 3D Studio Max is definitely high end, though graphics designers shouldn't blink at the hardware needs (see the following list). Note that the hardware listed meets only the package's basic requirements for creation of simple 3-D images and scenes. When tested on a system that met but in no way exceeded these requirements, performance was incredibly slow. On a Pentium 133 with 128MB of memory and plenty of hard disk space, Kinetix 3D Studio Max ran like a dream. Here are the hardware requirements:

- Pentium 90 PC (Ideal: Pentium Pro based PC)

- Microsoft Windows NT Workstation 3.51

- 32MB RAM (Ideal: 64-128MB)

- 100MB Hard Disk Swap Space (ideal: 200-300MB)

- PCI or VLB based graphics card supporting $800 \times 600 \times 256$ colors under Windows NT (Recommended: $1024 \times 768 \times 256$ colors [3-D hardware acceleration supported.] Ideal: $1280 \times 1024 \times 24$-bit double buffered 3-D accelerator)

- Windows NT-compliant pointing device

- CD-ROM drive

Export/Import File Format Options

If any drawback can be found in Kinetix 3D Studio Max, it's the limits to file imports and exports. Currently, the application can save files in the inherent .MAX format, .3DS, and .DXF (3-D AutoCAD) formats. Images within the 3-D space can be saved to virtually any image format available and certainly to those supported by VRML and Web browsers. The entire space can be archived as a unit and exported to another format through a third-party conversion program (many of which are available as shareware on the Internet). With the powerful API interface and plug-in supported architecture, you can bet a file format conversion plug-in is on the way.

remember *An entire site can be ported directly to VRML 2.0 at the touch of a button. Here again, remember complexity means time to end users. Developers must, therefore, devise a strategy to balance detail against end user frustration when deciding on use of textures, level of detail, number of elements and light sources, and other aspects of a scene graph, which add complexity or file size.*

Project Needs vs. Developer Capability

For all its complexity and power, Kinetix 3D Studio Max includes an intuitive interface, an outstanding collection of tools and features, and it is easy to learn and use. Within 20 minutes, our developers understood how to use most basic functions; after a few days, they were able to use the application effectively.

The only real drawback with Kinetix 3D Studio Max is its price; for instance, it costs around $2,500 to upgrade from 3D Studio Release 4 to the current version, Release 5. Outright purchase of a new copy can cost as much as $10,000.

VRML Version Compliance

Touting itself as the first VRML tool development tool to support VRML 2.0, Kinetix 3D Studio Max is a powerhouse of the most exciting features of 2.0, namely animation and multimedia.

Features

If StudioPro is feature rich, Kinetix 3D Studio Max offers an embarrassment of features. From basic rendering features found in most 3-D development packages to complex and animated object development, as well as full lighting control, Kinetix 3D Studio Max has too many features to name. VRML developers will find more functionality than they need.

In keeping with this generation of applications, Kinetix 3D Studio Max is networkable, enabling one copy of the program to reside on a server accessible by multiple clients. This allows separate developers to manage different pieces of a virtual space; the project is maintained on a server in its entirety.

AutoDesk includes a network queue manager with detailed network analysis capabilities as part of MAX 3D. This enables network administrators to manage network rendering processes remotely over the Internet. The queue manager can also schedule rendering servers' availability at specified times.

Kinetix 3D Studio Max supports a fully functional API, which allows software developers to enhance and expand the functionality of the application. A Kinetix 3D Studio Max Software Developer Kit, with extensive online documentation and source code examples, is included in the product, allowing developers access to over 75,000 functions through the MAX API. This developer kit is based on C++ 4.x; it includes extensive online documentation and source code examples.

Five Points Check

On the Five Points check, Kinetix 3D Studio Max comes out way ahead of StudioPro or any other run of the mill 3-D developer package. Its graphics and spaces are surprisingly easy to create. Kinetix 3D Studio Max is limited to Windows NT and, for some VRML developers, it may be financially prohibitive. But for creating high-end VRML worlds, unmatched by any but the Silicon Graphics' applications, Kinetix 3D Studio Max is a good value for its high cost.

Object Creation and Shaping

Kinetix 3D Studio Max supports all forms of rendering and several hundred options for object creation and manipulation. Aside from standard tools, object modifiers allow the deformation of standard polygons, turning models into "virtual clay." These objects are morphable within their own coordinate systems, with a special time tracking function, which allows changing objects to continue to morph over a specific time period. These modeling operations can be manipulated further as "objects" in their own right. Some of the object modifiers included are Bend, Taper, Twist, Skew, and Wave, to name a few. These animation sequences are supported only as translation animations when ported to VRML 2.0, giving a dynamic view of an object's morphing life cycle. The user interface for all of these functions is GUI oriented, originating from tool bars across the top of the display window. All features supported by Kinetix 3D Studio Max are accessed through the tool bar and enable the most relevant operations as specific objects are selected. How's that for intuitive?

Shading and Lighting

MAX 3D's light control options are even more numerous than its object creation tools. The standard light types included are Ambient, Directional (sun), and Target Spot, as well as Omni and Free Spot, which give more dynamic lighting options. Lights can be set to exclude or include certain parameters, to control object illumination, shadow-casting, or both. Using spotlights, of which an unlimited number can exist, it's possible to control their color, cone shape, umbra (determination of the width of the light beam and how quickly it widens), distance, and shadows cast by the light. These shadows can be either mapped or raytraced. Raytracing shadows makes them crisply colored, yet transparent.

By using the Place Highlight function, the position of a light may be automatically set, based on the part of an object the developer selects with the mouse, as determined by the current viewpoint. Lights can also be animated, and even controlled, with regard to shape, setting the light to oval or rectangular, with ratios for slit lighting, as well.

With the number of light controls supported in VRML 2.0, Kinetix 3D Studio Max offers the richest tools available for putting enhanced virtual worlds online.

Perspective

The perspective of a viewed image, object, or scene is totally controlled and set by the developer, allowing the finest details to be added, through a variety of functions.

Some of the modeling view options available from the user interface include Perspective; Current Construction Grid, which gives a bird's eye view; views from camera positions or spotlight positions; and straight-on views of an object or scene from its front, back, left, right, and top. Each viewport can be assigned a certain view, which updates automatically whenever any of the others are changed. Likewise, rendering options can be defined for each viewport, either updating independently of the rest of the view or set to update all views automatically.

From a VRML standpoint, this not only allows a development team to customize its development environment, but also ensures the overall virtual space remains consistent with any changes made from a single view. As per our requirement, this keeps image, lighting, and shading integrity at its highest. With the animation options available, a camera may be animated as a walk-through display or allow the VRML viewer to step through various view way points.

Texture Libraries

Several hundred combinations are available for texture mapping objects within a space. Individual textures, of which several hundred built-ins exist, may be rendered, shaded, or otherwise manipulated as independent objects. All textures can be modified and viewed—in real time within the virtual space—and new textures can be created using a texture creation tool. The amount of reflected or absorbed light, translucence, and even object self-illumination, is controllable from the texture editor. All images and textures are portable to VRML and Web browser readable formats.

Object Libraries

Although no complex objects are included in Kinetix 3D Studio Max's libraries, a host of normal polygons exist, which may be combined or shaped into complex objects. Also, Kinetix 3D Studio Max fully supports file imports from major modeling tools, such as AutoCAD, and objects obtained through third-party programs may be translated into a file format supported by the application.

Kinetix 3D Studio Max Summary

For production-quality, fully realized VRML worlds, Kinetix 3D Studio Max could be considered overkill. With its plethora of features, options, creation tools, and its support of VRML 2.0, Kinetix 3D Studio Max makes the job of creating virtual worlds much easier. The only real drawback a developer must face is the type of system needed to run the application so it will function acceptably. The program's limited file format import and export options are more troublesome. As stated earlier, third-party conversion programs can make the file format problem easy to work around, but it certainly makes it less convenient. But as more plug-ins for Kinetix 3D Studio Max are developed, you can bet a format conversion plug-in will soon appear to mitigate this shortcoming.

For a full-featured, 3-D rendering package, Kinetix 3D Studio Max is an excellent candidate. With its networking options, a powerful API that can extend the application's functionality through plug-ins, its rich rendering features, and easy to master interface, Kinetix 3D Studio Max has everything a 3-D graphics development team needs to create realistic virtual worlds and objects.

Summary

Rendering packages can greatly enhance a VRML development team's output, while they minimize the time it takes to create 3-D objects and spaces. Important things to look for in any rendering software are the ability to create complex objects within a virtual space; to morph, light, and shade those objects, relative to the point of the observer; and to transport the final product easily to a specified version of VRML. Additional features, such as light quality and behavior controls, animation, texture and object libraries can save time and give developers additional tools to create realistic 3-D objects and spaces for VRML publishing.

part 3

A Self-Extending VRML Resource Kit

T H E last section of the book provides the final pieces of the VRML puzzle. The first is Chapter 11, "Working with Surface Textures," which examines surface textures, explains what makes a good texture map, describes how to work with various graphic formats. It also provides some resources for texture maps, including clip art, graphics CDs, scanned images, commercial texture libraries, and a few Web sites that provide good examples of texture map use.

Then, we move on to Chapter 12, "Using Object Libraries," which explores the advantages of pre-built objects, describes how to work with objects from rendering and CAD programs, investigates some resources for object libraries, and shows a few good examples of object library use.

After that comes Chapter 13, "VRML Worlds for WWW Navigation," which tells you how to make a map of your Web site and how to present information effectively. In addition, we tell you how to know when to go 2-D and when to go 3-D, and provide some example sites using a VRML world for navigation.

The final chapter is Chapter 14, "Using Web Applications with VRML," which explores what a Web application can make VRML do, describes how to deliver VRML with your Web application, and then explains how applets that create VRML worlds on-the-fly on the client machine ultimately have more benefits than server-side CGIs. In conclusion, we provide some example sites that use VRML with Web applications.

building

VRML

World

chapter 11

Working with Surface Textures

G O O D VRML creation takes considerable time and a host of good tools. At this point, you have learned about packaged solutions, rendering applications, and VR server tools. Here, you will delve into some nuts and bolts tools that can make VRML worlds easier to create, detail, and publish. In particular, this chapter covers surface textures. As with reality, all objects within a virtual space have certain characteristics, such as shape, dimension, angle, shading, and color. The material component of an object, and how this material is displayed to users, is one of the most important properties that make a virtual object seem real; this is where surface textures come into play.

Texture maps are nothing more than image files which, when applied to a surface within a virtual space, automatically copy to cover that entire surface, or some portion of that surface, as determined by its designer. Not only does this supply a quick method for covering broad spaces within a virtual world, it also preserves system resources by requiring only one copy of a surface texture image on the hard disk. So, once an image is obtained for use as a texture for one object, the same image can be used as textures for other objects without the need for multiple copies of the image. The actual display of the finished image is a function of the VRML software: It requires neither multiple physical copies of the surface texture information nor of all the objects being instanced therein.

Surface texture libraries can be included with the development package chosen for constructing a virtual world, such as Virtual Home Space Builder or StudioPro, or they may be obtained either as shareware from the Internet or from a commercial source. A fourth option for compiling a collection of surface textures is to develop them yourself. Covered in this chapter are the needs and elements of style for surface textures within a virtual space, a variety of file formats for surface textures, tools for creating, altering, and converting images to serve as such textures, resources for ready-made textures, and some rules for "good use" of texture within a virtual space.

The Making of a Good Texture Map

As with any tool or resource, a "good" texture map depends on the project and the whims of its developers. Overall, the texture of an object should not only fit the mood of the space, but it also should fit the object upon which it will be displayed. Thus, if a VRML space created represents a tropical island, swirling green for forests, shades of yellow for sandy beaches, and gray and blue images for water and sky would be appropriate. There are times when surface textures are appropriate and when an object could be better served by using simple colors and straightforward rendering. For a cartoonlike ambiance, more sophisticated textures would clearly be out of place, as would complex shading or other attempts to enhance realism (because this is beside the point in a cartoon world).

Knowing when to use a texture, to determine how complex the pattern should be, and how to blend textures and objects are some of the most difficult aspects of VRML development as it's practiced today. Those VRML builder tools available are, indeed, intuitive and easy to master but, contrary to common belief, mere proficiency is not enough; a sense of style is also important. This primer for VRML style tries to pin down some elements that can make particular uses of surface textures "good" or "bad."

Elements of Style: VRML and Texture Use

A certain element of style exists that should be followed when dealing with VRML development and with any sort of visual design. To begin, VRML is a form of artwork; don't let a programmer persuade you otherwise! In an era of easy-to-use tools and easier interfaces, the need for code bashing has been replaced by the requirement to exercise your creativity.

This trend also has become prevalent in Web page design. When Web pages were in their infancy, the details of the underlying technology and its limitations overshadowed many developers' creative abilities. Web pages were produced with plain gray backgrounds, a jumble of images, and obscure text. Now, with the advancement of both the medium and related tools, Web pages have witnessed a renaissance of style. Artistic images, succinct text, and well-planned layouts complement the content and keep users coming back for more. VRML should follow this same trend as it is further deployed throughout the Internet. This makes a concern for style central to successful development, rather than an afterthought or add-on. Figure 11-1 shows a great sense of the dramatic, in addition to a unique and interesting sense of style.

Choosing a Theme

Before choosing a texture and even before developing a virtual space, a theme for the world it represents should be established. Every object and texture within the space should complement and enhance this theme. If certain objects or textures conflict with the theme, a good reason should exist why—shock value or to call attention to a certain aspect of the piece. This theme, and all the images and objects that embody and play off it, should reflect whatever mood the developer wants to convey to the viewers. Figure 11-2, for instance, illustrates a distinctive desert theme.

If a virtual mall is the kind of world under construction, then images, textures, and the interface should be kept simple. The main reasons for this are twofold: First, a virtual mall is a place where viewers come to spend money. Fancy, multitextured, or complex objects and surfaces will take a

FIGURE 11-1

This 3-D scene depicts a dragon about to eat a Viking ship for lunch (note the exquisite use of textures).

FIGURE 11-2

One of the more original VRML sites, found at StarDog's Web site, depicts a desert theme (www.teleport.com/~ stardog/vr.html).
■

long time to download and view; if users have low-end machines, such files may even crash their systems. This will frustrate and daunt potential customers. Second, by making elements of the virtual world simple—that is, the interface, common objects, and textures—the attention of the viewer will more naturally focus on other, more complex, objects, such as product displays or related information, as well as purchase directions.

If viewers spend too much time admiring the textures of the walls, ceilings, and floors, or looking at an animated fountain, they aren't looking at what's for sale. Some elaboration is good, but going overboard only defeats the purpose of a commercial space. In real-world terms, people go to stores to look at merchandise, not at the stores; a virtual implementation should emulate those characteristics.

Although this is a hypothetical situation, the function of a space should always be understood when developing themes for a virtual world. Always consider the circumstances of the audience because this is who the space will affect most. In keeping with this, make nonessential textures, such as ceilings and floors, simple. Use complex images, textures, and objects only for the foci of the space. This keeps file sizes and subsequent download times manageable; it also allows developers to direct viewers' attention to the important parts of the space.

Textures and the Theme

Many themes are possible for virtual worlds—from virtual malls to space ports. The textures within these spaces should convey and enhance the basic mood they're meant to create, rather than overshadow or conflict with the main images or objects displayed. Here are a few general guidelines to integrate textures into a space:

- Large areas should be covered by simple textures or a single nonconflicting color. Normally, large areas of a virtual space merely serve as background; they are not meant to overpower the foreground. As a result, simple patterns or unobtrusive colors should cover such areas as floors and ceilings, and possibly even walls. If options exist for a backdrop or background image for an outside scene, these should not draw the eye away from the objects or pictures most important to the space. In addition, ceilings, walls, and floors should be textured or colored differently, either in a different shade or color. This helps define a space and prevents these surfaces from blending into a single confusing image.

- Individual objects' textures should fit the theme. If the space's theme is a European-style pub, the objects displayed within that space should be textured accordingly. Walls, ceilings, and floors should be in dark wood textures, as should the bar and, possibly, the tables and chairs. Complex objects, such as doors and windows, can be tastefully decorated and likewise textured. An ornate mirror over the bar and well-rendered shelves of glasses will add to the ambiance. Possibly a large fireplace textured in fieldstone or brick, with an animated blaze within and some soft lighting, could round out the space. In contrast, a spaceport with objects, such as moving robots and information kiosks, as well as loud signs and garish colors, would make a great theme. Here, the use of textures would take a technological slant, although they should still be used only as needed.

- Style is totally subjective. The tasteful use of textures is relative to the point of view of the person or persons designing a space. If you would love to see a miasmic funky pattern on the walls of your virtual house, feel free to use one. VRML is a creative medium and virtual spaces need not blandly reflect reality. Even when developing commercial spaces, feel free to add artistic touches through the use of textures. Don't be afraid to texture: Some great textures could keep Web surfers coming back. Be careful, however, not to swamp your main objects or messages with too much "background noise."

Graphic Formats

The textures used in VRML are nothing more than single images copied over a selected surface, be it an object, the face of an object, or another surface, such as walls and floors. Such images are stored with the VRML file in a format readable by a VRML browser or a VRML Web browser plug-in. Most Web browsers support only compressed image formats for inline display, such as GIF or JPEG, but with VRML, virtually any image format can be used.

Image Format Considerations

The main points to remember when you choose an image file format are size and quality. The larger the image file, the longer it takes to download and display and, if storage space is a consideration, the more disk space the graphic consumes. GIF (.GIF) and JPEG (.JPG) images are in a compressed format, while Windows Bitmap (BMP) and PC Exchange (.PCX) formatted images are uncompressed. Thus, with a compressed image, developers can use a more detailed image and still conserve disk space.

Uncompressed formats such as Windows Bitmap (BMP) and PCX files average about 150 percent the size of GIF images, although in some cases, the file size of a BMP image is ten times the size of a JPEG and about three-and-a-half times the size of the GIF. In this example, the JPEG weighs in at 6KB, as a GIF, it would be 17KB, and as a Windows Bitmap rendition of this image, it would be a whopping 61KB.

This is a significant difference, especially when you consider a virtual space with several texture maps and a collection of other display images could become intolerably large (and correspondingly slow to download and view) fairly quickly when you use uncompressed image formats. Image quality as a factor is not so dependent on size as it is dependent on resolution of the original bitmap. JPEGs are generally the best quality image files, as they are always in 24-bit true color, while GIFs are limited to 256 displayable colors. JPEG image sizes vary with the amount of *lossyness* or compression applied to the image; this factor also ultimately affects the image quality.

Image Conversion Tools

The question the preceding section automatically provokes is: "How do I create textured images in the right formats?" Image conversion programs are the answer. Widely available as shareware and freeware, these applications are popular and full of useful functions. A few of the more popular image converters include LView Pro and PaintShop Pro for the Windows platform, GraphicsConverter for the Macintosh, and DeBabelizer for either platform, available at their respective addresses as follows:

LView Pro:

```
http://www.lview.com
```

PaintShop Pro:

```
http://www.jasc.com/pspdl.html
```

GraphicsConverter:

```
ftp://mirror.apple.com/mirrors/mac.archive.umich.edu/util/graph
icsutil/
```

DeBabelizer (Info only):

```
http://www.novaint.se/Nova_USA.html
```

An image converter translates image files in one format to other formats. In addition, most such programs support a core set of other graphics manipulation functions, such as adjustments to color balance and contrast. Typically, they can also convert color images to grayscale (black and white); some, like LView Pro, enable designers to alter the appearance of images through the use of filters. Using such filters, images can be softened or sharpened and details can be brought more into focus or faded.

Once images have been altered and converted, they may be imported to a rendering or VRML world-building application's texture library for easy drag-and-drop access. Most of these applications simply assign a directory where texture map files reside. Once they're ready, converted image files that are copied or moved to this directory could then appear in the application's texture toolbox or its equivalent.

Commercial graphics packages, such as Adobe Photoshop for both the Macintosh and the Windows platforms, not only allow the conversion of images, but also include more complex filtering, palette reduction, and other graphics creation and alteration tools. For the serious VRML or any Web development project, a package like this should be considered standard.

Graphics conversion programs are a great help to designers because they make building personal texture map libraries much easier. For instance, a wood grain texture map could be pulled into an image conversion program, darkened slightly, then saved to a separate file. Now the developer can use two wood grain images, of slightly different shades, in different parts of a virtual space. The following two images could even be used to differentiate between a paneled wall and a similarly textured floor.

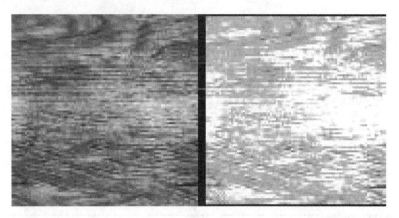

remember   *Not only does this technique create possibilities to convert on-hand images into correct formats for inclusion in a VRML world, it also allows designers to customize images to whatever project they're working on without requiring expensive commercial graphics packages. Furthermore, by permitting a single image to be altered for multiple reuse, it ensures consistency among related textures and adds more coherence to the scenes in which they appear. For this reason, we strongly recommend you shop around for VRML development tools that support this kind of flexibility when it comes to importing and exporting textures, as well as images of other kinds.*

Texture Mutation Tools

Texture Mutation tools take an existing texture and create variations automatically; they're extremely fun to use and useful for generating random texture files on-the-fly. The best-known example is Virtus' Alien Skin Texture Shop. Taking a single image, Texture Shop randomly adjusts colors, shading, contrast, and a whole host of other parameters, producing images ranging from slightly to radically different from the original.

For those at a loss for texture ideas or looking for something a little different, this application is a must-have. The Alien Skin Texture Shop has only one drawback: limited file export formats. Currently, the application only exports image files to PICT format, the Macintosh default. But this limitation can easily be overcome if you use one of the third-party graphics conversion programs previously covered, in addition to this outstanding product. To see what this product can do, check out Figure 11-3. For more information on Alien Skin Texture Shop (developed by Alien Skin Software, but owned and sold by Virtus Corporation), visit this Web site:

`http://www.virtus.com/textures.html`

No similar tools currently exist for Windows, except those included with most rendering packages.

Far from the random generation of textures created automatically by TextureShop, these integrated tools require manual alteration of various color and contrast parameters, much like the controls supplied with a graphic conversion program, including those mentioned in the preceding

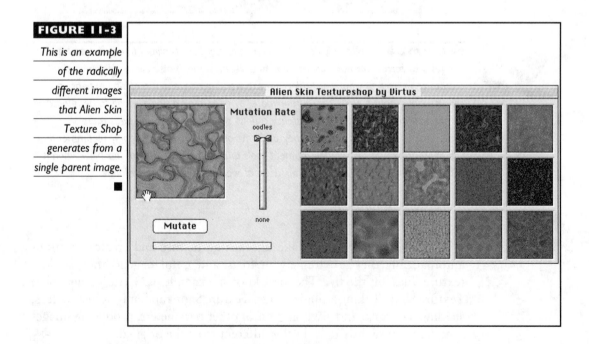

FIGURE 11-3

This is an example of the radically different images that Alien Skin Texture Shop generates from a single parent image.

section. Texture creator applications may be obtained from the following Web sites:

Adobe Texture Maker:

```
http://www.adobe.com/prodindex/texturemaker/main.html
```

Specular TextureScape:

```
http://www.specular.com/products/texturescape/
```

Resources for Texture Maps

Some believe the hardest part of building effective texture map libraries is finding the resources. This is not so! A plethora of options are available, depending on the need and expertise of your VRML development staff. Texture images may be bought in a commercial package or included with 3-D or other graphics design applications, obtained as freeware or shareware from the Internet or electronic bulletin boards, or custom textures can be created by your development staff using graphic design applications, scanned photographs, or digital images. Any one of these options is valid: Each option has its own advantages and drawbacks.

Obviously, purchasing a texture library saves the development staff considerable time, but this can cost anywhere from ten to hundreds of dollars. In-house development takes time and requires a certain level of application expertise, which your VRML development staff may or may not have. The Internet offers a ready solution in the form of shareware and freeware images, many of which were designed for texture mapping. Numerous free resources exist on the World Wide Web; good starting points for a search for these are provided in a later section in this chapter. Chances are good you'll obtain materials from one or all of these sources.

Commercial Packages

Many commercial texture map libraries are available in today's market. With the surging need for good background images for Web pages and computer desktops, the market for texture images has soared. Depending on the needs of your project, textures for VRML have some basic requirements, previously detailed in this chapter. Adherence to the theme of a VRML space, proper file formats, and the ability to customize images using third-party conversion programs easily are musts.

tip *Most commercial texture map libraries are generic in appearance and format options, but developers should ensure a prospective package fits their needs before purchasing any such library. Make certain any library you consider includes a money-back guarantee or purchase the library using a major credit card, which will give you time to return your purchase. This way, if you hit any compatibility snags, you can always return the library for a full refund.*

On-Board Application Libraries

Most rendering packages and VRML world builder tools include basic texture maps. These maps are stored in formats that the application can use. If this software can export its files directly into VRML format, it should support image formats, which are also supported by VRML. These texture images are generally in four styles: Wood Grain, Metal Textures, Tiles (i.e., Bathroom), and Miscellaneous, including technological, artistic, and abstract textures.

Although image alteration may not be supported within the application (most provide at least limited support for alteration), these textures can be altered in third-party conversion application, such as LView Pro or Graphic Converter. Such built-in textures are generally stored in a directory specifically addressed by the application's texture library. You should be able to address other images saved to the same directory in the same way, provided the images are in a format readable by the application.

Clip Art and Texture Libraries

Although most clip art is not generally suited for background images, this depends on the scope of a VRML project. Papering a wall with some cartoon or with generic clip art images may be useful to convey some mood or to enhance the theme of a space. An important concern with clip art libraries is the export formats supported and the platform for which the library is intended. Clip art for MacWrite Pro will not be useful for Windows NT developers; converting these images may either be more work than they're worth or impossible.

tip   *Pure texture libraries, on the other hand, are almost always stored in some format that's useful for cross-platform work. Generally, such images are stored in standard GIF or JPEG formats and they are specifically designed for use as textures. Some commercial texture packages usually come in an uncompressed 32-bit format, such as Targa or .txr.*

Alteration and conversion of these images with third-party conversion applications is easy and you can save them directly to your VRML development tool's texture library directory.

Graphics CDs

Image collections sold on compact disks normally include various images, both backgrounds and standalone pictures. Any of these can be used for texture maps or altered to fit the needs of your project; for example: a swatch from the image of a tiger could be cut out to use as a texture for a couch or another surface.

tip   *Here again, these collections should be checked for system and file format compatibility because many are limited to specific formats. Even if they don't directly support what you need for your VRML world, as long as they can deliver a workable format acceptable to one of your third-party conversion tools, you'll probably be able to make good use of these CDs.*

The World Wide Web

Surely the richest field for any VRML development tool or resource, the Web is home to countless collections of images, textures, and conversion or alteration tools. Sometimes all of these will occur together on one well-organized Web page; at other times, these items will be scattered randomly, spread across many pages and sites.

remember   *If you query any major search engine using the parameter "texture," this will help you get your search well underway. When dealing with images obtained from the Internet, keep in mind many images are copyrighted by their creator. These images may either be shareware (require a minor fee, plus legal permission to reproduce) or freeware (may require permission from, and acknowledgment of, their creators). A word of advice: Always pay shareware fees or comply with the creator's wishes. These images represent many hours of work and these creators feed the spirit of creation and sharing on which the Internet is based. Please give credit (and payment) where it's due.*

Shareware and Freeware

A cursory query on any major search engine will produce several hundred Web pages where extensive texture libraries or smaller collections reside. Likewise, other images and backgrounds obtained from Web pages across the Internet are useful to VRML developers because almost all images are already in GIF or JPEG formats.

tip *On a Windows-based browser, while holding the mouse pointer on an image or background and clicking the right mouse button or, on a Macintosh, while holding down the mouse button, an option should appear to view or save the image selected. This makes obtaining ready-to-use textures (and images) easy and fun. Before using any copyrighted images obtained in this manner, it's advisable to consult with their creators.*

Most of the major library collections are freeware, which may be downloaded and used in exchange for proper acknowledgment. Note: Place images downloaded from the Web into a transient folder or directory for review, prior to exporting them into you VRML world builder or 3-D graphics rendering application. This can save a lot of administrative time later because these images can be evaluated and discarded if they do not suit the needs of your project.

An especially good source for shareware and freeware is the Virtual Shareware Library. Its collection of pointers is available at:

`http://www.shareware.com`

To use this wonderful resource, point your browser at the URL, select the platform for which you need materials, and use "textures" or "texture software" as your search string. Once the reply to your query returns, you can select any of a number of download sites from which to obtain the resulting software or library items.

Surfing for Collections

The World Wide Web can be a huge storehouse of images and texture maps waiting to be viewed and downloaded. A development team should seriously consider this route to obtain good texture maps for a VRML project before spending any money for commercial collections or too many person hours on in-house image development.

In-House Graphics Development

Although development of images for use as texture maps may be time consuming, it could be necessary for the scope of the project. Like purchasing texture libraries, the importance of the textures used within the VRML piece must be determined. If textures are an integral part of the theme, then custom in-house development may be the solution. If textures play a small role in an overall virtual space, it may be best for the development team to consider other, less expensive, alternatives (in both dollars and time). With custom image creation, as with any sort of development, certain tools will be required depending on the method of creation desired and the importance of the final product. Some of these tools are listed, along with some probable paths a development staff might follow when they decide to create their own textures.

Graphic Art Development

Graphic art development is the most time-consuming and expensive method for capturing and customizing images to the needs of the VRML project, but it's also the most certain to produce the best results. Should a design staff seek to develop images and textures completely from scratch, some serious tools and time should be allocated to the task. Applications such as Adobe Photoshop and Fractal Painter are prime examples of the tools needed to produce high-quality custom textures. Both of these applications, and others of this ilk, can export and import images to formats useable in VRML. Likewise, both applications require significant amounts of time to enable designers to take best advantage of their inherent features and rich capabilities.

Development of texture images need not be approached so aggressively, however, because many options exist to produce effective textures for VRML publishing quickly and efficiently. It's unnecessary to do everything from scratch, except for truly big-budget operations. Both Photoshop and Fractal Painter can import existing images and alter such images to meet designers' needs.

Often, a combination of "home-cooked" textures and modifications to existing images may provide a sufficiently customized solution to fit the needs for custom textures and rapid image development.

Customizing Existing Images

One of the most popular—and the smartest—ways to build a library of texture maps is to take existing images, obtained from various sources, and alter them to fit the needs of your project. Adobe Photoshop and numerous other graphics packages are specifically designed for this use. Most textures used in a VRML space are fairly generic; customization is most often needed simply to distinguish one space or surface from another or to invoke or enhance a theme.

Digital Cameras

Digital cameras are fairly new to the graphics design world and they offer an easy method to obtain real-world, complex textures for VRML space enhancement. Most digital cameras output standard uncompressed image formats, such as PCX and BMP; many allow images to be stored onto a photo CD. These images, once obtained, may then be dumped directly onto a developer's hard drive, altered, saved to appropriate directories, and used immediately as textures. What more could you ask for in texture map development?

Digital cameras can be purchased as inexpensively as $600, while a fully professional rig (similar to a high-end professional optical camera) can cost as much as $15,000. Your world's resolution and design requirements should help you decide where your image needs hit this continuum, but outstanding results can be obtained from low-end cameras, plus subsequent image editing and manipulation.

Scanned Images

Scanning images provide an alternative to digital cameras, when you use the real world as a source of raw material. Again, with any equipment issues, the need of the project at hand should dictate how texture map images are obtained and at what cost.

Scanners cost from less than a hundred to several hundred dollars; the quality of output can vary as much as the price. Most scanners allow the production of a high resolution image and will output these images to TIFF format (uncompressed). Most scanners also come packaged with some image conversion program for easy reduction, changes, and file conversion to the scanned image, as needed. The good thing about scanned images is their use opens up a huge image resource: printed media. Scanned images, once obtained, can be evaluated, altered, and stored in your VRML development application's texture map directory for quick and easy use.

Examples of Effective Texture Map Use

These virtual spaces were included with Virtual Home Space Builder, and though very complex, they are visually stunning. Figure 11-4 shows an African temple, Figure 11-5 depicts a colonial theme, and Figure 11-6 shows an entire virtual art museum. All of these images use textures to good effect.

Summary

Although many options exist for obtaining, altering, using, and displaying textures within a VRML space, their use requires an appreciation of how these options fit within a virtual world. The world's overall theme, the tools, expertise, and systems available for its development, and your preferred development process will all affect how you obtain and use texture maps. Once you've built your collection of textures and the images are in the right formats, the rest is easy: Just drag-and-drop!

FIGURE 11-4

This example depicts an African temple, complete with rich textures.

Here is a colonial theme, with dark woods and low lighting.

A virtual art museum with abstract artwork and complex textures.

building

VRML

Worlc

chapter 12

Using Object Libraries

U

NLIKE texture map libraries, object libraries are a bit more difficult to obtain, even as shareware or freeware from the Internet. In addition, few resources exist through other media for obtaining 3-D objects that are easily portable into a virtual space.

Although most rendering and 3-D graphic programs include a host of simple polygons for building objects, they lack library-style resources for complex objects. Commercial object libraries are cropping up, though many are expensive and usually are used for animation programs. These objects can be used in VRML with polygon reduction, which reduces the size and detail of the object by reducing the number of triangles used to create it. Other resources for fully mapped VRML objects include VRML worlds themselves. In this chapter, the sparse Internet resources will be reviewed, as well as a few of the commercial package objects and some strategies for making the work of populating a virtual space with objects a little easier.

Why Object Libraries?

When faced with a large VRML development project, the main obstacle to overcome is time. In the past, VRML worlds were almost impossible to create and manage. Not only was the code somewhat difficult for the average programmer to learn, but the resulting files were huge, the medium simplistic, and the viewing software buggy and nearly unusable. VRML development environments now follow the same road as Web development—that is, the community now has access to easy-to-use development tools, a plethora of resources, and a viewing public that's armed with better computers, stable software, and a desire to interact with 3-D environments over the Internet.

With all these improvements to the lot of VRML developers, their biggest obstacle remains time. Time is still necessary to gather and learn to use the necessary tools and resources, and to plan and design spaces, to customize textures, to create and render objects and, finally, to publish a virtual world on the Internet.

By far, the biggest chunk of time required for building any VRML world is devoted to creating the objects that populate that world. Most 3-D development tools are intuitive and feature-rich, but few of them include built-in libraries of complex objects, ready to drag-and-drop into a working space, to be further customized by developers. Most of these tools include only a set of simple polygons and various tools to combine, shape, texture, and color those objects. This falls far short of the capability needed to speed the object definition phase of a VRML project.

Another concern for most VRML development teams is the expertise needed to create realistic objects that "fit" a virtual space. Creating complex objects is not easy, by any means. A team may have solid plans for the objects they need, and they may be entirely comfortable and conversant with VRML. But creating high-quality objects takes a certain amount of skill and time, especially when such objects must complement and coordinate with a particular space. Should your development team be faced with this problem, pre-fabricated objects may offer the easiest solution.

To speed the creation of quality objects for a world, developers must research avenues for obtaining common, fully rendered objects for export into their worlds-in-progress. This chapter seeks to clarify this aspect of the development process.

Working with Generic Objects

Ready-made object libraries can not only save your development team's time, they can also tend to empower a VRML site's overall theme by generating new ideas for the direction the space should take. The primary concerns addressed here include general strategies and procedures for implementing VRML objects libraries, file format and conversion issues, and the pros and cons of using model libraries compared to in-house development.

The Generic Object Strategy

The most time-consuming task regarding 3-D model libraries is locating the right objects. Once they're found, such objects may be imported to a 3-D development application and customized with textures, lighting, and rendering effects, then pasted into a working VRML space. Here are a few guidelines to follow when using generic objects:

- Start the search for objects on the Internet. Because VRML is an Internet-spawned phenomenon, this is the best place to start a search. Some of the newest and most comprehensive library sites are outlined later in this chapter.

- Gather the appropriate tools. To screen, download, and translate VRML objects properly (or 3-D models in any format), developers need the right tools. Obviously, an Internet connection is required, as well as a VRML-capable browser. The latter lets designers screen the objects for use without consuming valuable time and disk space to download and sort through a batch of models. In addition, a file conversion program may be required, depending on whether or not the 3-D development application supports the file format in which the object is rendered.

- Perform polygon reduction. Many times, the object for use is imported from a 3-D graphics or animation program. These objects tend to be very detailed and, thus, are unsuited for VRML development because the size of the object becomes unmanageable. Polygon reduction allows the developer to reduce the detail of an object, however, by removing the triangles that make up its geometry. This reduces the detail of the object considerably, depending on how many triangles are removed.

- Detail the Generic Model. Once imported to the world-building application, objects must be detailed and customized to fit their virtual spaces. Most 3-D models are simple shapes with no color or texturing (though some will be fully detailed).

- Fit the Model into the Space. When detailing is complete, an object is ready for placement into its VRML world. This may be handled best by saving or moving a copy of a detailed file into the 3-D application's library file. Then, only a drag-and-drop is required to place the object into the working space (this procedure depends entirely on the application).

tip *Always keep a copy of an undetailed original object, especially if it's generic enough for reuse elsewhere. VRML library sites represent some of the highest turnover sites on the Internet. When you return to find an original object, it may be gone. Keep your own copy!*

Another less desirable method to import VRML object files from one file to another entails copying and pasting VRML code. Each object within a VRML file is compartmentalized, which means all attributes for an object occur in one section of the code. This code may be copied and pasted like any other type of text. Naturally, this requires that both the export and the import file are VRML-formatted (a .wrl file). Once imported in this way, the new file may be opened by a 3-D graphics program and the individual objects may be manipulated individually. Although this method is not for the faint of heart, it is not too difficult to master.

Whatever method is chosen to import ready-made 3-D models to a VRML world, the savings in time and headaches outweigh the costs when gathering tools and objects.

File Formatting and Conversion

When dealing with 3-D graphical libraries, a main concern is portability. Most 3-D rendering tools and VRML authoring applications support some form of file import and export, but many accept only a small set of proprietary formats. Naturally, the project will need some tools—whether they are built into the application or created by a third party—to get files into the work space and out into a VRML world. Luckily, several brave souls already exist who had a need for tools such as these and the knowledge and resources necessary to create them.

Many of these utilities are shareware or freeware; a limited number are commercial applications. Commercial 3-D graphic conversion tools often allow greater freedom when importing and exporting files, permitting such things as textures, colors, and other object attributes to stick with an object during its "conversion experience." Some shareware and freeware applications are not so accommodating. Likewise, commercial applications are generally more stable than shareware utilities and companies that produce them offer better technical support and upgrade options.

Drawbacks to commercial programs usually include their price and a possible lack of support for a specific platform or file format needed by your development team. But, when weighing which 3-D conversion utility to use, the overall needs of the project should be carefully evaluated and compared to the capability of all the available tools.

Commercial Graphic Conversion Utilities

The following subsections detail many 3-D graphic conversion utilities available on the Internet, beginning with commercial alternatives and continuing with freeware and shareware options.

INTERCHANGE FROM SYNDESIS CORPORATION Interchange supports import and export of over forty graphics file formats, including: 3D Studio (.3DS), AutoCAD (.DXF), Inventor (.IV—export only), and VRML 1.0. Although available only for Windows, SGI IRIX, and Amiga, Interchange supports full import and export (for most file formats) of textures, and dependent files (either parent or child to the object, such as attached objects, sounds, or other functions). This utility is available for purchase via e-mail or telephone, and ordering information is available on the Web site. No demonstration version exists, but Syndesis also offers a variety of 3-D object libraries and often bundles such libraries with a purchase of Interchange.

You can reach the Syndesis Web site at:

```
http://www.threedee.com
```

CALIGARI'S TRUESPACE TrueSpace, an industrial strength 3-D graphics creation application, supports 3-D object imports of Encapsulated Postscript (.EPS), PostScript (.PS), 3D Studio (.3DS), AutoCAD (.DXF), Caligari Object Format (.COB), and many others, although it exports only to .COB, .DXF, and .ASC. TrueSpace also supports import and export of these two-dimensional image files: .BMP, .TGA, .JPG, and .AVI. Caligari TrueSpace and Pioneer may be found at:

```
http://www.caligari.com
```

Freeware and Shareware Utilities

An excellent source for a variety of conversion utilities is located at the Construct, Inc. Web site:

```
http://vrml.arc.org/tools/
```

Conversion applications here translate specific file types to VRML, such as DX2VRML, for AutoCAD .DXF files, and IVtoVRML, for SGI's Open Inventor format. These shareware programs are usually format-specific; many are platform specific. Some have only limited import and export options, especially regarding texture maps and hierarchical objects.

Resources for Objects

Few resources exist that specialize in predefined objects for VRML publication, which means designers must improvise and know which file import formats their development tool supports. Many applications, such as StudioPro for the Macintosh, support a wide range of file formats for import from other 3-D development packages. Likewise, conversion programs support many such formats for translating one type of 3-D object format to another. When trolling for objects for VRML libraries, designers must be both creative and diligent! File size and reduction are also considerations, as most objects produced with 3-D graphics and animation packages are very detailed, and are, thus, very large. This section outlines a few resources to begin the search process.

VRML Object Libraries on the Internet

As you might expect, the Internet is the most useful resource for VRML objects. Some sites specialize in VRML objects and offer them for download and use, free of charge. Other resources include VRML worlds themselves. Once a VRML space is downloaded and ported to a 3-D development application, its constituent objects may be manipulated, copied, and used in other spaces.

warning   *As with textures and anything on the Internet developed by someone else, to avoid any type of copyright infringement, please contact the designer or owner of any VRML file or object to request permission to use it. VRML object design takes a lot of time and designers deserve compensation, even if that's just public recognition for their efforts.*

Freeware VRML Object Libraries

Although they are scarce, free VRML objects are cropping up all over the Internet. The excitement over the recently released VRML 2.0 has created a resurgence of interest in the media. Developers worldwide are hustling to build and publish new virtual spaces. In the wake of this effort, object libraries are being generated and offered, most of them free of charge, to the VRML development community.

Here are some of the better Internet resources for VRML object libraries:

THE VRML OBJECT SUPERMARKET   Located in the U.K., the VRML supermarket has a huge collection of simplistic and more complex objects for use with VRML. Most of these were converted from other 3-D graphics formats, such as Open Inventor on the Silicon Graphics platform.

Check out this Web site:

```
http://www.dcs.ed.ac.uk/generated/package-links/objects/vrml.html
```

Browse for the objects depicted in Figures 12-1 through 12-3 and for other great VRML objects as well.

THE VRML MALL   The VRML Mall is a well-categorized site and it offers simple to complex images, divided into such genres as: Animals, People, Buildings, Chemistry, and even 3-D renderings of the creatures from the game DOOM.

The VRML Mall is located at:

```
http://www.ocnus.com/models
```

Figures 12-4 through 12-6 show a small sampling of the Mall's ample library:

CONSTRUCT, INC.   Construct's Web site is a stylish example of Web design and features a small collection of VRML objects. In addition, they offer a collection of avatars, used as 3-D representations of users within a multiuser VRML environment. Construct also includes a group of generic 3-D envi-

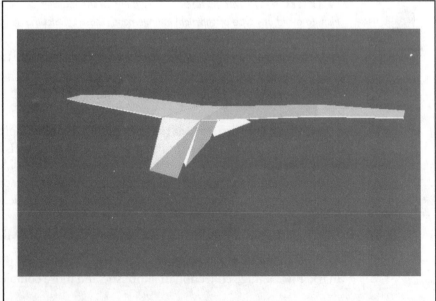

FIGURE 12-1

This object was supplied to the VRML Object SuperMarket by the VR-Art archive at the Design Research Center; it depicts a simple bird in flight.

FIGURE 12-2

An odd half-column and wall arrangement ready for porting to a 3-D graphic library!

■

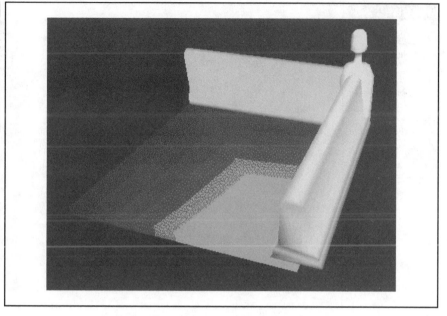

ronments, where designers can begin placing objects as they tackle the long and arduous task of creating a virtual world.

FIGURE 12-3

A nice virtual office is depicted in this .wrl file developed by IICM.

■

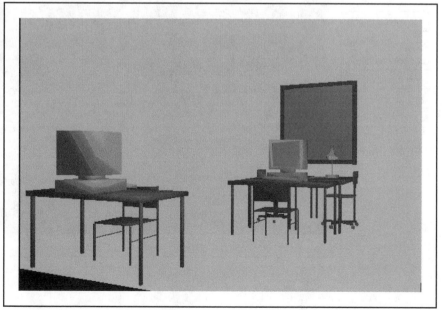

Stunning, yet simple, renderings such as these dolphins, can be downloaded, textured, and fit into VRML worlds with ease. ■

This M1A2 Main Battle Tank is textured in a camouflage pattern and needs only a few details, such as antennae, to make it realistic. ■

FIGURE 12-6

Models such as this AH-64 Apache Helicopter take hours of design time to depict accurately such details as the weapon racks and rotor blades.

Construct, Inc. can be accessed at:

`http://vrml.arc.org/`

Figures 12-7 and 12-8 depict a few samples of their object repertoire.

Commercial Libraries

With any development project, the team must consider whether or not to purchase tools or resources to get the job done. With VRML, this consideration is equally valid. While commercial libraries of VRML formatted objects exist, these are more sparse than free libraries. These commercial libraries are generally quite expensive but, otherwise, they are very detailed.

Some of the more popular sources for commercial 3-D models also provide VRML compliant files. One of these sources is ViewPoint DataLabs. Their Web site contains both free and for-a-fee 3-D objects for VRML and other 3-D graphics formats. ViewPoint DataLabs certainly represents one of the better libraries available, with over 30 objects available for download, ranging from quite simple to complex models.

ViewPoint DataLabs is located at:

`http://www.viewpoint.com`

FIGURE 12-7

A complex molecule system could be used for anything from a chemical diagram to an interesting navigational map for a VRML site. ∎

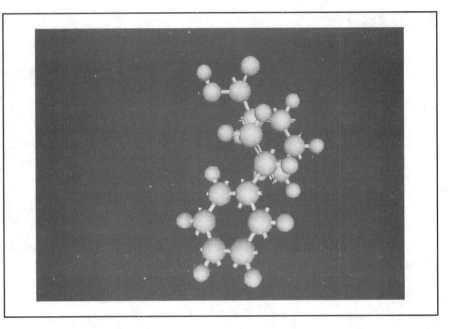

At this Web site, developers fill out a short form, whereupon they are granted access to a library of objects, including VRML models. Figures 12-9 through 12-11 show a small sample of some of their more interesting objects.

FIGURE 12-8

Avatars are the newest peripheral development in interactive VRML worlds. This particular avatar has vibrant colors and an . . . interesting design. ∎

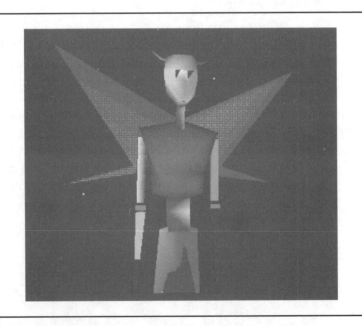

*This Hughes
MD-500 helicopter
is rendered, but
undetailed, waiting
for the right
textures, lighting,
and animation.*

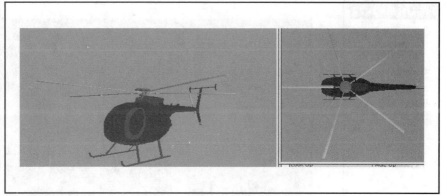

Other commercial sources for 3-D models should not rule out 3-D graphics and animation packages, such as Caligari TrueSpace modeler, which includes over 600 objects, and Trispectives by 3D/EYE, Inc., which includes over 1,000 objects! Again, these objects will require some work, as they were not specifically designed for VRML publication; thus, they must be converted to VRML and have excessive detail reduced to make them useable.

*This fully rendered
and colored angel
can either be used
as an avatar or
retextured as a
lifelike statue.*

VRML Library Development

Probably the least desirable option for most developers is in-house design of complex objects, primarily because this is the most time-consuming option. But with the level of complexity possible in most 3-D-rendering applications, complex, custom structures can be developed, which will not only add value to a VRML site, but can also be a good starting point for 3-D model libraries for future projects. Because these objects are portable between applications, for the most part, simultaneous development of multiple 3-D graphics projects is possible. For example, a 3-D animated model of the company logo made for a CD presentation designed in AutoDesk's 3D Studio MAX could be ported to a VRML 2.0 project.

note   *Always try to leverage as much existing work as possible in such projects or try to team up with other groups with similar needs and objectives.*

Rather than tackling development of a complete object library, you might further seek to modify public domain objects or those purchased from a 3-D graphics vendor. For example, you could take a simple 3-D rendering of a car and modify its body design to match a specific car needed for a project. Although this is still time-consuming, the recycling approach takes less time and is less resource consuming than building a car from scratch. Also, most objects when imported to a rendering tool, can be "stripped down" to a wireframe rendering, which makes moving the model easier and less processor consuming.

All in all, in-house 3-D graphic development should mirror the importance of the objects within the space. If the objective is to create a fairly generic space with a few simple objects—such as a parking lot full of cars—your needs may best be served by collecting public domain objects and detailing them individually.

If a customized set of objects is required, such as a rendering of a specific tool or machine part, in-house development is often the only viable solution. The main thing to remember when populating an object library is to weigh the need of the project against the resources already available.

Summary

Object libraries, while still sparse (even on the Internet), are ready resources for quick VRML development. These objects, regardless of the file format, provide easy-to-use sources for objects to populate a VRML space. The tools and resources to turn them to your best advantage are available, but finding the ones that fit your project will be the key to a successful VRML development experience.

building

VRML

World

chapter 13

VRML Worlds for WWW Navigation

A slow shift is occurring in Internet information presentation from simple graphics, text, and document links to complex, interactive 3-D environments. Although those Web sites that currently employ VRML technology on their sites are not numerous, we believe this will change over time.

Throughout this book, strategies for building virtual worlds have been covered, with a focus on key tools, resources, and general structure of VRML creation. What's left? Actual implementation of a true 3-D information site.

A new school exists of information gurus who are breaking ground in cutting edge Internet technologies, such as Java and VRML. Animation, multimedia, and three-dimensional information presentation are the future of online data; VRML 2.0 is the first step into this frontier. Implementing a VRML site is a science and must be approached as such. A driving theme, appropriate tools and equipment, and an expert development staff are the keys to any publishing venture, virtual or real. This chapter deals with these issues and the overall VRML project as an information engine for general World Wide Web consumption.

On the First Day: Preparing for World Creation

VRML worlds are not just for computer scientists anymore. With the appearance of VRML-specific publishing tools, growing resource libraries, and the desire of the general Internet public for 3-D interaction, virtual worlds for World Wide Web (WWW) navigation are cropping up slowly, but surely, all over the Internet. What it takes to use this technology effectively is the same as any large-scale development project: a solid plan, the right tools, and an expert staff. The first step to accomplishing these goals is the plan. Because the information to be published is on hand, the real hurdle is forming the idea for 3-D presentation and gathering the appropriate resources. Simple, right?

Brainstorming and Researching

Ideas drive any creation process; this is where any project of this nature begins. Starting with a stack of information and an order for the final product is how a Web designer usually enters such a project. Deciding how to present the information best, in a cohesive, linear nature, while maneuvering within the confines of the technology, is the first hurdle. With VRML, the constraints of the media are even greater than simple HTML creation because of the limited amount of bandwidth available on the Internet today. It takes far less bandwidth to transmit an HTML document than one enhanced with VRML.

Still an infant language and tool, VRML nevertheless offers a broad medium for information presentation. Knowing how to use this technology effectively requires creative ideas, which can be gained through benchmarking and researching.

The two greatest attributes of the Internet are its worldwide nature and its sizable virtual population, which provide any developer with a huge library of ideas, resources, implementation examples and, overall, a place to start. VRML is an Internet technology; therefore, the place to begin developing an idea for a VRML project is online. Other sources of ideas include 3-D perspective applications, such as computer games, multimedia presentations (a good source of balancing style and content), and any other 3-D graphics implementation, such as movies or commercials, in which theme and information are paramount.

Internet Resources

The Internet is rich in VRML implementation, but not necessarily in the marriage of information and 3-D presentation. Sites are cropping up daily that use VRML for these purposes but, still, these sites are few and far between. Something as simple as a group of objects in an object library or 2-D image displays on a Web site could spur an inventive idea for 3-D representation. Places to begin Internet research are Yahoo, Excite, or any of the other search engines publicly available. A simple search on the keyword "VRML" will yield everything from backwater developer sites stacked with forgotten objects and half-built worlds to fully functional virtual communities.

Sorting the "Net noise" from the useful information is the real problem, but this is inherent with any Internet research. As stated, information-intensive sites using VRML as a primary vehicle are still sparse, but with VRML publishing applications like Caligari's Pioneer Pro and Paragraph's Virtual Home Space Builder, you can expect such sites to blossom in no time.

With these applications in mind, example worlds at both Caligari and Paragraph's home pages offer another good Internet resource for ideas, as well as an indication of the sites to come. Virtual Home Space Builder includes several "bare-bones" worlds and some fully developed VRML sites, on both the CD and its Web site. One of the best examples of VRML 2.0 for information implementation is the Gourd CD Music Hall, which depicts a virtual music store where the client may navigate the hall, listen to tracks from a CD, read about the company from image placards and, generally, interact with a 3-D space as if it were real. Ideas for commercial spaces could be extrapolated from this quite easily. Gourd's CD Music Hall (see Figure 13-1) is available at:

```
http://vrml.paragraph.com/3dspaces/bluemusic/gourd.wrl
```

Gourd's CD Music Hall is an excellent example of use of VRML 2.0 technology with audio clips of displayed artists. Likewise, good use of text placards throughout the space removes the need to support HTML documents, which would detract from the 3-D experience.

Multimedia Resources

3-D graphics are everywhere these days—from first-person perspective interactive games to flashy commercials to stunning special effects in movies. Of course, such complex multimedia displays are far from possible in VRML. Sources such as these can generate ideas, however, and when scaled down, they offer possibilities for innovative VRML sites.

The game DOOM from ID Software has become a cultural phenomenon for many computer enthusiasts. Many VRML developers have dreamed of creating games such as DOOM on the Internet, games with multiuser, fully interactive capabilities. Of course, this dream is far from fruition, due to the limits both in VRML and end-user resources, but some have taken the vanguard and imported images and functions from such games and begun this long quest.

```
http://www.ocnus.com/models/doom.html
```

Movies are also a source for VRML inspiration. *Star Wars* models, such as the X-Wing fighter, were some of the first objects developed with VRML and still are popular today. Other more recent movies, such as *Independence Day*, actually used 3-D modeling when creating the special effects. Figure 13-2 shows a VRML representation of the *Millennium Falcon* that could be used as a virtual space for science fiction hobbyists and enthusiasts. By imbedding links around the outside structure, users can enter other virtual spaces showcasing the history of science fiction.

3-D graphics use is so widespread that ideas for VRML are sure to follow. Remember, high-end 3-D graphics rendering and VRML are far from synonymous, but as the Internet matures—meaning its users and technology—look for more intensive implementation of 3-D graphics through VRML. VRML 2.0 is already leagues ahead of its predecessor; as the demand for the medium grows, developers will respond with better tools and a more stable development environment.

FIGURE 13-1

Gourd's CD Music Hall

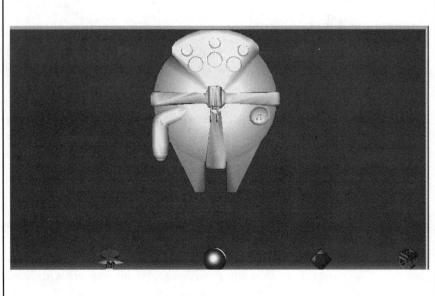

Themes, Plans, and Tools

Once ideas are spawned, a frantic time begins of building these ideas into a theme for the VRML piece. Tools that will serve the needs of the project, such as object libraries and VRML development applications, must be evaluated and obtained. Once all this is finished, the overall plan—from the first pixel in a virtual space to publication of a fully functional world—must be mapped out carefully. VRML development is far from easy, even with such applications as Virtual Home Space Builder. Creating objects, displaying surface textures, and translating the on hand information to 3-D representation all take a good amount of time. With a theme and a plan to guide the project and with all the right tools, VRML creation is well on the road to success.

Information and Theme

VRML creates a graphical representation of data in a virtual space. These data can be anything from a company's products to a virtual art gallery. VRML 2.0 provides a fast-moving medium for interactive 3-D information, all delivered over the Internet. For a successful VRML project, the developer must use the virtual space both to interest and entertain the end user. The best way to do this is by developing an overall theme for the piece. The simplest theme could be a virtual mall with storefronts around certain interactive artistic displays, all with the ever-familiar "mall music" background. But the subject of theme is unlimited when you deal with 3-D graphics. Although the virtual space has a limit to its complexity before it becomes unusable, such strategies as linking groups of smaller worlds, polygon reduction of objects, and effective use of surface textures all work together, both to build the theme and to keep the VRML world at a manageable size.

GRAPHIC INFORMATION   How to display information graphically has been the problem of many artists for thousands of years. Building a virtual world that conveys graphic information to the target audience, captures their attention, and functions as it should is the real challenge with VRML, as well. Creativity and innovation are the keys to 3-D graphics' displays. Choices must be made for the virtual world as a whole, in that some information may be better suited in 2-D or HTML format, while other information is best presented in audio streams; still other information could be conveyed with 3-D object displays. The balance among all of these, the theme, and the overall goal of the virtual world should be reflected in the overall plan for the VRML site.

DEVELOPING A THEME   Developing an underlying theme for any graphic display project is key to its success and the most difficult development stage. The following are a few simple steps to develop a VRML theme:

- **Look at the Information**   What information will be displayed? Geometrically simple products, such as computer monitors, have been effectively used in VRML display for some time. Basing the theme on the information at hand is the most effective way both to interest the target audience and to provide a better scope of the project.

- **Think About the Space**   You have a stack of information. Where do you place it in space? Using the previous computer monitor example, a brainstorming session may reveal the need to differentiate this product, or group of products, from similar VRML sites on the Internet. An interesting space might be a sandy beach with static displays of monitors sitting on palm stumps or hovering above rock sculptures.

- **Fit the Information into the Space**   The space is conceived, the information you want conveyed is at hand. How do you marry the two effectively, in keeping with the developing theme? This is where decisions must be made about the integration of HTML documents and multimedia options, such as sound and animation. Does the information work better in one of these forms than in a three-dimensional representation? From the continuing example, the virtual beach store front could use background sounds—the ocean, wind, or Hawaiian music—to enhance the theme. Although many people want specific information on monitors, such as data sheets, these could be handled simply by linking each monitor to a second VRML file, displaying the individual monitor itself with an appropriate image on its virtual screen, and a flat data sheet nearby with relevant information, such as refresh rates, dot pitch, display sizes, etc.

- **Details and Theme** Themes of any type are built on subtle details which, when noticed, both convey the message of the piece and may surprise the target audience, keeping their attention. Extending the beach side monitor gallery motif, audio streams could direct browsers to specific features of selected monitors or, using the previously mentioned data sheet idea, could actually read the data sheet when selected. An animated graphic on the virtual screens of all the monitors could round out the piece, giving life to an otherwise static scene.

Getting the Job Done 1: Applications

VRML development applications, whether specifically designed for VRML or not, have been well covered in preceding chapters. But the right tool for the job is essential; this cannot be stressed enough. On one hand, a VRML application designed for a hobbyist, such as Virtual Home Space Builder, would not suit the scope of a project spanning several VRML files that needs complex geometry for its objects. On the other hand, a 3-D graphics rendering package like AutoDesk's MAX 3D Studio would not be useful for a simple commercial site, which needs only a few basic objects and some functionality.

VRML DEVELOPMENT TOOLS New applications promoting ease of use in VRML development are cropping up every day. The following list includes VRML development packages, divided by platform and technical level. Some of these applications have previously been reviewed in full in this book, while others are new entrants into the VRML development world. More information about these applications can be found at their respective URLs.

- **Low-End Packages**   Not rich on features or capabilities, these authoring tools are for users who want to add VRML functionality to a Web page or to find out what VRML is all about. These sorts of packages may or may not support all functionality of VRML 1.0 and they probably don't have VRML 2.0 capabilities yet.

- **VRML Express 1.0.5**   This is a text-based VRML editor (from Model Works Software) with support only for Windows 95 or Windows NT 3.51 or later. VRML Express supports all VRML 1.0 features and has a handy VRML syntax error checker, which points out problems within a VRML file. A demo can be obtained from the Model Works Web site:

  ```
  http://www2.csn.net/express/
  ```

- **Mid-Level VRML Authoring Tools**   These kinds of packages are good for almost any project and a combination of such tools could help compensate for features that are lacking between new product releases. The best feature of these mid-grade VRML authoring tools is their price and functionality. Most are priced at under $200 and they are packed full of features. Again, for complex object creation, full VRML 2.0 compliance and other high-end features, rendering packages may be the best bet for the project.

- **Virtual Home Space Builder**   Paragraph started with a good idea and expanded on it, much to the delight of its users. Home Space Builder, reviewed earlier, is a solid application for producing fully interactive 3-D environments. Home Space Builder's only drawback is a distinct lack of object modeling capabilities, such as spheres and other curved objects. Offsetting this drawback are Home Space Builder's full VRML 2.0 compliance and rich development environment. Home Space Builder is available for Windows OSs of all flavors.

- **3-D Website Builder**   Virtus's VRML authoring tool, 3-D Website Builder, is everything you need to create 3-D environments for the World Wide Web. This fast and easy 3-D modeling program features a drag-and-drop WYSIWYG approach to create your own worlds for the Internet (and your desktop). 3-D Website Builder exports to VRML 1.0, with no support slated yet for a 2.0 version. 3-D Website Builder includes a core set of libraries, with simple polygon objects and texture maps to get the project underway. 3-D Website Builder is available for Windows 3.1, Windows 95, and the Power Macintosh. For a demo and more information on this application, contact the Web site at:

http://www.virtus.com

- **Workstation VRML Authoring Tools** Definitely for the high-end developer, VRML authoring tools for workstations, such as the SGI or DEC Alphas, use the processor power and capabilities of their platforms to produce stunning VRML graphics in no time. These packages are feature-rich, expensive, and many are used for general 3-D graphics rendering for other media, such as movies and virtual reality games.

- **EZ3D** Available for the SGI, Sun, HP-UX, IBM-AIX, and DEC Alpha Intergraph, EZ3D is a fully functional 3-D rendering graphics package, which includes the utility application EZ3D VRML Author. Specifically designed for VRML creation, EZ3D VRML Author includes features such as Level of Detail Editors and Polygon Reduction tools. EZ3D VRML Author is conscious of the need to reduce complex graphics, which may run fine on an SGI workstation, but may be practically unusable on a PC. EZ3D currently only supports VRML 1.0 and no indication has yet been seen of a 2.0 version in the works. Check out EZ3D at:

http://www.radiance.com/Ez3d-VRPro.html

3-D GRAPHICS RENDERING PACKAGES Projects that require such high-end graphics production are usually disappointing in the final product because graphics with complex details must be reduced significantly to make them useable in VRML publication. Features such as processing distribution across a network, found in MAX 3D Studio, are powerful but, in some cases, are unnecessary for VRML development. Should such packages already be on hand for other 3-D graphics work, then all the better. Overall these packages are overkill, but a VRML developer will not lack features.

LIBRARIES Gathering texture and object libraries could be the most difficult stage of preparing for VRML publication. Many publicly available archives exist for both objects and textures on the Internet; many are complex, as outlined in earlier chapters. Building a personal library for the ongoing project is time consuming but, when combined with altered, publicly available libraries, VRML spaces can be easily populated and detailed.

Planning for VRML Implementation

Implementing a VRML Web site is a study in Internet and computer capabilities. A dedicated Web server with a dedicated high-speed T1 connection is obviously desirable but, if the project's budget won't accommodate this optimal setup, then other options must be considered.

HARDWARE, INTERNET CONNECTION, AND PROMOTION   Any computer suitable as a Web server is ideal for VRML publication. For a complex virtual world, many cross-linked worlds will reside on the server; for a VRML world implementing Java, complex scripts, or other programs, a large hard drive (1Gb or higher) and plenty of memory (16MB or higher) are always a necessity.

Because none of the actual processing of the VRML file takes place on the Web server, no other specialized hardware is required. All you need is a standard Web server setup with an Internet connection.

VRML files are large, so they require a lot of bandwidth to transfer. If heavy traffic is expected to the VRML site, a server hosted on a shared T1 is optimal. For fairly simple sites, with average traffic, a shared Web server on a T1 or on a 128K ISDN link is sufficient.

Promotion of a VRML Web site is best handled by publishing the link to the site on the various search engines across the Internet. Announcements to newsgroups and message boards across the Internet are also good ways of promoting the site. Local or nationwide press releases for innovative or special sites is a good idea, as well. Sites such as Virtual Vegas are VRML success stories, getting press in magazines and television news worldwide. Promotion of the VRML site is the only way to get to your target audience.

Getting the Job Done 2: Developers

As with any programming project, expertise is the key. Finding the right people who have enthusiasm for the VRML project and the skills to make it work is a job in itself. Familiarity with the Internet, VRML, and 3-D graphics design are essential qualities in a development team. A plus is at least a working knowledge of 3-D graphics packages and VRML development tools.

VRML DEVELOPERS   The most successful VRML developers have an enthusiasm for the technology and the ability to think in 3-D. VRML is not a difficult language to learn, but effective integration of information into a 3-D space is. These key skills will go far to get the VRML project through the development stages and out onto the Internet.

MULTIMEDIA EXPERTS   With the advent of VRML 2.0, a new variable has been added to Internet virtual reality: multimedia. Developers skilled in integrating animation and sound into a VRML space will be essential in the years to come, as the language matures. Effective use of these features will not only enhance the underlying theme of the VRML piece, but also enable the information displayed to reach more of the target audience. Why read about your product when a potential customer can click on an interactive display that promotes your product for you?

INTERNET GURUS   A fundamental area of the VRML team is the Internet guru. VRML is an Internet animal and it needs the special attention and expertise only an Internet expert can give. Knowing the right connection strategy can make the VRML world that much better.

Electronic Darwinism and Target Audiences

As always, when planning a project using a technology like VRML, the target audience must be considered. VRML is far from a widespread phenomenon, even after two years of use on the Internet. Although the proliferation of VRML viewing tools is finally a reality, with such HTML browser plug-ins, such as Live3D for Netscape, the general Internet public still sits at a connection and hardware level only barely able to handle fairly simple VRML worlds. The quickness of HTML overshadows VRML and makes those casual Internet surfers move on to easier pages if a VRML file takes longer than a few minutes to download or, by chance, crashes their system during operation. This trend is changing, though. More Internet users have access to and demand for high-speed connections, such as ISDN. And more Internet users possess top-of-the-line desktop computers, which easily handle even the most complex virtual worlds. The demand for interactive 3-D Web pages is growing; the VRML developer would be well advised to keep an ear to the rails.

On the flip-side, if the target audience is a specific group of users, such as those on an internal network or those who possess T1 level access to the Internet, the VRML worlds created should reflect this. If a simple world is created with no interaction and little to catch the audience's eye, then the project will fail just as easily.

Balancing the scope and theme of the project against the intended target audience is a fine line to walk for a VRML development team. An easy way to circumvent disappointment is to use what many HTML sites offer today—choices. Something as simple as an option from a main page, for those with both high-speed and low-speed connections, will go far in making the VRML site more popular across the technological board and disseminate the information presented to more than just a specific group of users.

The Hammer and the Anvil: Banging Out a Virtual World

The plan is made, the themes are developed, and the team is assembled. Now, the project is under way. Decisions must be made along the way for maximizing the effect of the overall project, while minimizing the amount of resources needed. Information display methods must be considered such as integrating HTML to the virtual space and using such technologies as Java, scripting, and other Internet standards. These choices are best made in the planning stages. Plans change, however, as any project manager knows, and new ideas crop up. Here are some ideas on how to implement these options to their fullest potential.

Strategies for Linking Worlds

Most VRML sites are not standalone, which means certain supporting VRML worlds, HTML documents, and programs and functions exist, either internal to the site or elsewhere on the Internet, which add value to the site. The technical aspect of this process has been well covered, although a certain process occurs that cannot be ignored. Such strategies as dividing a VRML world into many linked spaces, as well as the integration of HTML documents, give the world a sense of completeness and convenience, which keeps the target audience attentive and generates repeat visits.

Satellite Worlds

A quick strategy for world building is to create many smaller worlds that are linked to a main world. This will not reduce the overall size of the site because each world will still contain the same amount of information—divided or whole—but it could reduce the load to the target audience, allowing them to visit areas of the VRML site in which they have interest.

An example of this would be a virtual facility tour. The theme is a virtual representation of a company's facility through which a customer can wander and, in doing so, link to more information about the company, its employees, and its products. Many facilities are either large or spread across several divisions in other states or countries. A sales office may be located in one area of the facility, a support office, a manufacturing area, etc. A good example would place a central room or site, which represents the main reception area, to provide general information about the company and links to other information. Thus, the user would link to the reception area and immediately be able to find product information. A link to the sales office would carry the user there, where links to specific product information would reside. From this virtual sales office, the user could access product information, see virtual representations of the products with technical specifications, order or purchase products, etc. Also, from this office, the user could link back to the main reception area, to product support, manufacturing, etc.

External links are also a good consideration because almost any company or site is related somehow to other sites on the Internet, be they vendors, supporting information on some technical aspect of a company's product, or other sites of general interest. The concept of the Internet, and particularly the World Wide Web, is based on easy navigation to information. Many sites—VRML or otherwise—do not effectively provide this but, with a VRML site in particular, linking both internal to the site and external is essential to the site's success.

Integration of HTML and VRML

In most cases, a VRML project is not strictly limited to the virtual world itself. Often the need exists for links within the space to supporting HTML documents, which either further explain the information presented or link to information on other sites. Smooth integration of HTML and VRML is easy, as embedded links within the space will function just as they do within an HTML document. These links can carry the browser to another VRML world or to another Web document. Knowing when to use HTML to enhance a VRML site is critical. Due to the limitations of VRML, such as file size and user-end capabilities, supporting HTML documentation is a good avenue to consider.

Using our company facility model, a VRML representation of the manufacturing area could have links from certain manufacturing areas that bring up HTML documents showing products manufactured in that area, outputs, employee information, etc. Other links could take the browser to specialized equipment vendors used in a manufacturing area or to spec sheets about the products produced there.

note *The most important question you must ask when you decide to use HTML documents to support VRML sites is "What is the best way to present the information conveyed?" This job is mostly handled in the overall planning of the site. If the information presented is primarily visual, such as an art gallery, a straight VRML site with minimal supporting HTML documents could easily serve the needs of the project. If the project needs considerable supporting text information, HTML documents are the best way to convey this. The role of VRML should be well defined before the project gets underway; then the role of HTML will easily fit into that model.*

Enhancing VRML Sites with Scripts and Multimedia

In this era of whiz-bang Internet technologies, such as Shockwave and Java, the need for enhancement of a VRML site is an attainable goal. Animation and use of sound are multimedia enhancements now possible with VRML 2.0 and they add value to a VRML site. Knowing when to use these features to enhance a VRML site depends upon both the purpose of the site itself and the expertise of the development staff. Implementation of complex scripts, such as Java, requires extensive resources, such as development staff expertise, hardware and software, and other considerations that will affect the final product and the target audience's ability to view it. Careful consideration must be made of the scope of the product before you decide to use such features.

To continue our VRML facility motif, the main reception area could have an animated receptionist that explains the features and links of the site. Links from various areas of the site could pull up standard HTML forms to record potential customer information. The human resources department could take online submissions of applications for employment. As you can see, the possibilities are endless. The need of the site, however, should dictate the use of such technologies and it should integrate seamlessly with the overall theme.

Example Sites

Examples of fully implemented and effective VRML sites are minimal at present. The technology itself is still in its infancy—even at the ripe old age of two years—and effective integration of VRML worlds has, until recently, not been considered an option. Reasons for this are numerous. The press given to VRML is sparse, tools for building worlds easily are a fairly recent development and, as stated earlier, many organizations cannot justify the overhead in development time of a VRML site, as the technological level of their target audience is still growing. Still, emerging and established sites exist out there. Here are a few for your enjoyment and, more specifically, for benchmarking and ideas for your own VRML project.

The Virtual Vegas site, shown in Figure 13-3, is a prime example of the integration of HTML and VRML, as well as other Internet technologies, such as Java and Perl scripts. With the running theme of a virtual casino, this site is a good one to benchmark when you decide to launch a VRML site that will need such supporting technologies. Virtual Vegas has been around for a few years and it was one of the first to use VRML effectively. Check out the site at:

```
http://www.virtualvegas.com
```

RealSpace has developed an extension to VRML 2.0, which is already considered revolutionary. The company has created a patent-pending panoramic image warping engine, capable of displaying full 360×180 degree panoramas. The examples on this site are only viewable with the Traveler plug-in, available for Netscape, Windows, and Macintosh platforms. The RealSpace site has the plug-in and everything you need to start into the world of VRML 2.0:

```
http://www.rlspace.com/
```

FIGURE 13-3

The Virtual Vegas site exemplifies integration of various Internet technologies, from VRML to Java, in one Web site.

The vrmLab at New College site contains a catalog example page, shown in Figure 13-4, which illustrates excellent use of HTML and VRML integration. By clicking on various areas of a product, in the following case of a Mark 2 Spider Internet bot, the bottom frame of HTML text changes to describe the selected part of the product—complete with product number and part functions.

For more information about vrmLab and a good directory of simple objects, look for them at:

```
http://www.newcollege.edu/vrmLab/
```

Summary

The key to any effective Internet publishing, especially with VRML, is planning, theme building, and development expertise. Building an effective VRML world carries the same requirements and careful considerations relating to the target audience's technical level; be sure to create a world that is meaningful to your target audience. The needs of the VRML site should dictate the necessity and use of such enhancements as supporting HTML

FIGURE 13-4

This catalog example divides the browser screen using frames.

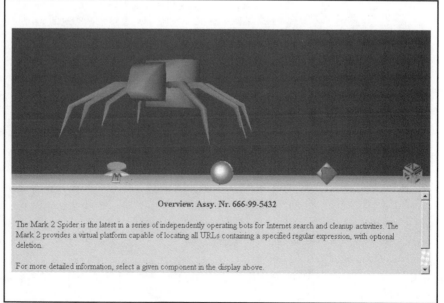

Overview: Assy. Nr. 666-99-5432

The Mark 2 Spider is the latest in a series of independently operating bots for Internet search and cleanup activities. The Mark 2 provides a virtual platform capable of locating all URLs containing a specified regular expression, with optional deletion.

For more detailed information, select a given component in the display above.

documentation, scripting, and multimedia. The possibilities for VRML development are endless, but realistic and professional implementation of a virtual world is always limited to the resources at hand.

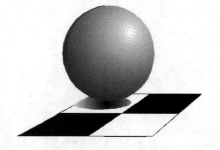

building

VRML

Worlc

chapter 14

Using Web Applications with VRML

W

H A T is a Web application? A *Web application* is just a catch-all term to describe a program that runs on either a Web server or client, which influences data sent via the Web on a Web server or client. Web applications have become a familiar sight on Web servers in the form of guestbook Common Gateway Interface (CGI) programs that take information provided by a visitor from an HTML form. Netscape Navigator users may be familiar with a JavaScript application that produces scrolling text at the bottom of their Web browser window. Server-side or client-side, Web applications have long been a good method to make HTML pages more dynamic.

VRML 1.0 worlds were mostly static. Nodes, such as MovieTexture, were unavailable to VRML developers at that time. One of the few ways to breathe life into a VRML world was with a Web application. Now, with VRML 2.0, Web applications have become a standard part of VRML.

tip *Although VRML creation tools have made world-building easier, script creation is still pretty much a hands-on endeavor. This chapter isn't intended to be a programming tutorial, so a specific programming language won't be covered in-depth. What will be covered are the best languages for creating Web applications and the best way to integrate these applications into a VRML world. Read this chapter, learn the language of your choice, then reread the chapter when you're ready to add the power of that language to your VRML world. No need to rush—programming Web applications for VRML is just like any other kind of programming—you'll need patience, perseverance, and a little luck!*

Server-side vs. Client-side Applications

Clearly, Web applications can improve the interactivity of a VRML world by enhancing movement and purpose. The question, then, becomes how and where to execute the Web application. A limited number of choices exist: The Web application can either be executed on a Web server, or on the client's Web browser or operating system.

On the Server-side: CGIs and APIs

For a few years after the birth of the Web, Web program execution was limited to software that actually executed on a Web server. These programs interact with Web browsers through a client-server specification known as the CGI, originally developed for NCSA's httpd Web server, but which became a global standard to pass programmatic input and output between a browser and a server. Because CGI is a method for client-server interaction, rather than a programming language in its own right, CGI programs can be written in whatever compiled or interpreted language the server supports: C++, Perl, Java, Visual Basic, whatever. The Common Gateway Interface provides a method to pass variables to a program and pipe the output back to the user. CGI applications have become familiar to most Internet users in the form of guestbooks and imagemaps, but they can be used to perform an incredible number of applications, from database queries to data modeling.

In addition to CGI, many Web servers support APIs. Web server APIs are program calls, which typically interact directly with the Web server software and its components. Depending on the server, the API calls can either be embedded with an HTML document or a CGI program. Web server manufacturers typically create APIs that enhance a server's multimedia capabilities, increase user authentication security, and allow easy integration with SQL databases.

Client-side Applications Break the Server Resource Barrier

As Web use has increased over the past few years, Web developers have found that requests to CGI programs can tax a Web server. If one person accesses a CGI program, which generates graphical statistics of Web site use, every 10 minutes, this may not create a problem, but if 20 people access a CGI program every 10 minutes, this could soak a server's CPU.

Also, although CGI programs and API calls somewhat expand the dynamics of a Web site, a demand has occurred for even more multimedia and interactivity on the Internet. It is impossible to get the same kind of slick experience you have using a CD-ROM computer game by using CGI programs: Every time you make a move that affects your environment, a request must be sent to the server; then you must wait for your client to download and process the data. If you're using a 28.8Kbps modem and accessing popular server, this experience would hardly be in real-time!

The solution to these problems has been the current trend in Web programming: client-side applications. With client-side applications, a script or *binary* is sent from the Web server to the client, where the script is run by the client's Web browser or operating system. The user must wait for the application to be downloaded but, once downloading occurs, execution time is dramatically decreased.

Client-side Application Languages

In the early days of the Web, client-side Web applications were Tcl/Tk scripts, which were delivered over the Web to clients who were operating in the X Windows UNIX environment. These scripts could be used to make simple programs with GUI interfaces, but they could only be run on a system that could interpret Tcl/Tk into its windowing software.

Then came Sun's Java, an architecture-neutral language, which can be run on any OS or Web browser that supports the Java runtime environment. Many Web developers feel this is the mold from which all other client-side Web programming languages should be made.

In addition to Java, other popular client-side languages have sprung up. Netscape's JavaScript is a simplified version of Java, which can be embedded directly in HTML code and delivered to a browser that can interpret it. Microsoft's ActiveX (currently limited to Windows systems, but Mac and UNIX versions are on the way) is being touted as Java's chief rival in the Web application language market. ActiveX and Java are actually slightly different. ActiveX takes a more holistic approach: Instead of creating another Web application language, Microsoft is attempting to create a Web application integration model, described as a "glue," which will link Web technologies (including Java) together.

Are Client-side Web Applications the Future of the Software Market?

Client-side applications are marked by their fluid behavior and user control so—not surprisingly—a large number of them are currently control panels and games. But as development progresses and issues, such as security and bandwidth, are tackled, more useful applications will be seen on the Web. Proponents of client-side Web applications are even envisioning a time when practically all the applications you run on your computer will be delivered via the Internet.

For VRML, Client-side Applications Will Prevail

A variety of exciting applications (apps) can enhance VRML worlds on both the server-side and client-side. Given the nature of how VRML works and what its uses are, the client-side applications are obviously a better choice for VRML interactivity. Here are some reasons why:

- VRML is rendered on the client-side. After a ".WRL" file is downloaded, the browser renders the objects within. Any modifications, movements, or other programmatic operations, consequently, should also take place on the client-side. Otherwise, the VRML-enabled browser must access the server any time an application must be accessed, which will slow down the experience considerably.

- Client-side apps are typically faster. When you access a server-run application over the Web, you share that server's resources with an untold number of other visitors to that site. You also access the site over a network or a series of connected networks, which might span the globe. When an application is executed client-side, you don't share your system's resources with anyone or have to make another network connection; the application will run faster and it will not destroy the "reality" of the world.

- The VRML 2.0 Script node: With VRML 2.0, client-side programs can be included into your VRML world using the Script node. Because the script is considered a node, it has the typical event and field attributes and behaviors that most nodes have. A Script node, however, can process events from nodes and send the results to other nodes. This concept of treating a script as an object means software effects can be included in your VRML worlds.

As you experiment with Web applications in your VRML worlds, you'll no doubt find instances where one execution method—server-side or client-side—makes more sense than the other. In this chapter, uses and implementation for both are explored.

Server-side Applications

The very first Web applications integrated with VRML were on the server-side. These applications generally come in two flavors: CGI and API. Most of these are back-end scripts that generate VRML on-the-fly from some given data set. Although the use of client-side applications with VRML has become more popular, some instances still exist where server-side applications make sense. Among these occasions are:

- The data set from which you are generating the VRML is quite large and the set is stored in the server (as in the case of a Web server log file or a large database).
- The Web application only needs to run once.

In most other situations, you may want to go with a client-side application. The network and CPU lag time that's inherent with communicating with a server destroys much of the dynamic feel and makes "moving worlds" with server-side apps nearly impossible.

Possible Uses for Server-side VRML Web Applications

Remembering the two occasions where using server-side applications was suggested, here are some possible uses for these applications:

- Generating a 3-D graph of historical data, such as stock trends.
- Creating a "one-off" world based on user input. The world could be built from scratch or just amended—for instance, a movie of the user's choosing could be shown on a wall.
- Creating a virtual filing cabinet based on a scan of the server's directory structure.
- Creating models of complex mathematical functions, such as fractal imagery.

Many other uses exist, of course. But server-side applications, although powerful at data massaging or number crunching, are too slow in their delivery for fluid motion.

Creating CGI Programs

As previously mentioned, CGI programs are the most common method used to run server-side applications. CGI is a paradigm for interfacing Web servers with programs and scripts and not a programming language in its own right. CGI programs themselves can be written in practically any programming or scripting language. Some of the more common CGI programming languages are C, Perl, Visual Basic, and AppleScript. Typically, you'll find UNIX Web servers running C and Perl CGI programs, Windows NT servers running Visual Basic CGI programs, and Macintoshes running AppleScript CGI programs. Which CGI programming language a developer chooses is based upon several factors: the speed of the language vs. the complexity of the program, how well the language is integrated into the operating environment, what APIs it includes, portability of the code, and how easy the language is to program.

Which Language Should Be Used with VRML?

For CGI programs that are interfaced with VRML worlds, which language you choose will depend on the complexity of the operation you wish to perform. If you're creating a VRML world from scratch using a large dataset, then you'll want to use a programming language with powerful mathematical abilities, such as C. If all you must do is modify an existing VRML file, then a language that specializes in file handling and text processing (Perl is a good example) would be your best choice.

Teaching the nuts-and-bolts of programming in any language is beyond the scope of this chapter so, in this section, the focus is on integrating CGI programs with VRML. For cases where an example is required, Perl is used as the represented CGI programming language. Perl is a good example because: Perl is easy to understand, Perl is one of the most prevalent CGI programming languages, and Perl is available for UNIX, Windows 95/NT, Macintosh, OS/2, and even for DOS.

NEW PROGRAMMERS SHOULD START SMALL If you're new to programming, select a language with which you're comfortable. UNIX users may want to begin with Perl, Windows 95/NT users with Visual Basic, and Mac users with AppleScript. Each of these languages essentially was created to simplify small application development for its corresponding operating system. If you're uncertain about which language to choose, we suggest Perl. The incredible Perl FAQ can help you begin:

```
http://www.perl.com/perl/faq/
```

Learn as much as you can, both about the language and CGI programming in general. Information on the CGI spec can also be found at the National Center for Supercomputing Applications (NCSA):

```
http://hoohoo.ncsa.uiuc.edu/cgi/
```

A Word About Web Server APIs

Web server APIs were previously mentioned as an alternative enhancement to CGI programs. Although APIs can perform some operations faster than CGIs, they are less a programming language than a way to access specific server functions, such as form-parsing or animation. APIs are also typically proprietary, with each Web server supporting its own API and possibly one or two others. Examples of servers with their own APIs are the Microsoft Information Server (ISAPI) and Netscape's suite of Web servers (NSAPI). As VRML grows in popularity, no doubt more VRML-specific server APIs will be seen.

Delivering VRML from Your CGI Programs

In this section, you won't learn how to generate an entire VRML world from a CGI program. The creation of VRML using a program poses different mathematics and algorithmic challenges, depending on the data set and the desired end result. Is it a sphere, the radius of which is based on some user input? Or is it a 3-D graph, based on years of weather data? Instead, the focus is on how to *deliver* VRML from a CGI program.

Delivery Basics

Because both VRML and HTML source files are text, CGI delivery of VRML code to a browser is similar to delivery of HTML. As with HTML, output of the VRML code should go through the Web server's standard output device. On UNIX systems, this is known as *stdout*. Two essential pieces of information exist that must be sent to the browser to deliver VRML over CGI: the MIME type and the VRML file header.

THE MIME TYPE   The most important bit of information to send to the Web browser is the VRML MIME type of *x-world/x-vrml*. If you don't send this MIME type *before* you send any VRML code, then the browser won't know what data type is coming and it will give an error, or default, to a certain MIME type.

remember   *You must send two newline characters after sending the MIME type, as per the HTTP specification.*

THE VRML FILE HEADER   So the browser knows which VRML specification it's about to receive, you should also send the VRML file header. This should come *before* sending any node or interface information. For VRML 2.0, the header is "#VRML V2.0 utf8".

The following bit of pseudocode outlines how to deliver VRML via CGI; comments are notated with two forward slashes (//):

```
// Send the appropriate MIME type and a 2nd newline
output "x-world/x-vrml"
output
// Send the VRML file header
output "#VRML V2.0 utf8"
// Next, perform some magic to generate VRML on-the-fly
// and store it in VRML_CODE
.
.
.
// Send the VRML output to STDOUT
while VRML_CODE exists then output VRML_CODE
```

This is, of course, just an example. The generated VRML code could either be sent directly to the standard output or stored in a file for later delivery.

VRML Generation

Exactly how you write your program to generate VRML will depend greatly on the size and complexity of your data set and how you want your world to look. Because of this, no easy way exists to cover all the possibilities for VRML generation. Instead, here is an example in Perl, which illustrates both how to generate and deliver VRML with a CGI program.

A Simple VRML Object Generator

In this example, an HTML form is created that takes radio-button input on what type of object you want to create (sphere, box, cone) and what color it should be (red, blue, green). Figure 14-1 is a screen-capture of this HTML form. The form then generates the object according to the specifications— such as the red cube in Figure 14-2, the green sphere in Figure 14-3, and the blue cone in Figure 14-4.

The program is called "vrmlgen.pl". The ".pl" extension is a common denotation for a Perl script. Instead of just listing the code with numerous comments, we step through it and insert text where commentary is appropriate. A single-code listing with embedded comments can often be confusing.

note *The script "vrmlgen.pl" was partially created using Sebastian Hassinger's "formgen.pl" CGI program. Sebastian's program allows for the simple creation of HTML forms online and it can combine the form and the form-handling Perl script to support it into one handy CGI.*

FIGURE 14-1

The HTML form for creating simple VRML objects in "vrmlgen.pl"

■

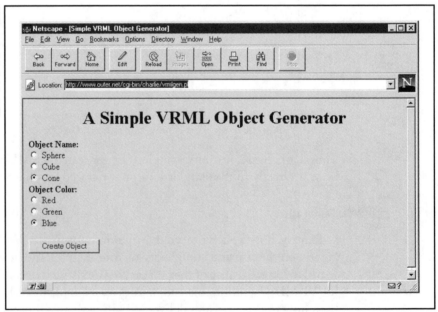

FIGURE 14-2

A red cube

generated by

"vrmlgen.pl"

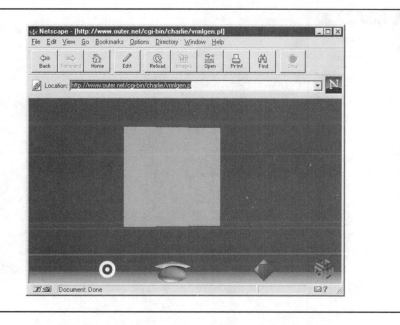

FIGURE 14-2

A red cube generated by "vrmlgen.pl"

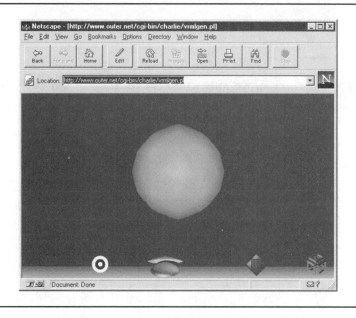

FIGURE 14-3

A green sphere generated by "vrmlgen.pl"

FIGURE 14-4

A blue cone

generated by

"vrmlgen.pl"

■

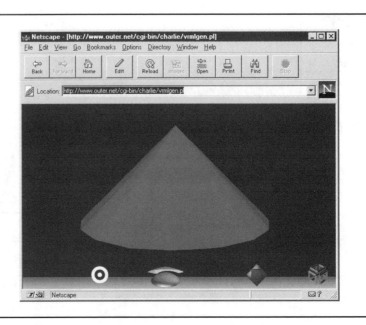

Vrmlgen.pl

CD-ROM

First, we must enter the location of our Perl program. In this case, it's "/usr/local/bin/perl". A few comments follow on the program itself, some variable declarations for form-handling.

```perl
#!/usr/local/bin/perl
# perl script to both supply and support the vrmlgen HTML form
# generated by http://www.outer.net/cgi-bin/formgen.pl
# on Mon Aug 19 19:23:37 CDT 1996
$| = 1;                  # output NOT buffered
$host = $ENV{SERVER_NAME};
$ENV{SCRIPT_NAME} =~ s/([a-zA-Z0-9\.\-_]+)$//;
$program = $1;
$scriptpath = $ENV{SCRIPT_NAME};
```

Next, the script decides whether or not this CGI has been called during a form POST (meaning data are being sent to it in a URL-encoded fashion). If so, the script will continue on with the VRML generation; if not, the script will jump down to the "else" condition, where the HTML form will be loaded.

```
## formlib stuff.
If (($ENV{REQUEST_METHOD} eq "POST") &&
    ($ENV{CONTENT_TYPE}   eq "application/x-www-form-urlencoded")){
```

What immediately follows are the form-handling algorithms, which put all of the form data into a name-value pair in an array called "%in".

```
# extract form data - borrowed heavily from
# Brigette Jellinek's formlib.pl
  read(STDIN,$input,$ENV{CONTENT_LENGTH});
  foreach (split("&", $input)) {
    /(.*)=(.*)/;
    $name = $1;
    $value = $2;
    $value =~ s/\+/ /g ;
    $value =~ s/%(..)/pack('c',hex($1))/eg;
    # unescape characters
    if (defined $in{$name}) {
      $in{$name} .= "#" . $value
    } else {
      $in{$name} = $value;
    }
  }
```

Here, it sends the VRML content-type of *x-world/x-vrml* to the browser, followed by the two carriage returns.

```
Print "Content-Type:\tx-world/x-vrml\n\n";
```

Next, the script makes a decision on what color to make the object, based on the input from the "Object Color" radio button, which is passed into the "$in{ObjectColor}" array. Then the color chosen (Red, Green, or Blue) is matched to the appropriate three-place RGB value as per the **SFColor** field type, and that value is stored in the "$ObjectColor" string.

```
If ($in{ObjectColor} eq "Red") {
    $ObjectColor = "1 0 0";
  } elsif ($in{ObjectColor} eq "Green") {
    $ObjectColor = "0 1 0";
  } else {
    $ObjectColor = "0 0 1";
  }
```

Then the VRML code itself is sent, starting with the VRML 2.0 header.

```
Print "#VRML V2.0 utf8\n";
```

Here, the first child node is set up, which contains the NavigationInfo node. The **headlight FALSE** turns off the headlight on the "walker." Instead, the DirectionalLight node is used to put a little light on the subject.

```
Print "Transform {\n";
print "children [\n";
print "NavigationInfo { headlight FALSE }\n";
print "DirectionalLight {\n";
print "direction 0 0 -1\n";
print "}\n";
```

The next child is the object itself: a Shape node with a geometry of Sphere, Box, or Cone. Which one is created depends upon whether the value of "$in{ObjectName}" is Sphere, Cube, or Cone, respectively.

```
Print "Transform {\n";
print "children [\n";
print "Shape {\n";
if ($in{ObjectName} eq "Sphere") {
  print "geometry Sphere { radius 2 }\n";
} elsif ($in{ObjectName} eq "Cube") {

  print "geometry Box { size 2 2 2 }\n";
} else {
  print "geometry Cone {\n";
  print "  bottomRadius 2\n";
  print "  height 2\n";
  print "}\n";
}
```

Finally, the object is given a little color, using the Appearance and Material nodes and **diffuseColor** field. The color used is the content of the "$ObjectColor" string, which was decided upon earlier.

```
Print "appearance Appearance {\n";
print "material Material { diffuseColor $ObjectColor }\n";
print "}\n";
print " }\n";
print "]\n";
print "}\n";
print "]\n";
print "}\n";
} else {
```

The rest of the program contains the information for the HTML form. If you are familiar with HTML form generation, you should be able to work your way through this and change items where desired. The NCSA's CGI site mentioned earlier has a good tutorial on forms. Note the <FORM> tag and the location of the script.

note *If you plan to modify this for your own use, you will need to change its URL to that of your CGI executable directory.*

```
Print "Content-Type:\ttext/html\n\n";
print "<!DOCTYPE HTML PUBLIC \"-//IETF//DTD HTML 2.0//EN\"><HTML>\n";
print "<HEAD>\n";
print "<TITLE>Simple VRML Object Generator</TITLE>\n";
print "</HEAD>\n";
print "<BODY>\n";
print "<!-- Form created by formgen.pl on Mon Aug 19 18:58:49 CDT 1996 \n";
print "<!-- For: charlie@outer.net →n";
print "<FORM ACTION=\"http://www.outer.net/cgi-bin/charlie/vrmlgen.pl\" METHOD=\"POST\">\n";
print "<H1 ALIGN=\"Center\">A Simple VRML Object Generator</H1>\n";
print "<B>Object Name:</B><BR>\n";
print "<INPUT TYPE=\"radio\" NAME=\"ObjectName\" VALUE=\"Sphere\" CHECKED>\n";
print "Sphere\n";
print "<BR><INPUT TYPE=\"radio\" NAME=\"ObjectName\" VALUE=\"Cube\">\n";
print "Cube\n";
print "<BR><INPUT TYPE=\"radio\" NAME=\"ObjectName\" VALUE=\"Cone\">\n";
print "Cone\n";
print "<BR>\n";
print "<B>Object Color:</B><BR>\n";
print "<INPUT TYPE=\"radio\" NAME=\"ObjectColor\" VALUE=\"Red\" CHECKED>\n";
print "Red\n";
print "<BR><INPUT TYPE=\"radio\" NAME=\"ObjectColor\" VALUE=\"Green\">\n";
print "Green\n";
print "<BR><INPUT TYPE=\"radio\" NAME=\"ObjectColor\" VALUE=\"Blue\">\n";
print "Blue\n";
print "<P>\n";
print "<INPUT TYPE=\"submit\" NAME=\"Create Object\" VALUE=\"Create Object\"><BR>\n";
print "</FORM>\n";
print "</BODY>\n";
}
```

Although this program isn't useful in and of itself, it is a good example on how to generate VRML from a CGI program. This program also is extensible: With the addition of a few more HTML form elements and variables, even more control over the VRML object could be given. You can create a HTML form and a CGI program that will allow users to create an entire VRML world from bits-and-pieces of their choosing.

Client-side Applications

Client-side applications are taking the Web by storm, spurred by the phenomenal acceptance of the platform-independent Java language and runtime environment. These Web "applets" are being used for everything from simple calculators and control panels to real-time arcade games and chat environments.

Client-side Web applications are still in their infancy. Although Java was introduced in 1992, it wasn't really used as a Web development language until a few years later with the release of the HotJava browser. Microsoft's ActiveX currently has only been around for a few months. Integration of client-side applications with VRML is even less well developed because VRML itself has only existed since 1994!

Consequently, client-side VRML Web application development is moving along at high velocity. What exists today are the templates needed to integrate client-side languages with VRML, mostly by way of VRML 2.0's Script node. In this section, you'll learn how to use the Script node and see specific examples of how to use it with Java and JavaScript.

Uses for Client-side VRML Web Applications

Many more possibilities ultimately exist in integrating client-side applications with VRML. Not only can you do much of what server-side applications can do—including on-the-fly VRML generation from user input—but you can also integrate them all with much more fluidity. Here are some examples of what can be done:

- Virtual chat rooms, similar to a 3-D multiuser dimension (MUD).
- 3-D games, using a Java control panel.
- VRML events based on other events. For example: "If the red button is pressed and the countdown timer has reached zero, then launch the rocket."

VRML client-side applications are a new frontier. As the VRML spec further develops and more languages create VRML APIs, the possibilities will only increase.

VRML 2.0's Script Node

When VRML 2.0's developers were crafting the specification, they realized to create "moving worlds," they must go beyond the "flip-flop" animation seen in many HTML pages. To accomplish this would mean the integration of event processing and logic into VRML, so a programmed event could influence the state of a scene. For example: IF the viewer is outside a building AND it's between 6 A.M. and 8 P.M., THEN the sun should be shining. For reasons already discussed, the decision was made that this processing should take place on the client-side of the connection; thus, the Script node was designed to handle this type of processing.

Because the script is considered a node, it has the typical characteristics of a VRML node: field characteristics that set it apart and input and output events. This status is what allows a Script node to interact easily with other nodes. In VRML 2.0 lingo, the Script node is categorized as a "Common Node," along with AudioClip, Shape, WorldInfo, and others. "Common Node" seems to be a catch-all for node types that don't fit nicely into other categories.

note *Even though a Script node is called "a Script node," the program to which it refers need not be a "script" per se. The program can also be a compiled binary, for which the VRML browser provides the runtime environment. For convenience, the convention of calling any executable program a "script" is followed here. The Script node is designed to be open ended; it does not require a VRML browser to support a specific scripting language. The script could be written in whatever language the browser supports, the most common being ActiveX, JavaScript, and Java.*

The Script Node Definition

The Script node's syntax has much in common with other VRML nodes, especially with its **field, eventIn,** and **eventOut** expressions. The definition of the node follows:

```
Script {
  exposedField MFString url            []
  field        SFBool   directOutput   FALSE
  field        SFBool   mustEvaluate   FALSE
  # And any number of:
  eventIn      eventTypeName eventName
  field        fieldTypeName fieldName initialValue
  eventOut     eventTypeName eventName
}
```

The **url** field is important because it specifies the location of the script (or scripts). You can actually specify multiple scripts within this field, separated by a comma. This location will mainly be on the server although, because some languages have their own protocol specification—such as JavaScript— you can include the code *within* the Script node (a trick you will see later). If the script is on a server, then the URL must include the fully qualified domain name of that server. Here's an example of **url** field usage with multiple scripts:

```
Script {
  url [ "http://www.vrmlurl.com/MovingWorld.class",
        "http://www.vrmlurl.com/MovingWorld.js" ]
}
```

The **directOutput** and **mustEvaluate** fields are Boolean variables (logical variables that are returned as true or false, depending on user response) that affect how the browser, the script, and the other nodes will interact. If **directOutput** is TRUE, then the script is allowed to send output directly to other nodes to which it has access. If **directOutput** is FALSE, then it can only affect other objects using **eventOut**. If the **mustEvaluate** field is set to FALSE, then the script can wait for input sent to it by the browser until the browser needs the resulting output from the script. With the **mustEvaluate** field set to TRUE, the browser must send input to the script, regardless of whether or not it needs the output.

note *For performance reasons always set **mustEvaluate** to TRUE, unless the script's execution has an output effect that the browser doesn't use. The **eventIn** field is used to tell the Script node where to gather information. The **eventOut** field allows the programmer to tell the script what type of information it can output.*

This combination of fields and events can be confusing when dealt with at this level of abstraction, but when a real scripting language is plugged into the equation, everything will become more clear.

Java and VRML 2.0

When Sun's Java first hit the scene, this language was hailed as the best thing to happen to the Internet since HTML. Finally, a way existed to make the Web more dynamic than just a series of pages and to move some of the processing burden of CGIs to the client-side. Java is a platform-independent, multithreaded, secure, general purpose programming language. With Java, you can add specialized "controls" to your Web pages, create animated scenes, and have self-generating pages based on user input and logical decisions. Java even allows you to create 3-D objects; in the trade press, hints were made of a "Java vs. VRML" war. In reality, though, these two languages were made for each other!

Java's Relationship to VRML

Java and VRML have two different ultimate goals: VRML's goal is to provide a descriptive language for modeling a three-dimensional scene composed of objects; Java's goal is to be a powerful programming language. Both Java and VRML share a similar subgoal as an accessible Web technology. Because of this shared goal, these two languages also share similar means to achieve this goal, including: adherence to the object-oriented paradigm (OO) and platform-independence.

THE OBJECT-ORIENTED PARADIGM Several important concepts exist in the OO paradigm to which both Java and VRML adhere. First is the idea of an *object* itself as the template for a container of information. In Java, this container is called a *class*; in VRML, this container is known as a *node*.

The second OO concept is instancing. The use of an object multiple times, each *instance* of which has its own internal attributes and does not alter the original object. For example, in VRML you can have multiple Sphere nodes in your VRML world; each Sphere node can have a different size, shape, and color. You can also reuse nodes by way of their DEF name. Similarly, in Java, you could have a class called "Horse" reused several times, each instance with a "Horse" of a different size, shape, and color.

The third OO concept is the idea that the parent-child relationship exists between objects in OO languages. In VRML, this is evident in the parent and child nodes, where the parent actually *contains* the child. In Java, a class can contain other classes in much the same way. In addition, this relationship is expressed in the derivation of a class from a class, also called *subclassing*.

PLATFORM-INDEPENDENCE The Internet isn't a homogenous group of computers using the same processor or operating system; therefore, for success on the Web, any Web technology should be independent of the client platform's architecture. VRML retains this independence by only *describing* what a 3-D scene should look like. VRML lets the browser worry about things like having the CPU perform mathematical calculations and telling the video driver to render it. In addition, the descriptive file VRML sends is in plain-text format, rather than a binary or encoded file.

Likewise, the Java language is platform-independent and can run on any system that supports a Java-capable browser or the Java runtime environment. Java is considered both a compiled language, as is C, and an interpreted language, as is Perl. You write Java source code using a plain-text editor, just as you write C source code. This program is then compiled into an *architecture-neutral* binary bytecode. This bytecode is interpreted by a platform-specific Java runtime environment. You only need to maintain one source code for any platform—a PC, UNIX, or Mac system—on which the bytecode will run. Examples of Java-capable browsers are Netscape 3.0 and Microsoft Internet Explorer 3.0, both of which can model VRML worlds with the appropriate plug-ins. The Java runtime environment is also available for many platforms and is included standard in the latest Linux kernels and in the newest version of OS/2, dubbed "Merlin."

The Java Nomenclature

To familiarize yourself with Java, understanding certain key concepts is important. The first is Java's template for an object, which is dubbed a class. Everything you program in Java is part of one or more classes; everything you program may also interact with any number of other classes and subclasses. OO programming, like any new paradigm, will take some adjustment. Some of its concepts may be difficult to grasp, even for seasoned programmers who are used to thinking linearly. To learn Java, pick up a book on Java or take a programming class; then study *lots* of examples from the Web. Here are some of the simpler Java concepts.

APPLICATIONS AND APPLETS Java jargon also makes the distinction between two different types of Java bytecode programs: applets and applications. This terminology split draws the line between Java programs, which are executed directly in the Java runtime environment (*applications*), and those that are executed within a Web browser via an embedded HTML call to the program (*applet*). Because the Java program used in a VRML world will be run by the VRML browser, this program is considered an applet. In HTML, applets are called with the <APP> tag; in VRML, applets are called with the Script node.

FILE EXTENSIONS Application or applet, Java source has the file extension of ".java" and Java programs have the file extension of ".class." For example, an applet you're including in your VRML world might have a source filename of "MovingWorld.java" and a bytecode filename of "MovingWorld.class." Although using ".class" isn't actually required for execution, its use will make everything easier for you and anyone else using your applet. Successful MIME delivery between a server and client often requires the standard extension be in place.

PACKAGES Java packages are collections of the interfaces of classes, which can be used and reused across multiple Java applets and applications.

Packages use certain procedures in a number of applications and, in this way, they are similar to the "include" files used in the C programming language. But packages are different in a fundamental way: *All* Java classes and interfaces are part of some package. To use a package in your Java application or applet, you access its contents using the **import** keyword. For example, to access a **vrml** package, use the following line at the beginning of your program:

```
import vrml.*;
```

The asterisk means to import all available public classes contained in the **vrml** package.

THE JAVA DEVELOPER'S KIT   Although Java source code is written in a plain-text format, you need the Java compiler to generate the architecture-neutral bytecode to be run on the Java-capable browser. All the tools you need are contained in Sun's Java Developer's Kit (JDK) which, along with the documentation, is available free for download on the following Web site:

```
http://java.sun.com/
```

Currently, versions of the JDK are available for Solaris, MacOS, Windows 95, and Windows NT. The source code is also freely available and developers are invited to port the JDK to other platforms.

Inclusion in VRML

To include a Java applet in your VRML world, use the Script node. To include this easily, put the Java class you wish to execute in the **url** field of the Script node. For example, to call our "MovingWorld.class" bytecode, we would have the following Script node in our VRML world:

```
Script {
        url "http://www.vrmlurl.com/MovingWorld.class"
        eventIn SFBool start
    }
```

This example is deceptively simple. Successful use of Java for VRML event processing requires the use of the VRML Java API.

The VRML API for Java

Introduced with VRML 2.0, the Java API for VRML creates the interface between VRML nodes and Java classes. Any Java programmer who wishes to process events generated by VRML Script nodes or to send processed output to VRML Script nodes must use these bindings. The formal description of this API can be found in Appendix C of the VRML 2.0 Specification at:

```
http://vrml.sgi.com/moving-worlds/spec/part1/java.html
```

THE VRML PACKAGES   The API is actually contained in three Java packages: **vrml**, **vrml.field**, and **vrml.node**. These packages contain all the classes necessary to integrate Java with VRML. The **vrml** package contains classes for, among other things, interfacing with the VRML browser. The **Browser** classes from the **vrml** package can be used to obtain and work with information regarding the browser's name and speed. The **Browser** classes also contain objects and methods to command the browser to create a VRML world or load a URL.

The **vrml.field** package holds the classes for access to VRML's single and multi-field fields, such as **MFColor** and **SFString**. Essentially, the **vrml.field** package makes a Java-equivalent object for each of these VRML fields. The **vrml.node** package contains all the classes relevant to the Script node and it *must* be imported to use the Script node with a Java applet.

RULES AND REGULATIONS   Running a Java applet within VRML isn't a simple matter of putting a Java class into the **url** field of a Script node. When a Java applet is executed via the Script node, two conditions must be met:

1. The Java applet must contain a class definition that has the exact name as the body of the filename.

2. The new class must be a subclass of the **Script** class defined in the **vrml.node** package.

For example, for the "MovingWorld.class" class to meet these conditions, its source ("MovingWorld.java") must look like this code:

```
import vrml.*;
import vrml.field.*;
import vrml.node.*;
class MovingWorld extends Script {
  // This area includes class attributes and other items...
  public void processEvent (Event e) {
    // This area is executed when an event is received from "eventIn"...
  }
}
```

All in all, Java is one of the most exciting Web technologies to integrate with VRML. VRML 2.0 worlds that use Java are already popping up and development tools for using Java with VRML will undoubtedly multiply.

JavaScript and VRML 2.0

On the heels of Java came Netscape Communication Corporation's Java Script language. JavaScript was intentionally designed as a loose interpretation of the Java language. JavaScript resembles Java in many ways, but it is neither as strict nor quite as versatile. The complete specification for JavaScript, as well as examples, can be found at Netscape's JavaScript info page:

```
http://home.netscape.com/comprod/products/navigator/version_2.0/
script/script_info/
```

JavaScript Isn't Quite Java

JavaScript's main function is to allow the fast and easy development of client and server applications. JavaScript is less concerned about execution speed than it is about allowing a user to create simple applications quickly. Whereas Java is compiled into a binary bytecode, JavaScript source is run directly by a JavaScript interpreter. You don't need any type of developer's kit to write JavaScript code. JavaScript code itself is platform-independent— only the interpreter on which it runs is platform-specific.

JavaScript doesn't require you to declare a variable type before using it (for example, calling it an **int** or a **boolean**). Instead, JavaScript limits the functions of what you can do with any given variable to numeric, Boolean, or string operations. In this way, JavaScript is more like Perl, whereas Java is more like C. JavaScript is built around a simple object model. You can use objects built-into the language, as well as those you create yourself. Java Script isn't a class-based object model, however, and there is no inheritance.

Typical Uses for JavaScript in Web Pages

Netscape Navigator allows you to run a JavaScript program directly from your HTML page. The JavaScript source code is actually embedded in the HTML document itself. When the Navigator sees text delimited by <SCRIPT></SCRIPT> tags in HTML, it knows it should parse and execute that text as a JavaScript program.

JavaScript provides an easy means to extend HTML documents and to access browser functions directly (such as opening windows, scrolling text, and creating special buttons). JavaScript is often used to add simple animation and accompanying audio to Web pages. On the Net, you can find JavaScript widgets for everything from calculators to adventure games.

How JavaScript can Enhance VRML

Although it began as an extension to HTML pages, there's no reason why JavaScript can't be implemented in VRML as well. Currently, JavaScript is probably one of the simplest ways to use VRML's Script node. JavaScript is especially useful for creating simple events, such as: "IF this happens THEN do that." Use of JavaScript does, of course, require your VRML browser to support JavaScript. If you're using Netscape Navigator with a VRML plug-in, then you should not have a problem.

The VRML specification doesn't require a VRML browser to support any specific language for use by the Script node. Appendix D of the VRML 2.0 spec does, however, include a reference for integrating JavaScript with the Script node:

```
http://vrml.sgi.com/moving-worlds/spec/part1/javascript.html
```

Using JavaScript with the Script Node

Two ways exist to call JavaScript applications from within the VRML Script node: The first way is to refer to the JavaScript application as a URL with a fully qualified domain name; the second way is to include the JavaScript code inline within the Script node reference. Which one you choose will depend on how long your JavaScript program is and how often you call the program. If your JavaScript is rather long, then use a URL to keep your VRML source uncluttered. If you use JavaScript numerous times within a VRML world or a series of worlds, then you should also use the URL; this way you'll only have to maintain one copy of the script. If neither condition is true, then putting the script inline is fine.

CALLING A JAVASCRIPT URL   To call a JavaScript using the VRML Script node, place the location of the JavaScript in the **url** field, much in the same way as with Java. The standard filename extension for a JavaScript program is ".js", so a Script node using JavaScript would resemble this example:

```
Script {
  url "http://www.vrmlurl.com/MovingWorld.js"
}
```

In this example, "MovingWorld.js" is a plain-text JavaScript program residing on the server "www.vrmlurl.com".

INLINE JAVASCRIPT EXECUTION Netscape Navigator can treat JavaScript as a supported protocol, the same way it does "file:", "http:", "ftp:" and others. The protocol designator for JavaScript is simply "javascript:". Using this protocol allows you to run JavaScript programs directly from Navigator, without having to embed them in the HTML with the <SCRIPT> tag.

Using the "javascript:" protocol with VRML browsers that support JavaScript allows you to place the JavaScript code inline within the VRML source. The entire JavaScript code portion is inside the Script node's **url** field. For example:

```
Script {
  url "javascript: function MovingWorld() {
                   // Perform some operation within
                   // this JavaScript function....
  }"
}
```

In this example, the JavaScript function **MovingWorld** is executed directly from its source contained in the **url** field of the Script node.

JAVASCRIPT EVENT INPUT Handling VRML event input (**eventIn**) with JavaScript is relatively straightforward. Remember one rule, though: The name of the JavaScript function that should occur *must* be the same name as the variable in the **eventIn** field. For instance:

```
Script {
  eventIn SFBool moveWorld
  url "javascript: function moveWorld(value, timestamp) {
        // Code for our mythical MovingWorld program
  }"
```

In this example, the input event is a Boolean data type; the script will be accessed whenever an event is received. The event is given a name of "moveWorld", which executes the JavaScript function of **startClock**. When the script is called, it is passed two arguments. The first, **value,** is the given value of the **eventIn**. In this case, because the value is a Boolean, it will either be TRUE or FALSE. The second is **timestamp**—the time at which the event was generated—expressed in terms of VRML's **SFTime** field.

While JavaScript isn't the solid application language Java is, JavaScript is still suitable for many VRML scripting needs. If nothing else, JavaScript is a good way to get your feet wet programming for VRML.

Summary

The possibility of adding programmatic actions to VRML worlds is an exciting one. Finally, a technology exists that allows a developer to generate on-the-fly worlds or to add realistic behaviors to a scene. Server-side applications, typically in the form of CGI programs, are good for one-off worlds and generating objects from large data sets. Client side applications, usually Java applets, are best suited for object-to-object interaction and for event processing. Java and JavaScript have lead the way in VRML client-side programming by developing their own APIs. Soon more applications will be seen with VRML-based interfaces, which may increase VRML's acceptance as a navigation tool and bring a new way of thinking about the Web.

part 4

Appendixes

building

VRML

Worlc

appendix AA

Glossary

.gz. an abbreviation for GNU zip, a (primarily UNIX-based) file compression format; a common file extension for files compressed using the GNU zip tool.

.tar. An abbreviation for tape archival, *tar* is the UNIX compression command that creates ".tar"-formatted files.

.vrml. A non-standard, but commonly used, file extension for VRML world files. You should include this extension in your MIME-types definitions so that your VRML browsers will know what to do with such files.

.wrl. The file extension required by the VRML specification for VRML world files. You should include this extension in your MIME-types definitions so that your VRML browsers will know what to do with such files.

.Z. A format designator associated with the UNIX compression program. You use the UNIX uncompress program to decompress .Z-formatted files.

3-D (three-dimensional). The optical illusion of depth in a graphic rendered onscreen.

abstract. A brief summary of the contents of a file or document.

AFF (A File Format for the Interchange of Virtual Worlds). This file format consists of tags that possess specific properties, and end up composing a 3-D virtual world (e.g., a material, shape, or texture map). *AFF* is a precursor to VRML.

algorithm. A step-by-step, programmatic recipe for producing a certain set of results in a computer program.

alias. A computer system name that points at another name, rather than to an underlying object. Most Web URLs are either wholly or partly aliases (to protect the underlying file system on the Web server).

alpha. A way of rating the completion status of a piece of software, *alpha* indicates that it's still in the internal testing phase, and has not yet been released outside its development organization.

ambient light. A resemblance to the illumination caused by the reflection of light from objects within a VRML scene.

anchor. An HTML term for the destination end of a hyperlink; it may, however, sometimes be used as a synonym for hypertext links of all kinds.

animation. Moving sequences of images created with the use of computer graphics; or, any graphic method where the illusion of motion is created by rapid viewing (at least 16 frames per second, usually 30) of individual frames in a sequence.

ANSI (American National Standards Institute). One of the primary standards-setting bodies for computer technology in the United States.

API (Application Programming Interface). Usually, a set of interface subroutines or library calls that define the methods for programs to access external services.

application-independent. A format or facility that works in multiple environments, and doesn't require a specific application to understand or use its contents.

Archie. A program that catalogs files on over a thousand anonymous FTP servers worldwide. *Archie* lets users search against this database using interactive queries, e-mail, gopher, or a Web browser.

ASCII (American Standard Code for Information Interchange). A standard encoding for text and control characters in binary format.

asynchronous. Literally, "not at the same time," the term refers to computer communications in which sender and receiver do not communicate directly, but rather through accessing a common pick-up/drop-off point for information, such as an FTP server or via e-mail.

attribute. A named component of an object or term, with specific value typing, element definitions, requirements, and default status.

authentication. A way to identify a user prior to granting him or her permission to access, change, or delete a system or network resource. It usually depends on a password or some other method of proving that "JohnBoy" really is "JohnBoy."

authoring tools. A software application that generates formal code (like VRML), based on how the author manipulates the tool's or system's interface. This is much easier than writing VRML by hand, so we expect that most VRML development will occur within authoring systems.

avatar. 3-D objects that represent live participants in a shared virtual world.

back end. Computerspeak for a service that runs on a computer elsewhere on the network, usually driven by an interface or query facility from another machine elsewhere on the network (the front end).

behavior. Characteristics that determine motion, response, or action in response to other actors or objects. Establishing *behavior* is a programmatic method for determining how an object or node "acts" within a virtual reality.

beta. A way of rating the completion status of a piece of software, *beta* indicates that the software has been released outside its development organization, but only to a hand-picked group of testers who will use it to try to catch (so the developers can fix) remaining bugs before the commercial release.

binary. Literally, this means that a file is formatted as a collection of ones and zeros; in reality, however, it means that a file is formatted to be intelligible only to a certain application, or that it is an executable file.

BIND (Berkeley Internet Name Domain). The most popular implementation of the Internet Domain Name Service in use today. *BIND* supplies a distributed database capability that lets multiple DNS servers cooperate to resolve Internet names into correct IP addresses.

bitmap. A two-dimensional map of binary digits (bits), destined for use in a one-to-one mapping with a display device's pixels.

boot. The process of starting up a computer from its powered-off state.

bottleneck. A part of a computer or a network where things slow down due to limited bandwidth or processing power.

boundary error. In computer programming, errors can occur within the range of the expected data, outside that range, or right on the edge of the expected range. If an error occurs at the edge of the expected range, it is a *boundary error* (for example, if a number between 1 and 100 is acceptable, what happens with 1 or 100?).

bounding box. For VRML, the minimum rectangular volume that can contain a node is a *bounding box*. It defines a region of operation that limits the range and complexity of calculations for rendering purposes.

breakpoint. A marked location in a program, usually set with a debugger, at which the program halts execution so the programmer can examine the values of the program's variables, parameters, settings, and so forth.

browser. An application that lets users access WWW servers in order to surf the Net or view local files. Environments like SGML also use browser programs to render markup into viewable information onscreen. In this book, we use the term to match common usage.

BSDI (Berkeley Software Distribution, Inc.). BDSI remains one of the major flavors of UNIX available today, except that now it's distributed by a spin-off business and not the University of California at Berkeley.

bug. An error, problem, or "unsolved mystery" in a computer program.

C. A programming language created by two of the developers of UNIX, Brian Kernighan and Dennis Ritchie.

C++. Developed by Bjarne Stroustrup, C++ is a successor to the C language. It is an object-oriented (OO) implementation of C.

CAD (Computer-Aided Design). A computer system designed for creation, engineering, and testing of models and objects.

camera. A VRML node that defines the point of view for a scene graph.

Cartesian projection. Developed by the French mathematician, René Descartes, *Cartesian projection* is a method for organizing breadth, height, and depth in a three-axis graph, where the axes are known as x, y, and z, respectively.

case-sensitive. Upper- and lowercase letters do not have the same value (for example, UNIX filenames are *case-sensitive*; "TEXT.TXT" is not the same as "text.txt").

CD-ROM (Compact Disk-Read-Only Memory). A read-only computer medium that contains computer data.

CGI (Common Gateway Interface). The parameter passing and invocation technique used to allow Web clients to pass input to Web servers (and to specific programs written to the CGI specification).

child. An object contained within another object; in VRML, this means a *child* node is contained within another (group) node.

class. A method for defining a set of related objects that can inherit or share certain characteristics.

clickable image. A graphic in an HTML document that has been associated to a pixel-mapping CGI on the server; users can click on different locations of the graphic and thereby be linked to an associated URL.

client. Can be (a) a synonym for Web browser (or Web client), or (b) a requesting, front-end member for a client/server applications (like the Web).

client pull. A Netscape method where a Web client can instruct a server to send it a particular set of data, such as client-initiated data transfer.

client/server. A computing paradigm in which processing is divided between a graphical front-end application running on a user's workstation, and a back-end server that performs processing tasks in response to client service requests.

close. Refers to a session teardown and termination, usually at the end of a networked information transaction.

compiler. A software application that reads the source code for a programming language and creates a binary executable version of that code.

compliant. Conforms to a defined standard.

connection. A link between two computers for the purposes of communication.

content. The information contained in a document.

Content-Type. The MIME designation for file types that are to be transported by electronic mail and HTTP.

data content model. The notation that describes what markup is legal within the context of a specific markup element.

DBMS (Database Management System). A set of programs and utilities used to define, maintain, and manage access to collections of online data.

debugger. A tool used to control the execution of programs under development so that they can be halted and queried at any point during execution, to locate errors or "bugs."

delimiter. A text character that indicates a record or field boundary within a text stream, rather than being interpreted as part of the text itself.

development environment. A collection of tools, compilers, debuggers, and source code management resources used in the software development process.

Digital Actor. The placement of a user within a virtual reality, represented as some kind of virtual object.

directional light. A light source that is defined by a direction vector and a light color.

directory structure. The hierarchical organization of files in a directory tree.

DNS (Domain Name Service). The Internet service that maps symbolic names to IP addresses, via queries across the available pool of *DNS* servers.

document annotation. The process of attaching information to a document (usually with annotation software for electronic copy).

document root. At the base of a Web server's document tree, the *root* defines the scope of all the documents that Web users may access (for example, access is allowed to the root and all its children, but not to any of the root's peers or parents).

editor. An application used to edit a file.

document tree. The collection of all directories underneath the document root, with all the documents that each such directory contains.

element type. The value that an element can take (for example, text, number, and tag).

element. A basic unit of text or markup.

e-mail (electronic mail). The service that allows users to exchange electronic messages across a network; the major *e-mail* technology in use on the Internet is based on the Simple Mail Transfer Protocol (SMTP).

encoding. Describes how to express values according to a particular notation, such as binary, ASCII, and EBCDIC.

environment variables. A value passed into a program or script by the runtime environment on the system where the program is running.

error checking. Examining input data to make sure it is both appropriate and accurate.

exception handling. If a program behaves abnormally, encounters unexpected input, or detects an anomaly, it must react; this is called *exception handling.*

extensibility. A description of how easy it is to write applications that build upon core mechanisms, to add functionality, new methods, or subclasses (depending on the paradigm).

extension language. A programming language that extends the functionality of programmable languages or interfaces.

FAQs (Frequently Asked Questions). A list of common questions and their associated answers, maintained by most of the special interest groups on the Internet. These lists lower the frequency of basic technical questions.

field. A named component of a record and its associated values in a database; or, a named input widget or text area and its associated value in an HTML form.

file mapping. Similar to an alias, *file mapping* is a method of supplying a filename to outside users that does not reveal the internal file structures involved.

filtering. How you remove certain objects from a document. For example, removing processing instructions that are important to a specific scheme not used in a general markup scheme eliminates unintelligible materials.

flat shading. The simplest form of shading, in which each face is seen in the same color.

floating-point. A method for storing and calculating numbers in which the decimal points do not line up as in fixed point numbers.

front end. The client or user interface side of a client/server application, the *front end* is what users see and interact with to gain information from a server.

FTP (File Transfer Protocol). An Internet protocol and service that provides electronic file transfers between any two network nodes that have file access rights.

gif (also GIF, Graphics Interchange Format). A compressed graphics file format patented by Unisys. This format is widely used in HTML documents for inline graphical elements.

Gouraud shading. A shading technique developed by Henri Gouraud in which lighting calculations are performed once per vertex; the resulting colors are then blended from one vertex to another.

GPL (GNU General Public License). A scheme for the mandatory distribution of source code with software, devised by Richard Stallman of the Free Software Foundation. GNU tools are very popular in the development community because source code is always available.

grab and twist. An interactive manipulation technique used in virtual reality interfaces, usually with a data glove, to manage user interaction.

group. A node that contains one or more other (child) nodes.

GUI (Graphical User Interface). Any computer interface that uses graphics, windows, and a pointing device, such as a mouse or trackball, instead of a purely character-mode interface. Windows, Mac OS, and X11 are all examples of GUI interfaces.

gzip (GNU zip). A UNIX-based compression program that produces ".gz" compressed file formats.

helper applications. Applications, also called plug-ins, that are invoked by a Web browser to render, display, or play-back data types that the browser cannot handle in and of itself (such as video or multimedia files).

HTML (HyperText Markup Language). Derived from SGML, *HTML* is the text-based descriptive markup language used to describe documents for use on the Web.

HTTP (HyperText Transfer Protocol). The TCP/IP-based communications protocol that defines how clients and servers communicate over the Web.

httpd (HTTP daemon). The daemon (or listener) program running on a Web server, listening for and ready to respond to requests for Web documents or CGI-based services.

hyperlink. An electronic link between one object and another. (See also hypertext.)

hypermedia. Any of the methods of computer-based information delivery that can be interlinked and treated as a single collection of information, including text, graphics, video, animation, and sound.

hypertext. A method of organizing text, graphics, and other kinds of data for computer use that lets individual data elements point to one another.

IICM (Institute for Information Processing and Computer Supported New Media). A part of the team that built the VRWeb VRML viewer, the *IICM* is Graz University's team of talented graphics and Internet programming wizards.

imagemap (also called clickable image, or clickable map). A graphical image that has an associated map file that lets users select links by clicking on certain portions of the image, *imagemaps* are identified by the <ISMAP> tag.

inheritance. Describes how objects that are subordinate to parent objects or classes obtain attributes or properties from superordinate objects (they *inherit* them from elements higher in the object hierarchy).

instance. An incarnation of an object, class, or record, *instances* include the data for one single item in a collection of data.

interactivity. The ability to interact with, or to be in a conversational mode with, a computer.

interface. Subroutines, parameter passing mechanisms, and data that define how two systems (which may be on the same or different machines) communicate.

international standard. A standard that is honored by more than one country; in practice, this refers to an International Standards Organization (ISO) standard.

Internet. The worldwide, TCP/IP-based networked computing community that electronically links government, business, research, industry, and education.

interpreter. A software program that reads source code from a programming language every time it is run, to interpret the instruction it contains.

IP (Internet Protocol). The most widely used network protocol in the world, *IP* is the primary network layer protocol for the TCP/IP protocol suite.

ISP (Internet Service Provider). An organization that provides Internet access to a consumer, usually for a fee.

jpeg (also JPEG, Joint Photographic Experts Group). The highly compressible graphics format designed to handle computer images of high-resolution photographs efficiently.

keyword. A term that can be used to search indexed data.

kludge. A workaround or an inelegant solution to a programming problem.

LAN (Local Area Network). A network with a span that is generally less than one mile linked by physical cables.

library. A collection of programs or code modules.

link. A hypertext method for jumping from one point in a document to another point in the same document, or another document anywhere on the Internet.

Lisp (LISt Processing language). A programming language for which all operations are defined through the evaluation of a list of functions.

Mac/OS. The Macintosh Operating System.

mail server. A class of Internet programs (e.g., *majordomo, listserv,* and *mailserv*) in which users participate in ongoing data exchanges or file retrieval via e-mail.

mailing list. The list of participants who exchange e-mail messages regularly, generally focused on a particular topic.

map files. The boundary definitions for a clickable image, used to assign URLs to regions on an image for user navigation.

markup. A special form of text that is embedded in a document that describes elements of document structure, layout, presentation, or delivery.

material binding. The process of associating a material with a node to indicate its composition or other properties.

MEME (Multitasking Extensible Messaging Environment). An interactive development package that allows programmers to create virtual worlds and act within them.

Mesa. An X Window System-based graphics library that supports OpenGL's and Open Inventor's implementation aspects and capabilities.

metalanguage. A formal language, such as SGML, used to describe other languages.

MIDI (Musical Instrument Digital Interface). A standard protocol for the interchange of musical information between computers.

MIME (Multipurpose Internet Mail Extensions). Extensions to the RFC822 electronic mail message format that permits more complex data and file types than plain text. Some MIME types are: sound, video, graphics, PostScript, and HTML.

mirrored servers. The process of completely copying heavily used file archives, Web servers, or other network servers, to lower the demand on any one server and to reduce long distance network traffic. When one server acts as a full copy of another, the second server is said to be a *mirror* of the first.

mirrored site. See mirrored servers.

modularity. A program that is broken into components, each of which supplies a particular function or capability, is a *modular* program.

MOO (or MUD, Object-Oriented). A multiuser, text-based virtual reality.

Motif. A UNIX-based graphical user interface.

Moving Worlds. Another name for the VRML 2.0 specification.

MUD (MultiUser Dungeon). An Internet-based role-playing game, where users gather and interact through typed-in text.

multithreaded.   A runtime environment that uses a lightweight process control mechanism, called *threading*, to switch contexts among multiple tasks.

MUSH (MultiUser Shared Hallucination).   A "Textual Reality" zone where you can chat with other inhabitants and visit rooms they've created.

navigation.   In VRML, the process of moving around in a virtual space.

NCSA (National Center for Supercomputing Applications).   The place where the Mosaic browser was originally developed, *NCSA* is an arm of the University of Illinois.

net-pointers.   URLs, FTP addresses, or other locations on the Internet where you can go to get data.

network services.   The collection of shared files, printers, data, or other applications (e.g., e-mail and scheduling) that is accessible across a network.

network utilization.   The amount of network usage, usually expressed as the percentage of bandwidth consumed on the medium, for a specific period of time.

newsgroups.   Groups that exchange regular message traffic, such as topic areas on USENET, that are a great source of information for technical topics of all kinds.

node.   A VRML object; each VRML *node* defines a tool that can be used to help create a 3-D virtual world. A node may be a movement, a texture, or a specific geometric shape, such as a sphere or a cube.

normal.   A common technique used to estimate the light reflecting off a surface back at the viewer.

NULL.   Denotes a missing or empty value.

object-oriented (OO).   A programming paradigm that concentrates on defining data objects and the methods that may be applied to them.

OIF (Open Inventor File format).   An ASCII-based file format that supports all of the graphical elements and operations specified in the initial VRML requirements document.

OO. See object-oriented.

Open Inventor.   Created by Silicon Graphics, Inc., *Open Inventor* is the 3-D graphics description technology that shaped much of VRML and its capabilities as a language (see also OIF).

OpenGL (Open Graphics Language).   A graphics language, administered by the Architecture Review Board, that defines syntax and structure for 3-D graphics that informs much of VRML.

orientation.   Specified as yaw, pitch, and roll; defines how an object is oriented.

padding. Additional null values added to the end of a data or byte stream, usually to make sure it is an even number, or some other specified minimum number of bytes.

parameter. Whenever code components communicate with one another, a *parameter* value is passed into or out of a program, subroutine, or across an interface.

parent. Indicates that an object contains, or is superordinate to, another, either by inheritance or inclusion.

parse tree. The designation of, and relationships between, tokens or lexical elements in an input stream after that stream has been parsed, shown in a graphical representation.

pattern matching. A computerized search operation in which input values are treated as *patterns*, and *matches* are sought in a search database.

Perl (Practical Extraction and Report Language). Developed by Larry Wall, *Perl* is an interpreted programming language that has string-handling and pattern-matching capabilities. *Perl* is a favorite among Web programmers for CGI use.

pitch. The slant from back to front.

pixel (PICture Element). The most primitive individual element for controlling graphics (it's also how image maps are measured and specified).

placeholder. An ideal example of a *placeholder* is a parameter, because it is a symbolic representation to be manipulated by a program, but only when it's running and an initial input value is defined. While code is being written, all parameters are placeholders.

platform-independent. A program or device that is said to be *platform-independent* works on any computer, irrespective of make, model, or type.

plug-in. Also called a helper application, a *plug-in* is an application that is called by a Web browser to handle a specific application or file type.

point cloud. A collection of points with no geometric relation between its members.

point light. A light source that is defined with a position and a color, which produces an effect similar to a naked light bulb.

polygon. The basic visual units that VRML uses to define surfaces, and to combine them to represent all kinds of visual objects.

port (short for transport). Porting code is the act of taking a program written for one system and altering it to run on another.

port address. The socket identifier that a program or a service seeks to address for a specific type of communication; for example, HTTP's *port address* is 80.

PostScript. A common format for exchanging nicely formatted print files, *PostScript* is a page description language defined by Adobe Systems. *PostScript* files usually carry the extension ".ps" in the UNIX world.

primitive. A graphics element that is used as a building block for creating images, such as a line, point, or sphere.

processor-intensive. An application is said to be *processor-intensive* if it consumes lots of CPU cycles (i.e., runs for a long time). Good examples include heavy graphics rendering, such as ray-tracing, animation, CAD, and other programs that combine lots of number-crunching with intensive display requirements.

properties. The values of an object's attributes endow an object with *properties* that distinguish it from other objects.

proprietary. Technology that is owned or controlled by a company or organization, and that may or may not be widely used. *Proprietary* software is the opposite of public domain software.

protocol suite. A collection of networking protocols that defines a complete set of tools and communications facilities for network access and use (for example, TCP/IP, OSI, and IPX/SPX are all *protocol suites*).

pull and manipulate. An interactive manipulation technique used in virtual reality interfaces, usually with a data glove, to manage user interaction.

push and pop. Operations used to manipulate a programming structure, called a stack, that uses a "Last-In, First-Out" priority order. When you add an element to a stack, it's called a *push*; when you remove an element from a stack, it's called a *pop*. This is how the VRML separator manages stateful information for nodes in a scene graph.

query string. The parameters passed to a Web-based search engine, usually using the GET method.

QuickDraw and **QuickDraw 3D**. Apple Computer Corp.'s built-in two- and three-dimensional graphics packages, included with the Mac OS.

QuickTime. Apple Computer Corp.'s video- and animation-rendering library, included with the Mac/OS, but also available for other platforms, such as Microsoft Windows.

radian. A measurement of the arc of a circle, defined by the angle of the radii that define the beginning and end of the arc.

ray tracing. The creation of reflections, refractions, and shadows on a graphics image.

reflection. The amount of light which bounces off an object's surface, allowing it to be seen.

remote location. A site or machine elsewhere on the network; also, a machine that is intermittently connected to a network, usually via a dial-up connection.

render. The process of interpreting the contents of a document, image, or other file for display or playback on a computer.

replication. The duplication of information to multiple servers, usually according to some strict synchronization protocol or scheme, so that a copy can be said to be an exact replica of the original.

repository. A location where data is kept, such as a file archive, database server, or document management system.

request. A network message from a client to a server that asks for a particular item of information or service.

request header. The preamble to a request that identifies the requester and provides authentication and formatting information where applicable. This lets servers know where to send a response, whether that request should be honored, and what formats it can take.

response. A network message from a server to a client that replies to a request for service.

response header. The preamble to a response, it identifies the sender and the application to which the response should be supplied.

response time. The amount of time that elapses between a request and the arrival of the response.

reusability. The degree to which programs, modules, or subroutines have been designed and implemented for multifunction use. The easier it is to take preexisting code and employ it in new applications, the more *reusable* it is.

roll. The angle of rotation about the lengthwise axis.

rotation. A VRML node's motion around a defined axis, indicating its front-facing orientation.

runtime variables. Program input or output values that cannot be assigned until the program is running.

scale. The size of a VRML node, relative to the viewing volume and other objects on display in a scene graph.

scene graph (or more simply, scene). The hierarchical file that dictates the order in which VRML nodes are parsed and rendered.

script. A synonym for *program*; programmers usually refer to their work as a *script* when it is written in an interpreted language. This is because, like a script, it is read all the way through each time it's run.

search string. The input passed for keyword search and pattern matching.

separator. A VRML programming construct used to isolate the state of one node from another state that occurs earlier in a scene graph's node order.

server. The software on a computer that lets other computers contact it and request information or services via client software. Also, the computer that runs the server software.

server push. A technique designed by Netscape that lets a server initiate data transfer, especially useful for time-sensitive data like voice or video, in which quick delivery is crucial for continuity.

signal to noise. The ratio of good information to irrelevant information in a newsgroup or mailing list.

snail mail. The antithesis of e-mail, *snail mail* requires envelopes, stamps, delivery vehicles, and personnel, and takes a whole lot longer to arrive at its destination.

source code. The original text files that contain instructions in a programming language that programmers write when creating software. The ability to view and understand source code gives you a good shot at understanding what a program is and how it works.

specification. The official requirements, inputs, outputs, and capabilities of a protocol, service, language, or software program (a kind of "blueprint" for a computer system or service of some kind).

spotlight. A light source, defined by a position, a direction vector, a drop-off angle, a spread angle, and a color, that produces a cone of light.

standard. A program, system, protocol, or other computer component that is *standard* may be the subject of an official published standard from some standards-setting body, or it may simply have acquired that status through widespread or long-term use.

standards-aware. Software that understands standards and can work within their constraints.

standards-compliant. Software that rigorously implements all of a standard's requirements and capabilities.

state. How a VRML node is affected by nodes that occur earlier in a scene graph's node order.

stateless. A stateless protocol needs no information about what has happened in the past, or expected to happen in the future, regarding communications between sender and receiver.

step-by-step execution. When debugging a program, *step-by-step execution* allows developers to locate the exact line of code where an error occurs, which is essential to detecting and fixing the problem.

stepwise refinement. A phrase coined by Edsger Dijkstra that indicates the repeated respecification and analysis of program elements to create elegant designs and implementations.

string. A sequence of characters.

surface. A shape that defines an area, but has no volume.

symbolic link.   A mechanism in which one name points to another name in a system, rather than directly to an object. Symbolic names are common for Web servers, document roots, and other system objects, to protect the internal structure from outside view.

synchronous.   A method of communications in which all communicating parties interact with one another at the same time.

syntax.   The rules that govern the structure of a language statement, *syntax* specifies how words and symbols are put together to form a phrase.

system administrator.   The individual responsible for maintaining a computer system, managing the network, setting up accounts, and installing applications.

Tcl (Tool Command Language, pronounced "tickle").   A simple scripting language for extending and controlling applications.

TCP/IP (Transmission Control Protocol/Internet Protocol).   Protocol suite upon which the Internet runs.

telnet.   A TCP/IP protocol and service that allows a user on one computer to emulate a terminal attached to another computer.

template.   An example or pattern for a program or document which acts as a predefined skeleton that only needs to be filled in to be complete.

texture.   The appearance of the surfaces of objects in a VRML world.

texture binding.   The association of the node that defines a particular texture with a node that defines a shape or a collection of surfaces.

texture map.   Image files which, when applied to a surface within a virtual space, cover the surface, or some portion of the surface, as determined by the designer.

toolset.   A collection of software tools that perform certain tasks, such as CGI input handling or image map creation.

transform.   VRML nodes that apply mathematical functions to control the visual orientation or presentation of the nodes that follow them in a scene graph.

translation.   A transformation on a node that occurs parallel to the coordinate axes, and contains no rotation or scaling.

transparency.   The effect of transmitting light through a non-opaque surface.

tree.   A hierarchical structure for organizing data or documents, such as file system directories, object hierarchies, and family trees.

troff.   A UNIX-based text formatting program that employs procedural markup.

UNIX.   The operating system developed by Brian Kernighan and Dennis Ritchie as a form of recreation at Bell Labs in the late 1960s.

URI (Uniform Resource Identifier).   Any of a class of objects that identify resources available to the Web; both URLs and URNs are instances of a URI.

URL (Uniform Resource Locator).   The naming scheme used to identify Web resources, *URLs* define the protocols, the domain name of the Web server where a resource resides, the port address to be used, and the directory path to access a named Web document or resource.

URL encoding.   A method for passing information requests and URL specifications to Web servers from browsers.

URN (Uniform Resource Name).   A permanent name for a Web resource (seldom used in today's Web environment).

USENET.   An Internet protocol and service that provides access to a vast array of named newsgroups. (See also newsgroups.)

USENET hierarchy.   The way newsgroups are organized is hierarchical.

vector.   A line segment described by two vertices; or location coordinates in a Cartesian space.

version control.   The ability to associate particular versions of documents or programs together (which may be necessary to maintain a production version and a development version).

vertex.   A point at the corner of a face or line set.

viewing volume.   The bounding box that defines the space being rendered from a VRML scene graph.

virtual world.   An environment created using a virtual reality modeling tool of some kind.

VRML (Virtual Reality Modeling Language).   A language for describing multiparticipant interactive simulations—virtual worlds networked via the global Internet and hyperlinked with the World Wide Web.

W3.   The World Wide Web.

Webification.   The process of turning complex electronic documents into HTML.

Webmaster.   The individual responsible for managing a Web site.

Webspace.   The total of all sites, resources, and documents available on the Web.

wireframe.   A style of rendering a solid model only by its outlines, rather than using shaded or textured surfaces.

X Windows.   A windowed graphical user interface governed by X11.

X11.   The GUI standard that governs X Windows.

Yahoo (Yet Another Hierarchical Officious Oracle).   A database written and maintained by David Filo and Jerry Yang. Yahoo is one of the best search engines on the Web.

yaw.   The spinning of a boat or place about its vertical axis.

building
VRML
World

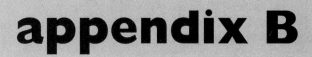

appendix B

Resources

T H E following lists contact information for all of the products mentioned throughout the book.

Abaco Systems
510-494-0690
Fax: 510-494-0893
http://www.abaco.com

Adobe Systems, Inc.
1585 Charleston Rd., PO Box 7900
Mountain View, CA 94039-7900
800-833-6687; 415-961-4400
http://www.adobe.com
Direct sales: 800-642-3623
Fax: 415-961-3769

Alien Skin Software
800 St. Mary's St., Ste. 100
Raleigh, NC 27605-1457
919-832-4124
http://www.catalogue.com/alienskin
Fax: 919-832-4065

Apple Computer, Inc.
1 Infinite Loop
Cupertino, CA 95014
800-776-2333; 408-996-1010
http://www.apple.com
Direct sales: 800-538-9696 (Hardware);
            800-325-2747 (Software/Claris Corp.)
Fax: 408-996-0275

Autodesk, Inc.
111 McGuinness Pkwy.
San Rafael, CA 94903
800-879-4233; 415-507-5000
http://www.autodesk.com
Direct sales: 800-964-6432
Fax: 415-507-5100

Axial Systems, Inc.
12901 Saratoga Ave. #4
Saratoga, CA 95070-4162
408-996-3100
Fax: 408-996-3381

Black Sun Interactive, Inc.
50 Osgood Place, Ste. 330
San Francisco, CA 94133
415-273-7000
http://www.blacksun.com
Fax: 415-273-7001

Caligari Corp.
1955 Landings Dr.
Mountain View, CA 94043
800-351-7620; 415-390-9600
http://www.caligari.com
Fax: 415-390-9755

Digital Equipment Corp. (DEC)
146 Main St.
Maynard, MA 01754-2571
800-344-4825; 508-493-5111
http://www.dec.com
Direct sales: 800-642-4532 (Digital PC/PCs Compleat)
Fax: 508-493-8780

Dimension X, Inc.
235 Pine St., Ste. 1300
San Francisco, CA 94104
415-243-0900
http://www.dimensionx.com
Fax: 415-243-0997

IBM (International Business Machines)
Old Orchard Rd.
Armonk, NY 10504
800-426-3333; 914-765-1900
http://www.ibm.com
Direct sales: 800-426-7255

Integrated Data Systems
6001 Chatham Center Dr., Ste. 300
Savannah, GA 31405
912-236-4374
http://www.ids-net.com/ids/index.html
Fax: 912-236-6792

InterVista Software, Inc.
45 Liberty St.
San Francisco, CA 94110
415-648-2749
http://www.hyperion.com/intervista

JASC, Inc.
PO Box 44997
Eden Prairie, MN 55344-0997
800-622-2793; 612-930-9800
http://www.jasc.com
Fax: 612-930-9172

Kinetix (division of Autodesk, Inc.)
111 McInnis Pkwy.
San Rafael, CA 94903
800-879-4233; 415-507-5000
http://www.ktx.com
Fax: 415-507-5314

Macromedia, Inc.
600 Townsend St., Ste. 310 W
San Francisco, CA 94103-4945
800-326-2128; 415-252-2000
http://www.macromedia.com
Direct sales: 800-945-9085
Fax: 415-626-0554

MetaTools, Inc.
6303 Carpinteria Ave.
Carpinteria, CA 93013
800-972-4025; 805-566-6200
http://www.metatools.com
Fax: 805-566-6385

Microsoft Corp.
One Microsoft Way
Redmond, WA 98052-6399
800-426-9400; 206-882-8080
http://www.microsoft.com
Direct sales: 800-MSPRESS
Fax: 206-93-MSFAX

**National Center for Supercomputing Applications
(Software Development Group)**
605 E. Springfield Ave.
Champaign, IL 61820-5518
217-244-3473
http://www.ncsa.uiuc.edu

NEC Technologies, Inc. (Internet Business Unit)
110 Rio Robles Dr.
San Jose, CA 95134
800-668-4869; 408-433-1200
http://www.privatenet.nec.com

Netscape Communications Corp.
501 E. Middlefield Rd.
Mountain View, CA 94043
800-NETSITE; 415-254-1900
FAX: 415-528-4124
http://home.netscape.com

ParaGraph International
1688 Dell Ave.
Campbell, CA 95008
408-364-7700
http://www.paragraph.com
Fax: 408-374-5466

Power Computing Corp.
Austin Operations Center, 2555 N. Interstate 35
Round Rock, TX 78664
800-999-7279; 512-388-6868
http://www.powercc.com
Fax: 512-250-3390

RealSpace, Inc.
4320 Stevens Creek Blvd., Suite 285
San Jose, CA 95129
http://www.rlspace.com

Silicon Graphics, Inc.
2011 N. Shoreline Blvd.
Mountain View, CA 94043-1389
800-800-7441; 415-960-1980
http://www.sgi.com
Fax: 415-961-0595

SONY Electronics, Inc.
3300 Zanker Rd.
San Jose, CA 95134-1901
800-352-7669; 408-432-1600
http://www.sony.com
Fax: 408-943-0740

Specular International, Ltd.
7 Pomeroy Lane
Amherst, MA 01002
800-433-SPEC; 413-253-3100
http://www.specular.com
Direct sales: 800-213-3314
Fax: 413-253-0540

Spyglass, Inc.
1230 E. Diehl Rd.
Naperville, IL 60563
800-647-2201; 630-505-1010
http://www.spyglass.com
Fax: 630-505-4944

Strata, Inc.
2 W. St. George Blvd., Ancestor Sq., Ste. 2100
St. George, UT 84770
800-869-6855; 801-628-5218
http://www.strata3d.com
Direct sales: 800-678-7282
Fax: 801-628-9756

Sun Microsystems, Inc. (JavaSoft Division)
2550 Garcia Ave.
Mountain View, CA 94043-1100
415-960-1300
http://java.sun.com

Syndesis Corp.
235 S. Main St.
Jefferson, WI 53549
414-674-5200
Fax: 414-674-6363

Tenet Networks, Inc.
3461 Camino Valencia
Carlsbad, CA 92009
619-736-8473
http://www.tenet.net
Fax: 619-736-4572

Viewpoint DataLabs International
625 S. State St.
Orem, UT 84058
800-DATASET; 801-229-3000
http://www.viewpoint.com
Fax: 801-229-3300

Virtus Corp.
118 Mackenan Dr., Ste. 250
Cary, NC 27511
800-847-8871; 919-467-9700
http://www.virtus.com
Fax: 910-460-4530

Visual Software Solutions, Inc.
3057 Coral Springs Dr., Ste. 203
Coral Springs, FL 33065
800-208-1051; 954-346-8890
Fax: 954-346-9394

Index

About the CD

The CD included with this book is a partitioned hybrid CD. This means that it contains both a long-filename partition that is readable on a Macintosh or UNIX system and an 8.3 ISO 9960 partition that is readable on any DOS or Windows system. The Macintosh/UNIX partition takes advantage of the long filenames that may have been used by the vendors. The DOS/Windows partition uses shortened 8.3 filenames (these are listed in parenthesis after the long filenames in the list that follows later in this section).

Additional Utilities

The files included in the software directory on the CD are all archived and compressed. Proper compression tools will be required to extract the original files from these archives. All of these tools can be located quickly using the search engine at C|Net's Shareware.Com at:

http://www.shareware.com

Windows

Most of the Windows software is archived with PKZip. You can use the original PKZip program to extract the files or a newer GUI-based decompression utility named WinZIP. The latest version of PKZip is 2.04G with the filename pkz204g.exe. Copy the PKZip file into an empty directory then execute it to extract the files. There is a detailed manual and readme file that explain how to use the software. The latest version of WinZIP can be downloaded from:

http://www.winzip.com.

WinZIP also includes complete installation and use instructions, which are also available online.

Macintosh

All the Macintosh archives are BinHexed (hqx) and/or Stuffed (sit). You can download the BinHex 4.0 software from:

ftp://ftp.bio.indiana.edu/util/mac/binhex.bin

This file is Macintosh executable. You can download the StuffIt Expander 4.0.1 from:

http://www.aladdinsys.com/

Complete installation details are available on the Aladdin Web site as well.

UNIX

There is only one UNIX compression file on this CD; it is a *tar* file. Most UNIX operation systems include an *untar* utility. For detailed instructions on the use of *tar*, read the manual page by typing **man tar** at any prompt. If your system does not display the *tar* page, then contact your system administrator. Without the access to the *tar* utility, you won't be able to access this archive. For WinZIP users, please note that it can handle *tar* formatted files, as well as zipped ones.

Installation Tips

Here are a few things we highly recommend when installing new software:

1. Back up your system.

2. Reboot your machine.

3. Move the file to be unarchived into an empty directory on your hard drive.

4. Test the extracted files for viruses before installing anything.

5. Read all the instructions before attempting to install new software.

6. [DOS/Windows only] Before starting any installation, unload any terminate-and-stay-resident (TSR) programs—especially anti-virus, memory managers, and memory-resident graphics drivers (this may require you to reboot). [Macintosh] users should turn off all unnecessary INITs or system resources.

Contents

The following information provides a listing of the contents of the CD, followed by a brief explanation of each item.

bvw.htm

This is the first document you should load in your Web browser.

urls.htm

This is a menued list of URLs from the text.

cp11.exe

This is the Caligari Pioneer 1.1 free trial version (Windows).

cpp11.exe

This is the Caligari Pioneer Pro 1.1 demo restricted version (Windows).

http-analyze1.9d.tar (HTTPANAL.TAR)

This is the http-analyze software for UNIX.

SProExamplefiles.sit.hqx (SPROEX.HQX)

These are StudioPro examples for the Macintosh.

StudioPro1.75demoPPC.sit.hqx (STRATA.HQX)

This is the StudioPro demo for Macintosh systems.

vhsbdemo.exe

This is the Virtual Home Space Builder demo for Windows.

3dwbdemo68k.sit.hqx (3DWBDEMO.HQX)

This is the 3-D WebSite Builder 1.0 demo for the Macintosh (68k).

3dwbdemoppc.sit.hqx (3DWBPPC.HQX)

This is the 3-D WebSite Builder 1.0 demo for the Power Macintosh.

3dwbw31.zip

This is the 3-D WebSite Builder 1.0 demo for Windows 3.1.

3dwbw95.zip

This is the 3-D WebSite Builder 1.0 demo for Windows 95.

pro2demo.exe

This is the WalkThrough Pro 2.0 demo for Windows 3.1.

pro2demo68k.sit.hqx (PRO2_68K.HQX)

This is the WalkThrough Pro 2.0 demo for the Macintosh (68K).

vrsi10.zip

This is the VRServer trial version for PCs.

vrsm10.zip

This is the VRServer trial version for MIPS.

Installation

The following information lists the installation instructions provided by the individual software vendors.

cp11.exe—Caligari Pioneer 1.1 free trial version (Windows) and cpp11.exe—Caligari Pioneer Pro 1.1 demo restricted version (Windows)

Execute the .exe file, this will initiate the installation. Follow the onscreen prompts.

http-analyze1.9d.tar (HTTPANAL.TAR)—http-analyze (UNIX)

A more detailed set of instructions is included in the archive. Once you have extracted the files, read the document entitled install.

1. Extract the files from the TAR archive. On UNIX systems, use one of the following commands:

   gzcat http-analyze1.9d.tar.gz | tar xvof -
   zcat http-analyze1.9d.tar.Z | tar xvof -
   tar xvof http-analyze1.9d.tar

2. This creates a directory called http-analyze1.9d, which contains all source files.

note *Before you can compile http-analyze, you have to compile the gd graphics library. See the installation instructions in the documentation of gd1.2 (http://www.boutell.com/gd/).*

3. Change into the directory http-analyze1.9d and edit the *Makefile* according to your needs.

4. Now, compile the program using the command *make all*.

5. Next, install it by issuing the command *make install*.

SProExamplefiles.sit.hqx (SPROEX.HQX)—StudioPro examples (Macintosh) and StudioPro1.75demoPPC.sit.hqx (STRATA.HQX)—StudioPro demo (Macintosh)

Extract the files, then read the installation documentation included in the archive. Basically, you will be executing a file called StudioPro 1.75 Install, then follow the prompts.

Paragraph's vhsbdemo.exe—Virtual Home Space Builder demo (Windows)

Extract the files by executing the .exe file. Once extracted, execute the vhsb.exe file to start the program, no other installation is needed.

Virtus' 3-D WebSite Builder

Macintosh—extract the archive files then execute the main file, labeled with the product name, follow the prompts.

Windows—extract the archive files, then execute the setup file, follow the prompts.

Virtus' WalkThrough Pro

Macintosh—extract the archive files then execute the main file, labeled with the product name, follow the prompts.

Windows—extract the archive files by typing **pro2demo.exe -d** at a DOS prompt or Run command line, execute the setup file, then follow the prompts.

vrsi10.zip—VRServer trial version (Intel) and vrsm10.zip—VRServer trial version (MIPS)

Extract the archive files, then execute the setup file, follow the prompts

Fine Print

....

The copyright for each of these software products is held by its respective vendor. Any restrictions on use or redistribution is covered in each software's license that is either included with the software or available from the vendor. Osborne/McGraw-Hill makes no additional claims, warranties, or guarantees about these software products including their use or misuse, merchantability, or fitness for commercial use.